VERGIL

Aeneid Book 1

The Focus Vergil Aeneid Commentaries

For intermediate students
 Aeneid 1 • *Randall Ganiban, editor* • *Available now*
 Aeneid 2 • *Randall Ganiban, editor* • *Available now*
 Aeneid 3 • *Christine Perkell, editor* • *Available now*
 Aeneid 4 • *James O'Hara, editor* • *Available now*
 Aeneid 5 • *Joseph Farrell, editor* • *Available 2012*
 Aeneid 6 • *Patricia Johnston, editor* • *Available 2012*

For advanced students
 Aeneid 1–6 • *Available 2012 (Single volume. Contributers as listed above)*
 Aeneid 7–12 • *Available 2013 (Available only as a single volume)*
 Contributors:
 Randall Ganiban, editor • *Aeneid 7*
 James O'Hara, editor • *Aeneid 8*
 Joseph Farrell, editor • *Aeneid 9*
 Andreola Rossi, editor • *Aeneid 10*
 Charles McNelis, editor • *Aeneid 11*
 Christine Perkell, editor • *Aeneid 12*

VERGIL

Aeneid Book 1

Randall T. Ganiban
Middlebury College

Focus Publishing
R. Pullins Company
Newburyport, MA
www.pullins.com

Vergil Aeneid 1
© 2008 Randall T. Ganiban

Focus Publishing / R. Pullins Company
PO Box 369
Newburyport MA 01950
www.pullins.com

Interior illustration by Sam Kimball

ISBN 13: 978-1-58510-225-9

Printed in the United States of America

14 13 12 11 10 9 8 7 6 5

1112H

Table of Contents

For Elizabeth

Preface

This volume is an introductory commentary on *Aeneid* 1 for use at the intermediate level or higher. It provides a generous amount of basic information about grammar and syntax so that students of varying experience will have what they need to translate the Latin. At the same time, it addresses issues of interpretation and style so that students at all levels will have a richer experience of the poem. Finally, it includes extensive bibliographic notes that will help readers pursue areas of special interest. I hope that this combination of information will offer a useful alternative to other student editions (often targeting the secondary school level), and will be particularly suited to intermediate (and perhaps even more advanced) Latin students at today's colleges and universities, who may benefit from an edition that helps them understand the Latin but also gives them a fuller experience of Vergil's style, themes, and the types of questions explored in contemporary Vergilian criticism.

This commentary takes as its starting point the still valuable school edition of *Aeneid* 1 by T. E. Page (1892), reprinted without vocabulary in his *Virgil: Aeneid 1-6* (1894). Page's notes have been pared down, revised, updated, or omitted, while new notes and introductory material have been added throughout. In addition, the general introduction, bibliography, appendices on meter and style, and general index are all new. In adapting Page's vocabulary, some definitions have been altered, and various changes made in the formatting and the presentation of word listings. I have also consulted a wide range of commentaries on book 1; those by Conington, Conway, Austin, and Williams were particularly helpful.

The Latin text used here is that of F. A. Hirtzel (Oxford, 1900) with the following differences in readings: 1.1a-d omitted; 2 *Laviniaque* for *Lavinaque*, 224 *despiciens* for *dispiciens*, 455 *inter* for *intra*, 599 *exhaustos* for *exhaustis*, and 708 *pictis* for *pictis*. (i.e. the period has been omitted). This edition places the Latin and commentary on the same page. A complete Latin text of *Aeneid* 1, however, may also be desirable for individual study or for use within the classroom, and has therefore been made available for download on the publisher's website. Please go to www.pullins.com for it as well as for information and updates on this volume and other *Aeneid* commentaries in the same series.

It is with pleasure that I offer thanks to a number of people who have read various portions of this edition and have given helpful advice: Elaine Fantham; the anonymous readers for Focus Publishing; my colleagues in the Classics Department at Middlebury College (Jane Chaplin, Pavlos Sfyroeras, Chris Star, and Marc Witkin); my collaborators on a larger *Aeneid* 1-6 commentary project for Focus (Joe Farrell, Pat Johnston, Jim O'Hara, and Christine Perkell); my intermediate Latin students in 2007 who tested parts of the commentary and gave me valuable feedback; several student research assistants (Matt Friend, Caroline Gersh, Sarah Miller, Rebecca Scholtz, and, in the final stages of manuscript production, especially Carrie Bryant), who have helped in various ways with this project and others related to it, and whose work was generously funded by Middlebury College; Claire Ennen Ganiban, who has made the project even more enjoyable; and Elizabeth Ennen, who, as always, has provided timely counsel and unceasing support. Whatever flaws or errors remain are mine alone.

Finally, I would like to thank the people at Focus Publishing. It was Ron Pullins' idea to create new *Aeneid* commentaries by using Page's editions, and he was kind enough to give me the opportunity to contribute this volume. Throughout the process he has been unceasingly generous, supportive, and patient. Cindy Zawalich carefully proofread the manuscript, and Linda Diering has cheerfully guided the manuscript through the twists and turns of production.

Randall T. Ganiban
Middlebury College

Introduction

Vergil's lifetime and poetry

Publius Vergilius Maro (i.e. Vergil)[1] was born on October 15, 70 BCE near the town of Mantua (modern Mantova) in what was then still Cisalpine Gaul.[2] Little else about his life can be stated with certainty, because our main source, the ancient biography by the grammarian Donatus (fourth century CE),[3] is of questionable value.[4] The historical and political background to Vergil's life, by contrast, is amply documented and provides a useful framework for understanding his career. Indeed, his poetic development displays an increasing engagement with the politics of contemporary Rome, an engagement that culminates in the *Aeneid*.

Vergil lived and wrote in a time of political strife and uncertainty. In his early twenties the Roman Republic was torn apart by the civil wars of 49-45 BCE, when Julius Caesar fought and defeated Pompey and his supporters. Caesar was declared *dictator perpetuo* ("Dictator for Life") early in 44 BCE but was assassinated on the Ides of March by a group of senators led by Brutus[5] and Cassius. They sought to restore the Republic, which, they believed, was being destroyed by Caesar's domination and intimations of kingship.[6]

---

1   The spelling "Virgil" (*Virgilius*) is also used by convention. It developed early and has been explained by its similarity to two words: *virgo* ("maiden") and *virga* ("wand"). For discussion of the origins and potential meanings of these connections, see Jackson Knight (1944) 36-7 and Putnam (1993) 127-8 with notes.

2   Cisalpine Gaul, the northern part of what we now think of as Italy, was incorporated into Roman Italy in 42 BCE. Mantua is located ca. 520 kilometers north of Rome.

3   This biography drew heavily from the *De poetis* of Suetonius (born ca. 70 CE).

4   Horsfall (1995: 1-25; 2006: xxii-xxiv) argues that nearly every detail is unreliable.

5   Kingship was hateful to the Romans ever since Brutus' own ancestor, Lucius Junius Brutus, led the expulsion of Rome's last king, Tarquin the Proud, in ca. 509 BCE, an act that ended the regal period of Rome and initiated the Republic (cf. *Aeneid* 6.817-18). In killing Caesar, Brutus claimed that he was following the example of his great ancestor—an important concept for the Romans.

6   For the reasons behind Caesar's assassination and the fall of the Republic, see the brief accounts in Scullard (1982) 126-53 and Shotter (2005) 4-19.

The assassination initiated a new round of turmoil that profoundly shaped the course of Roman history. In his will, Caesar adopted and named as his primary heir his great-nephew Octavian (63 BCE-14 CE), the man who would later be called "Augustus."[7] Though only eighteen years old, Octavian boldly accepted and used this inheritance. Through a combination of shrewd calculation and luck, he managed to attain the consulship in 43 BCE, though he was merely nineteen years of age.[8] He then joined forces with two of Caesar's lieutenants, Marc Antony (initially Octavian's rival) and Lepidus. Together they demanded recognition as a Board of Three (*triumviri* or "triumvirs") to reconstitute the state as they saw fit, and were granted extraordinary powers to do so by the Roman senate and people. In 42 BCE they avenged Caesar's murder by defeating his assassins commanded by Brutus and Cassius at the battle of Philippi in Macedonia, but their alliance gradually began to deteriorate as a result of further civil strife and interpersonal rivalries.

Vergil composed the *Eclogues*, his first major work, during this tumultuous period.[9] Published ca. 39 BCE,[10] the *Eclogues* comprise a sophisticated collection of ten pastoral poems that treat the experiences of shepherds.[11] The poems were modeled on the *Idylls* of Theocritus, a Hellenistic Greek poet of the third century BCE (see below). But whereas Theocritus' poetry created a world that was largely timeless, Vergil sets his pastoral world against the backdrop of contemporary Rome and the disruption caused by the civil wars. *Eclogues* 1 and 9, for example, deal with the differing fortunes of shepherds during a time of land confiscations that

---

7   See below.

8   By the *lex Villia annalis* of 180 BCE, a consul had to be at least forty-two years of age.

9   Other works have been attributed to Vergil: *Aetna, Catalepton, Ciris, Copa, Culex, Dirae, Elegiae in Maecenatem, Moretum,* and *Priapea.* They are collected in what is called the *Appendix Vergiliana* and are generally believed to be spurious.

10   This traditional dating, however, has recently been called into question through re-evaluation of *Eclogue* 8, which may very well refer to events in 35 BCE. See Clausen (1994) 232-7.

11   Coleman (1977) and Clausen (1994) are excellent commentaries on the *Eclogues.* For a discussion of the pastoral genre at Rome, see Heyworth (2005). For general interpretation of the *Eclogues*, see Hardie (1998) 5-27 with extensive bibliography in the notes, and Volk (2008a).

resonate with historical events in 41-40 BCE.[12] *Eclogue* 4 describes the birth of a child during the consulship of Asinius Pollio (40 BCE) who will bring a new golden age to Rome.[13] By interjecting the Roman world into his poetic landscape,[14] Vergil allows readers to sense how political developments both threaten and give promise to the very possibility of pastoral existence.

The *Eclogues* established Vergil as a new and important poetic voice, and led him to the cultural circle of the great literary patron Maecenas, an influential supporter and confidant of Octavian. Their association grew throughout the 30s.[15] The political situation, however, remained precarious. Lepidus was ousted from the triumvirate in 36 BCE because of his treacherous behavior. Tensions between Octavian and Antony that were simmering over Antony's collaboration and affair with the Egyptian queen Cleopatra eventually exploded.[16] In 32 BCE, Octavian had Antony's powers revoked, and war was declared against Cleopatra (and thus in effect against Antony as well). During a naval confrontation off Actium on the coast of western Greece in September of 31 BCE, Octavian's fleet decisively routed the forces of Marc Antony and Cleopatra, who both fled to Egypt and committed suicide

---

12   Octavian rewarded veterans with land that was already occupied.

13   This is sometimes called the "Messianic Eclogue" because later ages read it as foreseeing the birth of Christ, which occurred nearly four decades later. The identity of the child is debated, but the poem may celebrate the marriage between Marc Antony and Octavian's sister Octavia that resulted from the treaty of Brundisium in 40 BCE; this union helped stave off the immediate outbreak of war between the two triumvirs. For more on this poem, see Van Sickle (1992) and Petrini (1997) 111-21, as well as the commentaries by Coleman (1977) and Clausen (1994).

14   In addition to the contemporary themes that Vergil treats, he also mentions or dedicates individual poems to a number of his contemporaries, including Asinius Pollio, Alfenus Varus, Cornelius Gallus, and probably Octavian, who is likely the *iuvenis* ("young man") mentioned at 1.42 and perhaps also the patron addressed at 8.6-13.

15   For the relationship between Augustus and the poets, see White (2005). White (1993) is a book-length study of this topic. For an overview of literature of the Augustan period from 40 BCE-14 CE, see Farrell (2005).

16   In addition to the political conflicts, there were also familial tensions: Antony conducted a decade-long affair with Cleopatra, even though he had married Octavia, Octavian's (Augustus') sister, as a result of the treaty of Brundisium in 40 BCE (see n. 13 above). Antony divorced Octavia in 32 BCE.

in the following year to avoid capture.[17] This momentous victory solidified Octavian's claim of being the protector of traditional Roman values against the detrimental influence of Antony, Cleopatra, and the East.[18]

Vergil began his next work, the *Georgics*, sometime in the 30s, completed it ca. 29 BCE in the aftermath of Actium, and dedicated it to Maecenas. Like the *Eclogues*, the *Georgics* was heavily influenced by Greek models—particularly the work of Hesiod (eighth century BCE) and of Hellenistic poets[19] such as Callimachus, Aratus, and Nicander (third–second centuries BCE). On the surface, it purports to be a poetic farming guide.[20] Each of its four book examines a different aspect or sphere of agricultural life: crops and weather signs (book 1), trees and vines (book 2), livestock (book 3), and bees (book 4). Its actual scope, however, is much more ambitious. The poem explores the nature of humankind's struggle with the beauty and difficulties of the agricultural world, but it does so within the context of contemporary war-torn Italy. It bears witness to the strife following Caesar's assassination, and sets the chaos and disorder inherent in nature against the upheaval caused by civil war (1.461-514). Moreover, Octavian's success and victories are commemorated both in the introduction (1.24-42) and conclusion (4.559-62) of the poem, as well as in the beginning of the third book (3.1-39). Thus once again, the political world is juxtaposed against Vergil's poetic landscape, but the relationship between the two is not fully addressed.[21]

---

17   For the history of the triumviral period, see the brief accounts in Scullard (1982) 154-71 and Shotter (2005) 20-7; for more detailed treatments, see Syme (1939) 187-312, Pelling (1996), Everitt (2006) 16-185. For discussion of the contemporary artistic representations of Actium, see Gurval (1995).

18   This ideological interpretation is suggested in Vergil's depiction of the battle on Aeneas' shield (8.671-713).

19   See discussion below.

20   Recent commentaries on the *Georgics* include Thomas (1988) and Mynors (1990). For interpretation, see the introduction to the *Georgics* in Hardie (1998) 28-52 with extensive bibliography in the notes, and Volk (2008b). Individual studies include Wilkinson (1969), Putnam (1979), Johnston (1980), Ross (1987), Perkell (1989), and Nappa (2005). For allusion in the *Georgics*, see Thomas (1986), Farrell (1991), and Gale (2000).

21   The overall meaning of the *Georgics* is contested. Interpretation of the *Georgics*, like that of the *Aeneid* (see below), has optimistic and pessimistic poles. Otis (1964) is an example of the former; Ross (1987) the latter. Other scholars, such as Perkell (1989), fall in between by discerning inherent ambivalence. For discussion of these interpretive trends, see Hardie (1998) 50-2.

Octavian's victory represented a turning point for Rome's development. Over the next decade, he centralized political and military control in his hands. He claimed to have returned the state (*res publica*) to the senate and Roman people in 27 BCE.[22] His powers were redefined, and he was granted the name "Augustus' ("Revered One") by the senate. It is true that he maintained many traditional Republican institutions, but in reality he was transforming the state into a monarchy. So effective was his stabilization and control of Rome after decades of civil war that he reigned as *Princeps* ("First Citizen") from 27 BCE to 14 CE, creating a political framework (the Principate) that served the Roman state for centuries.[23]

Vergil wrote his final poem, the *Aeneid*, largely in the 20s, during the first years of Augustus' reign, when the Roman people presumably hoped that the civil wars were behind them but feared that the Augustan peace would not last. The *Aeneid* tells the story of the Trojan hero Aeneas. He fought the Greeks at Troy and saw his city destroyed, but with the guidance of the gods and fate he led his surviving people across the Mediterranean to a new homeland in Italy.[24] As in the *Eclogues* and *Georgics*, Vergil interjects his contemporary world into his poetic world. In the *Aeneid*, however, the thematic connections between these two realms are developed still more explicitly, with Aeneas' actions shown to be necessary for and to lead ultimately to the reign of Augustus. (See below for further discussion.)

Vergil was still finishing the *Aeneid* when he was stricken by a fatal illness in 19 BCE. The ancient biographical tradition claims that he traveled to Greece, intending to spend three years editing his epic there and in Asia, but that early on he encountered Augustus, who was returning to Rome from

---

22   Augustus, *Res Gestae* 34.

23   For general political and historical narratives of Augustus' reign, see the relatively brief account in Shotter (2005); longer, more detailed treatments can be found in A. H. M. Jones (1970), Crook (1996), Southern (1998), and Everitt (2006) 186-320. A classic and influential book by Syme (1939) paints Augustus in extremely dark colors. For broader considerations of the Augustan age, see the short but interesting volume by Wallace-Hadrill (1993) and the more comprehensive treatments by Galinsky (1996, 2005). For the interaction of art and ideology in the Augustan Age, see Zanker (1988).

24   For general interpretation of the *Aeneid*, see the recent overviews provided by Hardie (1998) 53-101, Perkell (1999), Anderson (2005), Johnson (2005), Fratantuono (2007), and Ross (2007). For the literary and cultural backgrounds, see Martindale (1997), Farrell (2005), and Galinsky (2005).

the East, and decided to accompany him. Vergil, however, fell ill during the journey and died in Brundisium (in southern Italy) in September of 19 BCE. The *Aeneid* was largely complete but had not yet received its final revision. We are told that Vergil asked that it be burned, but that Augustus ultimately had it published. While such details regarding Vergil's death are doubted, the poem clearly needed final editing.[25] However, its present shape, including its sudden ending, is generally accepted to be as Vergil had planned.

Vergil and his predecessors

By writing an epic about the Trojan war, Vergil was rivaling Homer, the greatest of all the Greek poets. The *Aeneid* was therefore a bold undertaking, but its success makes it arguably the quintessential Roman work because it accomplishes what Latin poetry had always striven to do: to appropriate the Greek tradition and transform it into something that was both equally impressive and distinctly "Roman."

Homer's *Iliad* tells the story of the Trojan war by focusing on Achilles' strife with the Greek leader Agamemnon and consequent rage in the tenth and final year of the conflict, while the *Odyssey* treats the war's aftermath by relating Odysseus' struggle to return home. These were the earliest and most revered works of Greek literature,[26] and they exerted a defining influence on both the overall framework of the *Aeneid* and the close details of its poetry. In general terms, *Aeneid* 1-6, like the *Odyssey*, describes a hero's return (to a new) home after the Trojan war, while *Aeneid* 7-12, like the *Iliad*, tells the story of a war. But throughout the *Aeneid*, Vergil reworks ideas, language, characters, and scenes from both poems. Some ancient critics faulted Vergil for his use of Homer, calling his appropriations "thefts." Vergil, however, is said to have responded that it is "easier to steal his club from Hercules than a line from Homer."[27] Indeed, Vergil does much more than simply quote material from Homer. His creative use and transformation of Homeric

---

25   We can be sure that the poem had not received its final revision for a number of reasons, including the presence of roughly fifty-eight incomplete or "half" lines. See commentary note on 1.534.

26   These poems were culminations of a centuries-old oral tradition and were written down probably in the eighth century BCE.

27   *...facilius esse Herculi clavam quam Homeri versum subripere* (Donatus/Suetonius, *Life of Vergil* 46).

language and theme are central not only to his artistry but also to the meaning of the *Aeneid*.

Though Homer is the primary model, Vergil was also influenced by the Hellenistic Greek tradition of poetry that originated in Alexandria, Egypt in the third century BCE. There scholar-poets such as Apollonius, Callimachus, and Theocritus reacted against the earlier literary tradition (particularly epic which by their time had become largely derivative). They developed a poetic aesthetic that valued sophistication in meter and word order, small-scale treatments over large, the unusual and recherché over the conventional. Hellenistic poetry was introduced into the mainstream of Latin poetry a generation before Vergil by the so-called "neoterics" or "new poets," of whom Catullus (c. 84-c. 54 BCE) was the most influential for Vergil and for the later literary tradition.[28]

Vergil's earlier works, the *Eclogues* and *Georgics*, had been modeled to a significant extent on Hellenistic poems,[29] so it was perhaps a surprise that Vergil would then have turned to a large-scale epic concerning the Trojan war.[30] However, one of his great feats was the incorporation of the Hellenistic and neoteric sensibilities into the *Aeneid*. Two models were particularly important in this regard: the *Argonautica* by Apollonius of Rhodes, an epic retelling the hero Jason's quest for the Golden Fleece, and Catullus 64, a poem on the wedding of Peleus and Thetis.[31] Both works brought the great and elevated heroes of the past down to the human level, thereby offering new insights into their strengths, passions and flaws, and both greatly influenced Vergil's presentation of Aeneas.

---

28 Cf. Clausen (1987, 2002), George (1974), Briggs (1981), Thomas (1988, 1999), and Hunter (2006) display these influences, while O'Hara (1996) provides a thorough examination of wordplay (important to the Alexandrian poets) in Vergil.

29 The *Eclogues* were modeled on Theocritus' *Idylls*; the *Georgics* had numerous models, though the Hellenistic poets Callimachus, Nicander, and Aratus were particularly important influences. See above.

30 For example, at *Eclogue* 6.3-5, Vergil explains in highly programmatic language his decision to compose poetry in the refined Callimachean or Hellenistic manner rather than traditional epic. See Clausen (1994) 174-5.

31 On the influence of Apollonius on Vergil, see the important book by Nelis (2001).

Of Vergil's other predecessors in Latin literature, the most important was Ennius (239-169 BCE), often called the father of Roman poetry.[32] His *Annales*, which survives only in fragments, was an historical epic about Rome that traced the city's origins back to Aeneas and Troy. It remained the most influential Latin poem until the *Aeneid* was composed, and provided a model not only for Vergil's poetic language and themes, but also for his integration of Homer and Roman history. In addition, the *De Rerum Natura* of Lucretius (ca. 94-55/51 BCE), a hexameter poem on Epicurean philosophy, profoundly influenced Vergil with its forceful language and philosophical ideas.[33]

Finally, Vergil drew much from Greek and Roman[34] tragedy. Many episodes in the *Aeneid* share tragedy's well-known dramatic patterns (such as reversal of fortune), and explore the suffering that befalls mortals often as a result of the immense and incomprehensible power of the gods and fate.[35] As a recent critic has written, "The influence of tragedy on the *Aeneid*

---

32   Ennius introduced the dactylic hexameter as the meter of Latin epic. Two earlier epic writers were Livius Andronicus who composed a translation of Homer's *Odyssey* into Latin, and Naevius who composed the *Bellum Punicum*, an epic on the First Punic War. Both Naevius and Livius wrote their epics in a meter called Saturnian that is not fully understood. For the influence of the early Latin poets on the *Aeneid*, see Wigodsky (1972).

33   See Hardie (1986) 157-240 and Adler (2003). The influence of the Epicurean Philodemus on Vergil (and the Augustans more generally) is explored in the collection edited by Armstrong, Fish, Johnston, and Skinner (2004). For Lucretius' influence on Vergil's *Georgics*, see especially Farrell (1991) and Gale (2000).

34   The earliest epic writers (Livius, Naevius and Ennius; see above) also wrote tragedy, and so it is not surprising that epic and tragedy would influence one another. Latin tragic writing continued into the first century through the work of, e.g., Pacuvius (220-ca. 130 BCE) and Accius (170-c. 86 BCE). Their tragedies, which included Homeric and Trojan War themes, were important for Vergil. However, since only meager fragments of them have survived, their precise influence is difficult to gauge.

35   Cf., e.g., Heinze (1915, trans. 1993: 251-8). Wlosok (1999) offers a reading of the Dido episode as tragedy, and Pavlock (1985) examines Euripidean influence in the Nisus and Euryalus episode. Hardie (1991, 1997), Panoussi (2002), and Galinsky (2003) examine the influence of tragedy, particularly in light of French theories of Greek tragedy (e.g. Vernant and Vidal-Naquet (1988)), and draw important parallels between the political and cultural milieus of fifth-century Athens and Augustan Rome. On tragedy and conflicting viewpoints, see Conte (1999) and Galinsky (2003).

is pervasive, and arguably the single most important factor in Virgil's successful revitalization of the genre of epic."[36]

The *Aeneid* is thus a highly literary work. By considering its interactions with these and other models, or, to put it another way, by examining Vergil's use of "allusion" or "intertextuality,"[37] we can enrich both our experience of his artistry and our interpretation of his epic. However, no source study can fully account for the creative, aesthetic, and moral achievement of the *Aeneid*, which is a work until itself.

The *Aeneid*, Rome, and Augustus

While Aeneas' story takes place in the distant, mythological past of the Trojan war era, it had a special relevance for Vergil's contemporaries. Not only did the Romans draw their descent from the Trojans, but the emperor Augustus believed that Aeneas was his own ancestor.[38] Vergil makes these national and familial connections major thematic concerns of his epic.

As a result, the *Aeneid* is about more than the Trojan war and its aftermath. It is also about the foundation of Rome and its flourishing under Augustus. To incorporate these themes into his epic, Vergil connects mythological and historical time by associating three leaders and city foundations: the founding of Lavinium by Aeneas, the actual founding of Rome by Romulus, and the "re-founding" of Rome by Augustus. These events are prominent in the most important prophecies of the epic: Jupiter's speech

---

36   Hardie (1998) 62. See also Hardie (1997).

37   See Farrell (1997) for a full and insightful introduction to the interpretive possibilities that the study of intertextuality in Vergil can offer readers. For a general introduction to intertextuality, see Allen (2000). For the study of intertextuality in Latin literature, see Conte (1986), Farrell (1991) 1-25, Hardie (1993), Fowler (1997), Hinds (1998), and Edmunds (2001). For Vergil's use of Homer, see Knauer (1964b), Barchiesi (1984, in Italian), Gransden (1984), and Cairns (1989) 177-248. Knauer (1964a), written in German, is a standard work on this topic; those without German can still benefit from its detailed citations and lists of parallels. For Vergil's use of Homer and Apollonius, see Nelis (2001).

38   Augustus' clan, the Julian *gens*, claimed its descent from Iulus (another name for Aeneas' son Ascanius) and thus also from Aeneas and Venus. Julius Caesar in particular emphasized this ancestry; Augustus made these connections central to his political self-presentation as well. See, e.g., Zanker (1988) 193-210 and Galinsky (1996) 141-224.

to Venus (1.257-96) and Anchises' revelation to his son Aeneas (6.756-853). Together these passages provide what may be called an Augustan reading of Roman history, one that is shaped by the deeds of these three men and that views Augustus as the culmination of the processes of fate and history.[39]

This is not to say that the associations among Aeneas, Romulus, and Augustus are always positive or unproblematic, particularly given the ways that Aeneas is portrayed and can be interpreted.[40] To some, Vergil's Aeneas represents an idealized Roman hero, who thus reflects positively on Augustus by association.[41] In general this type of reading sees a positive imperial ideology in the epic and is referred to as "optimistic" or "Augustan." Others are more troubled by Vergil's Aeneas, and advocate interpretations that challenge the moral and spiritual value of his actions, as well as of the role of the gods and fate. Such readings perceive a much darker poetic world[42] and have been called "pessimistic" or "ambivalent."[43] Vergil's portrayal of Aeneas is thus a major element in debates over the epic's meaning,[44] and

---

39   See O'Hara (1990), however, for the deceptiveness of prophecies in the *Aeneid*.

40   For general interpretation of the *Aeneid*, see n. 24 (above).

41   This type of reading is represented especially by Heinze (1915, trans. 1993), Pöschl (1950, trans. 1962), and Otis (1964). More recent and complex Augustan interpretations can be found in Hardie (1986) and Cairns (1989).

42   See, e.g., Putnam (1965), Johnson (1976), Lyne (1987), and Thomas (2001). Putnam's reading of the *Aeneid* has been particularly influential. Of the ending of the poem he writes: "By giving himself over with such suddenness to the private wrath which the sight of the belt of Pallas arouses, Aeneas becomes himself *impius Furor*, as rage wins the day over moderation, disintegration defeats order, and the achievements of history through heroism fall victim to the human frailty of one man" (1965: 193-4). For a different understanding of Aeneas' wrath, see Galinsky (1988).

43   For a general treatment of the optimism/pessimism debate, see Kennedy (1992). For a critique of the "pessimistic" view, see Martindale (1993); for critique of the "optimistic" stance and its rejection of "pessimism," see Thomas (2001). For the continuing debate over the politics of the *Aeneid* and over the Augustan age more generally, see the collections of Powell (1992) and Stahl (1998).

44   Indeed some readers also question whether it is even possible to resolve this interpretive debate because of Vergil's inherent ambiguity. See Johnson (1976), Perkell (1994), and O'Hara (2007) 77-103. Martindale (1993) offers a critique of ambiguous readings.

book 1 introduces us to Aeneas in important ways that will influence our understanding of him throughout the epic.

Book 1 within the context of the *Aeneid*

The *Aeneid* begins as Aeneas and the Trojans are sailing to Italy, about to reach the land that fate has promised them, when their nemesis Juno intervenes and sends a storm that shipwrecks them at Carthage. There, with some divine assistance, they are welcomed by Dido, the Carthaginian queen. At a feast at the end of book 1, she asks Aeneas to tell his story about the end of the Trojan war and its aftermath.

Aeneas agrees, and the next two books comprise his own flashback narrative that describes events that preceded the storm that brought him to Carthage. In book 2, he provides an eyewitness account of the fall of Troy. In book 3, he describes his often confused wanderings from Troy in search of Italy, and ends his narration with his arrival at Dido's city.

Book 4 then treats the tragic love affair that develops between Dido and Aeneas, whose desire to linger with the queen in Carthage is set against his duty to lead his people to Italy. Aeneas ultimately leaves Dido and, after a stop in Sicily (book 5) and a heroic journey through the Underworld (book 6), he reaches Latium in Italy (book 7). Upon his arrival there, however, he is immediately entangled in a troubling war that occupies the remainder of the poem.

Throughout the epic Aeneas appears as a complicated figure, whose strengths and weaknesses are always on display. Book 1 provides a powerful and programmatic introduction to his portrayal. In it, we see Aeneas at one of his lowest points, enduring seemingly unending travails and struggling to make sense of the gods and fate. In the process, we are introduced to the epic's most important ideas and motifs.

Structure and major themes of *Aeneid* 1

Book 1 plunges us into Aeneas' story *in medias res*. The goddess Juno sees Aeneas approaching Italy in fulfillment of his fate. In a fit of rage, she sends a storm that shipwrecks him and his fleet at Carthage. These events are modeled on *Odyssey* 5. There the sea god Poseidon observes Odysseus continuing his voyage homeward. In an outburst of anger he sends a storm that shipwrecks Odysseus among the Phaeacians. Such thematic and structural similarities with Homer occur throughout book 1 (and the *Aeneid* more generally). But in transforming Homer, Vergil also produces significant contrasts that set in relief ideas that will distinguish his epic. Indeed in creatively engaging Homer, *Aeneid* 1 masterfully introduces the major themes of the entire poem.

Book 1 makes clear that Aeneas will be a different type of hero. In *Odyssey* 5, Odysseus has already lost all of his companions on their journey from Troy, as he struggles to return home and reestablish his honor. Aeneas, however, is concerned less for himself than for his family and people: he strives to find a new country for them. Thus whereas Odysseus' heroism is defined by his resourcefulness and is rooted in personal glory, Aeneas' defining characteristic is his *pietas*, his devotion and duty toward his family, people, and gods (cf. 10 n., 378, and 544-5).

These differences are connected to the divine dimension of the poems. While Zeus' plan in the *Odyssey* primarily focuses on ensuring Odysseus' return to Ithaca (cf. *Odyssey* 1.76-9, 5.21-42), Vergil's Jupiter situates Aeneas and his sufferings within a much larger context, one that promotes an overarching fate that looks to the foundation of Rome and Augustus' reign (1.254-96). Vergil's addition of this historical dimension fundamentally transforms his Homeric models and opens a new plain on which Aeneas' story can have meaning. Vergil thus enables his story about the Trojan warrior Aeneas to be one ultimately about Rome.

In doing so, Vergil expands and transforms the Homeric role of divine wrath. Odysseus suffers because of Poseidon's personal anger that his son, the Cyclops Polyphemus, had been blinded by the Greek hero (cf. *Odyssey* 1.68-79; 5.286-90). Juno's wrath in the *Aeneid* has a personal dimension too (cf. 1.23-8), but it is also involved in the grand movement of history. Fate requires that Rome will destroy her favorite city Carthage centuries later (1.12-22). As a result, Juno becomes a figure of *furor* and *ira* who sends countless pains upon Aeneas (cf. the storm at 34-222), but her actions also have divine consequences, because they hinder Jupiter's will and the necessities of fate. Vergil's Juno poses a challenge to cosmic order in ways that Homer's Poseidon never does.

The opening sequence of book 1 enacts these concerns in brilliantly symbolic terms. Juno, in all her wrath, co-opts the aid of the wind god Aeolus not only to obstruct Aeneas' progress to Italy but also to challenge Jupiter's authority and Fate's plan. The storm must be quelled by Neptune, a figure of *pietas* and order, and the conflict between *furor* and *pietas* becomes a thematic building block of the epic (see 34-222 n.). In the process, we are also shown that Aeneas' story has a significant divine and historical component, one that is made especially clear in Jupiter's prophecy (1.254-96).

While the first half of book 1 primarily examines the divine realm and the struggles it entails for Aeneas, the second half explores more fully the human dimension of Aeneas' fate through his incipient relationship with the Carthaginian queen Dido. She has much in common with Aeneas, though she suffers from one devastating difference: the gods and fate are ultimately not concerned with her well-being (cf. 305-417 n.). In Dido, divine will (Jupiter, Venus, Cupid, and later Juno) will mix with the violence of human passion to pose a difficult personal test of character and resolve for Aeneas.

In short, book 1 explores what it takes to act heroically in a world in which the values and ideals of the Homeric poems are transformed into something decidedly Roman. A new type of heroism is necessary for a warrior who must assume the burden of a fate that far transcends his personal desires and individual glory. It will be Aeneas' challenge throughout the epic to figure out how to play this role.

For general interpretation, see Pöschl (1962) 13-24, Otis (1964), Quinn (1968) 99-112, Anderson (2005), Segal (1981a), Perkell (1999) 29-49, and Fratantuono (2007) 1-36. For the Homeric influences, see Knauer (1964a, 1964b), Otis (1964) 215-41, Johnson (1976), and Lyne (1987) 100-7, and Cairns (1989) 177-214. For the influence of Homer and Apollonius, see Nelis (2001) 67-112, 117-20. For the gods, see especially Feeney (1991) 129-42. For the differing conceptions of heroism, see Johnson (1999) 50-4 and Adler (2003) 252-79.

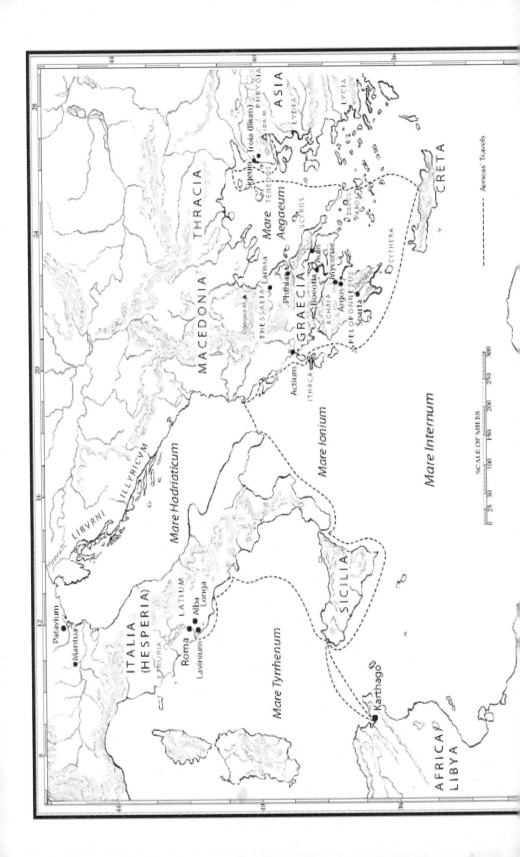

LIBER PRIMUS

Please note: when reference is made to a line in *Aeneid* 1, the number of the line is given (e.g. "cf. 229"); when the reference is to another book of the *Aeneid*, the number of the book is added (e.g. "cf. 4.229"). References to *Allen and Greenough's New Latin Grammar* ("AG"; see Mahoney (2001) in Works Cited) are provided by section number (e.g. "AG §290"). An asterisk marks terms that are listed in Appendix B.

Preliminary lines

The ancient commentators Donatus and Servius (fourth century CE) claim that the *Aeneid* originally began not with the famous *arma virumque cano* but with the following autobiographical passage, which Varius, Vergil's literary executor, deleted:

> Ille ego, qui quondam gracili modulatus avena
> carmen, et egressus silvis vicina coegi
> ut quamvis avido parerent arva colono,
> gratum opus agricolis, at nunc horrentia Martis

These lines connect the *Aeneid* (*at nunc horrentia Martis*) to the poet's two earlier works, the *Eclogues* (*Ille ego, qui quondam gracili modulatus avena/ carmen*) and the *Georgics* (*et egressus silvis vicina coegi/ ut quamvis avido parerent arva colono,/ gratum opus agricolis*). Most editions of the *Aeneid*, however, rightly reject this passage for a number of reasons. First, there is no clear evidence about it before the fourth century CE, and it is not included in any of the earliest and most important manuscripts of Vergil but is attested only beginning in the ninth century CE. Second, a number of Vergil's poetic successors quote *arma virumque* as the first words of the *Aeneid* (see Ovid, *Tristia* 2.533, Seneca, *Epistulae* 113.25, Persius 1.96, and Martial 8.56.19); these words also appear in graffiti from Pompeii. Third, the opening *arma virumque* points to the first lines of Homer's *Iliad* and *Odyssey* (see 1 n.), the most important poetic models of the *Aeneid*. Finally, it would be highly unusual to begin a Classical epic by intermingling biographical information with the introduction of the epic's hero. These are just some of the arguments. On the spuriousness of these lines, see, e.g., Austin *ad loc.* and Cairns (2003). Hansen (1972) argues for their authenticity.

1.1-33

ARMA virumque cano, Troiae qui primus ab oris   1
Italiam fato profugus Laviniaque venit
litora—multum ille et terris iactatus et alto
vi superum, saevae memorem Iunonis ob iram,
multa quoque et bello passus, dum conderet urbem   5
                              (IMP)

1-11. Vergil introduces the subject of his poem and invokes the Muse.

The opening immediately engages the Homeric poems and is particularly modeled on *Odyssey* 1.1-7. See notes below. For further discussion of the parallels, see Fredricksmeyer (1984), Hardie (1986), Cairns (1989: 190-4; 2003), and Braund (2004).

1. **ARMA virumque:** *arma* points to the *Iliad*, a poem about the Trojan war; *virum* to the *Odyssey*, which begins with Gr. *andra* or "man." (For Vergil's interaction with Homer, see "Vergil and his predecessors" in the Introduction.) **Troiae:** note the emphatic initial placement created by postponing the relative pronoun *qui*. The relative clause from lines 1-7 contains a summary of Aeneas' story, one that is bounded by the words *Troiae* and *Romae*, which introduce a thematic connection central to the epic (Braund (2004) 137-8). **primus:** "first." The Trojan Antenor, however, had actually settled earlier in Patavium (modern Padua; cf. 242-8). Vergil makes no mention of Antenor in the prologue, presumably since he is not connected to the *Aeneid*'s presentation of Rome's foundation, and Patavium in Cisalpine Gaul was incorporated into Italy only in 42 BCE. Aeneas is Rome's forefather, and the epic tells his story.

2. **Italiam:** emphatically placed; accusative of motion toward without preposition. **fato:** to be construed both with *profugus* and *venit* ("came by fate an exile to Italy"), though with *venit* it makes the larger point for the epic: it was Aeneas' "fate to reach Italy." **Laviniaque:** *Lavinia* is an adjectival form of *Lavinium*, the city Aeneas founds; it must be scanned as four syllables by construing the second *i* as a consonant. The adjectival form *Lavinaque* is also found in the manuscripts but is probably a "correction" for the more difficult *Laviniaque*.

3. **multum ille...multa quoque (5):** "much buffeted on land and on sea...having suffered much too in war ...." This pleonastic use of *ille* (i.e. *ille* is syntactically unnecessary here) is an archaism (Servius) and draws marked attention to the storm-tossed and war-worn hero. The passage echoes *Odyssey* 1.1-3: "the man, who was driven far off course after he sacked the holy city of Troy...and in his heart endured many pains at sea."

4. **superum:** Virgil commonly uses this contracted genitive in *-um* (sometimes written *om* when *v* precedes) with proper names (cf. *Danaum, Teucrum, Argivum*) or names describing a class of persons as here (cf. also *divum*; *socium* (5.174)). **Iunonis ob iram:** introduction of the theme of Juno's wrath, cf. 12-33 n. and 27 n. The motif of divine wrath also opens the *Iliad* ("Sing, Muse, of the wrath of Achilles...") and occurs at *Odyssey* 1.20-1 (Poseidon "raged unceasingly at godlike Odysseus until he reached his homeland.")

5. **multa quoque...:** cf. 3 n. **dum conderet urbem:** here *dum* with the subjunctive expresses the aim and object of all Aeneas' wanderings and sufferings; he endured everything "until he could found a city," which would be called Lavinium.

(imp)   *plural always*

inferretque deos Latio—genus unde Latinum
Albanique patres atque altae moenia Romae.
Musa, mihi causas memora, quo numine laeso
quidve dolens regina deum tot volvere casus
insignem pietate virum, tot adire labores   10

---

6. **inferretque deos Latio:** *Latio* is dative after the compound verb *inferret.* Aeneas famously conveyed the *penates* (household gods) out of burning Troy, as the end of Book 2 recounts. This deed is emblematic of Aeneas' *pietas* and of the religious and cultural connection between Troy and Rome. **unde …:** "whence," referring back to Aeneas and his struggles just described.

7. **Albanique patres:** Ascanius will assume power after his father Aeneas has died and will eventually found Alba Longa. See 267-77 with notes. **Romae:** note that Rome is the climax of the long sentence (1-7), mirroring the fact that the city is also the result, though distant, of Aeneas' struggles. Cf. 1 n.

8-11. The invocation of the Muse is traditional. Vergil, however, adapts the tradition. He "asks the Muse not for the story (as Homer does) but for the reasons behind the story" (Williams). Vergil thus raises a question that will plague Aeneas throughout the epic: Why should a pious man suffer Juno's anger so relentlessly? In an important sense, the epic explores the answer to this question by examining the nature both of divine wrath and of the quintessential Roman virtue *pietas.*

8. **quo numine laeso:** probably not "what god having been insulted?," for it is clear that Juno alone is referred to (cf. 9 *quidve dolens regina deum*). *Numen* must mean "her own divine power." Thus: "for what insult to her divine majesty?" (lit. "what divine majesty of hers having been insulted?").

9. **volvere casus:** "to endure continuously so many misfortunes." The idea expressed in *volvere* is that of a cycle of disasters that have to be passed through. The metaphor* is probably derived from the movements of the heavenly bodies and the seasons, cf. 234 *volventibus annis,* 269 *volvendis mensibus.*

10. **insignem pietate virum:** throughout the epic, Vergil defines Aeneas by his *pietas* (cf. *pius Aeneas* 378), though this virtue is never explicitly defined. It involves duty and affection for one's family (*parentes, propinqui*), country (*patria*), and gods (especially those of one's home or country). It is a defining component of both moral leadership and heroism (151 *pietate gravem et meritis…virum;* 544-5 *Aeneas…quo iustior alter / nec pietate fuit, nec bello maior et armis*). Aeneas is especially "pious" from his care of the Penates, and for having carried his father from the flames of Troy.

> impulerit. tantaene animis caelestibus irae?
>   Vrbs antiqua fuit (Tyrii tenuere coloni)
> Karthago, Italiam contra Tiberinaque longe
> ostia, dives opum studiisque asperrima belli;

---

11. **impulerit**: emphatic enjambment; "drove to endure" (*volvere* 9) and "to face" (*adire* 10). *Impulerit* takes an infinitive, as if it were a verb expressing a desire. The infinitive is so convenient a form, and the final dactyl or trochee which it provides so useful metrically, that the poets extend its use and introduce it after verbs where a subordinate clause would be more common. (Cf. 2.55 *impulerat foedare* and 105 *ardemus scitari*.) **tantaene animis caelestibus irae?**: *animis caelestibus* is dative of possessor. Such questioning of the gods' behavior by the poet contrasts with the openings of the Homeric poems. It is therefore startling but gets to the heart of Aeneas' difficult situation.

12-33: Juno's hatred of the Trojans

    The poet had asked in 8-11 why Juno so hates Aeneas; in this section we are given the reasons. Foremost among them is Rome's fated destruction of Carthage, Juno's favorite city, in the Punic Wars nearly a millennium later (cf. 20 n.). Thus Aeneas suffers not so much because of his own actions against Juno, but because fate has given him a role in events that the goddess will vigorously resist (cf. 32 n.): He is to lead the Trojans from their fallen city to Italy, where their descendants will eventually found the city of Rome, Carthage's future conqueror. For more on the nature of Juno's fury, see Johnston (2002) and Syed (2005) 107-13.

12. **antiqua:** "ancient" (i.e. from the perspective of Vergil's own day), but the adjective also conveys nobility (Servius). There may be a wordplay or paronomasia* here, since the city's name *Karthago* (13) means *nova civitas* in Punic (see Servius on line 366). For more on the possible wordplay and discussion of the theme of the ancient city in the epic, see Reed (2007) 129-47. **Tyrii:** "Tyrians." Carthage is a colony founded by Dido, who had to flee her city of Tyre. See 340-68 for this story. In the narrative time of the *Aeneid*, Carthage is just being built (see, e.g., 419-40). **tenuere:** *tenuerunt*. The alternative ending *–ere* of the third person plural perfect indicative active is used often in Vergil. Understand *eam* (i.e. *urbem*) as direct object.

13. **Karthago:** Carthage, a city in Northern Africa (in modern Tunis). **contra…:** "opposite," takes *Italiam* and *Tiberinaque…ostia* as objects, and should be understood in geographical and historical terms. Cf. 20 n., and 4.628-9. **Italiam contra…:** here the preposition follows its object, a stylistic feature called anastrophe* that Virgil employs frequently (e.g. 32, 218). *Karthago* and *Italiam* are opposed syntactically as they will be militarily. **longe:** construe with *contra*.

14. **dives opum:** "rich in resources," describing Carthage; the genitive follows adjectives that indicate want or fulness, cf. 343, 441. **studiis:** ablative of respect explaining how Carthage is (or will be) *asperrima*. *Dives opum* and *studiis asperrima belli* anticipate the greatness of Carthage, when the city will fight Rome in the Punic Wars (cf. 20 n.).

quam Iuno fertur terris magis omnibus unam   15
posthabita coluisse Samo: hic illius arma,
hic currus fuit; hoc regnum dea gentibus esse,
si qua fata sinant, iam tum tenditque fovetque.
progeniem sed enim Troiano a sanguine duci

w/ Samo having esteemed less

---

15. **quam:** object of *coluisse* (16); its antecedent is *Karthago* (13). **fertur:** "is said to…" With this use of the verb, Vergil suggests that he is relating traditional information. **magis omnibus unam:** lit. "alone more than all (other) lands," i.e. "far more than all other lands." Note that the *unam* is juxtaposed against and thus increases the force of *magis omnibus*, which is virtually a superlative ("more than all" = "most"). *Unus*, which has by itself a superlative force, is sometimes added to superlatives or expressions equivalent to a superlative to give emphasis, cf. 2.426 *iustissimus unus*, "most just of all men."

16. **posthabita...Samo:** ablative absolute. *Posthabeo* means "esteem less." *Samos* (f.), an island off the coast of Asia Minor, was home to one of the most famous buildings of the ancient world, the *Heraeum* or "temple of Hera" (= Juno). Cf. Herodotus 3.60. At Carthage, Juno was associated with the Carthaginian goddess Tanit, and was celebrated in Africa as Juno Caelestis. **Samo: hic:** note the hiatus, the "gap" (lit. "yawning") created when two syllables, which would normally be elided, are not, usually when the preceding syllable receives special emphasis, as here the final syllable of *Samo* coincides with the metrical ictus. (The *h* in *hic* was also possibly regarded as partly consonantal, cf. 5.735 *colo. huc*). Elsewhere in the first six books of the *Aeneid* instances of hiatus occur only in lines containing proper names, cf. 617 n., or for a special effect as in 4.667 *femineo ululatu*. (In 4.235 *spe inimica* is an exception.) **hic illius arma:** *fuerunt* must be understood from 17. *Hic* is the adverb "here" (i.e. at Carthage). Note that the genitive *-ius* has a short *i*, as often in poetry. **arma:** Juno was traditionally depicted with a sword and shield, emblems suggesting her warlike nature. Cf. 2.614.

17. **currus:** Juno's "chariot" is described at *Iliad* 5.720-32. **hoc regnum...:** "that this (*hoc* = Carthage) be an empire (*regnum*) to nations (i.e. hold sway over them) even then she makes her object and her care." *Hoc...esse* is an accusative and infinitive construction following the sense of "wish" or "desire" contained strongly in *tendit* and less strongly in *fovet* (cf. 18 n.).

18. **si qua fata sinant:** *qua* is long and is therefore the indefinite adverb (not the indefinite adjective modifying *fata*); *si qua* with the subjunctive expresses great doubt and almost despair of the result. **iam tum:** "already then," emphasizing the deep-rooted nature of Juno's love for Carthage. **fovet:** describes the "cherishing" care which a parent bestows on a child.

19. **sed enim:** "but indeed," an archaic combination of which Vergil was fond (Quintilian 9.3.14). The sense is: "but (in spite of her efforts she had her fears), for she had heard…" **duci:** "was springing," lit. "was being drawn out."

audierat Tyrias olim quae verteret arces;   20
hinc populum late regem belloque superbum
venturum excidio Libyae: sic volvere Parcas.
id metuens veterisque memor Saturnia belli,
prima quod ad Troiam pro caris gesserat Argis
(necdum etiam causae irarum saevique dolores   25

---

20. **Tyrias...arces:** note the artistic positioning, whereby the adjective ends at the strong caesura (i.e. the word break following the first syllable of a metrical foot; see Appendix A) in the third foot and the noun falls at line end. **verteret:** *verteret* ("overthrow") is subjunctive in a relative clause of purpose with *progeniem* as antecedent. Note the delay of the relative pronoun, common in poetry. The rivalry between Rome and Carthage led to the three Punic wars (264-241, 218-201, 149-146 BCE) and ended in the total destruction of Carthage (including Juno's temple) by the Roman general Scipio Aemilianus in 146 BCE. **olim:** "some day," construe with *verteret.*

21-2. **hinc:** i.e. from the race of Troy. **populum late regem...venturum (esse)...sic volvere Parcas:** the accusative and infinitive construction set off by *audierat* (20) continues. **populum...late regem:** "a people ruling widely" (i.e. Rome); the adverb *late* qualifies the noun *regem*, which is adjectival in force. Cf. 181 *prospectum late,* and Horace, *Odes* 3.17.9 *late tyrannus.* **superbum:** conveys Juno's hatred of Rome. Note that Anchises at 6.853 foretells that the Romans will *debellare superbos.* **venturum excidio Libyae:** double dative construction (AG §382), "would come for the destruction of Libya," i.e. be the ruin of Libya; cf. 298-9 *pateant...hospitio Teucris,* "may be open for lodging for the Trojans" (i.e. to welcome the Trojans). **sic volvere Parcas:** "thus the Fates decreed" (lit. "unrolled their plans," "spindles," or some other understood object of *volvere*). Cf. 262.

23. **id:** i.e. the prophesied greatness of Rome and destruction of Carthage. **veterisque...belli:** the "old war" (i.e. the Trojan war), objective genitive dependent on *memor.* **Saturnia:** see 47 n.

24. **prima:** she had "first" helped the Greeks in their war against Troy; this word is contrasted with the fresh attacks on the Trojans which her zeal for Carthage inspired. But *prima* can also mean "foremost" (i.e. among those attacking Troy); cf. Juno at the sacking of Troy (2.612-13): *hic Iuno Scaeas saevissima porta/ prima tenet.* **pro caris...Argis:** *Argis* is ablative masculine plural (though in Greek the city's name is neuter singular), and here stands for the "Greeks" more generally. Juno had a special connection to the Argives. Her most famous temple was at Argos, and in Homer she is given the epithet "Argive" (e.g. *Iliad* 4.8).

25. **necdum etiam...:** lines 25-8 interrupt the flow by including this parenthesis explaining the causes of Juno's hatred of Troy that precede even the Trojan war. At 29, the original flow of thought is resumed with the words *his accensa super,* and we are told of her present tormenting of the Trojans. **saevique dolores:** this phrase, describing Juno's pain that sets the epic in motion, is echoed by the *saevi monimenta doloris* (i.e. Pallas' sword-belt, 12.945) that incites Aeneas to kill Turnus at the end of the epic (see de Grummond (1981)).

exciderant animo; manet alta mente repostum
iudicium Paridis spretaeque iniuria formae
et genus invisum et rapti Ganymedis honores) —
his accensa super iactatos aequore toto
Troas, reliquias Danaum atque immitis Achilli,   30
arcebat longe Latio, multosque per annos
errabant acti fatis maria omnia circum.
tantae molis erat Romanam condere gentem.

26. **manet:** emphatic by position. **alta mente:** "in her deep mind," i.e. deep in her mind.
repostum: by syncope (lit. "cutting short"; the contraction of a vowel or syllable in the middle
of a word) for *repositum* ("stored away"), which metrically cannot be used in a hexameter.

27. **iudicium Paridis:** elaborated in the remainder of the line. **spretaeque...formae:**
appositional genitive (AG §343d) following *iniuria*, "the insult of her scorned beauty" (i.e.
the insult involved in the scorning of her beauty). The shepherd Paris was asked by Juno,
Minerva, and Venus to judge who was the most beautiful goddess. He decided in favor of
Venus.

28. **genus invisum:** the Trojans were also "hateful" to Juno because Dardanus, their ancestor,
was the son of Jupiter by Electra, of whom Juno was jealous. **Ganymedis:** genitive. While
hunting on Mt. Ida, Ganymede, son of Tros, was carried off by an eagle to become the cupbearer of Jove; a homoerotic aspect to their relationship developed as part of the tradition.
This story is embroidered on the cloak described at 5.252-7.

29. **his accensa super:** *his* = "by these things" (i.e. the things mentioned in lines 25-8; cf. 25
n.). *Super* can be taken as an adverb, "in addition" (to the things mentioned in 23-4, i.e.
the Trojan war and the fates of Carthage and Rome), and should be translated closely with
accensa.

30. **reliquias Danaum...:** lit. "the leavings of the Greeks" (i.e. those not killed by the
Greeks), in apposition to *Troas*. The first syllable of *reliquias* is lengthened by metrical
necessity (it is sometimes written *relliquias*). **Danaum:** *Dana(or)um*; cf. 4 n. **Achilli:** for
this genitive, see 120 n.

32. **errabant:** The Trojans suddenly become subject, as we are told of their wanderings as a
result of Juno's hatred. **acti fatis:** probably with two meanings — fate requires that the
Trojans travel across the Mediterranean to Italy, while fate has also turned Juno into their
enemy who makes them endure innumerable hardships. Cf. 2 *fato profugus*. **maria omnia
circum:** the preposition *circum* follows its objects, an example of anastrophe*.

33. **tantae molis erat:** "it was (of) such a great task to found the race of Rome." The phrase
tantae molis is genitive of description. Vergil thus concludes this section on the causes of
Juno's anger with memorable grandeur and thematic resonance for the poem. **condere:**
note that this verb, describing the founding of Rome, will also be used innovatively to
describe Aeneas' slaying of Turnus (*condit* 12.950). James (1995) 624 sees the connection
between these two passages (and others that use *condere* in depicting the deaths of Italian
warriors) as pointing to "the violence and fury beneath the founding of Rome."

34-222: Juno's shipwreck of the Trojans

In 12-33, we learned the causes of Juno's hatred of Aeneas; we now see that hatred in action. She persuades Aeolus (king of the winds) to send a terrible storm against Aeneas. Though Neptune ultimately quells it, the storm shipwrecks the Trojans at Carthage. Juno here acts as a figure of *furor*, who opposes Aeneas, the epic's figure of *pietas*, and thus dramatizes one of the recurring motifs of the epic. Throughout the *Aeneid*, we will see figures of *pietas* attempting to control *furor*, both their own and that of other characters. This particular manifestation of the theme has important divine and cosmic implications. By resisting fate (39) and by persuading Aelous to create a storm in violation of his duty to Jupiter (see 50-64 n.), Juno poses a significant threat to the stability of the cosmos and Jupiter's control of it.

The opposition between *furor* and *pietas* is central to the epic. In optimistic or Augustan intpretations, *pietas* prevails (e.g. Pöschl (1962) and Otis (1964); cf. Introduction). The opposition, however, becomes increasingly complex as the poem proceeds, since characters of *pietas* also act with *furor*. Most famously, Aeneas is *furiis accensus* (12.946), when he slays Turnus (see especially the discussions in Putnam (1965, 1995)).

This passage is closely modeled on *Odyssey* 5.282-493, where the god Poseidon (= Neptune) sees his enemy Odysseus sailing home peacefully from Calypso's island and is angered. He sends a storm that will ultimately be stopped by Athena but will leave Odysseus shipwrecked at Phaeacia. The contrasts between the two heroes are especially important because they establish a basic distinction that will run throughout the *Aeneid*. Odysseus is most concerned with his personal glory, while Aeneas will come to reject this heroic outlook and instead base his actions in the overall good of his community. Moreover, the contrasting actions of the sea god in these epics also signal the changed world of Vergil's poem: while Poseidon/Neptune had been the god of wrath who sends a storm in the *Odyssey*, in the *Aeneid*'s corresponding scene he functions as a force of calm and order.

For a general interpretation of the scene, see Pöschl (1962) 13-24, Otis (1964) 227-34, R. D. Williams (1965-66), Anderson (2005) 24-6, McKay (1989), Perkell (1999) 33-42, and R. A. Smith (2005) 12-20. On Juno and the gods, see Feeney (1991) 129-37. On Aeolus, see Phillips (1980). On the literary background, see Knauer (1964a); Hardie (1986) 90-7, 103-10, 180-3, and 237-40; Nelis (2001) 67-73.

Vix e conspectu Siculae telluris in altum   *[plowing?]*
vela dabant laeti et spumas salis aere ruebant,   35
cum Iuno aeternum servans sub pectore vulnus
haec secum: "mene incepto desistere victam
nec posse Italia Teucrorum avertere regem?
quippe vetor fatis. Pallasne exurere classem
Argivum atque ipsos potuit summergere ponto   40

34-49. Juno is outraged as she sees the Trojans set sail from Sicily for Italy and chastises herself for not doing more to stop them.

34. **Vix e conspectu…:** Vergil, like Homer, plunges at once "into the middle of things" (*in medias res,* Horace, *Ars Poetica* 148). The events described here pick up from the end of Book 3, where Aeneas concludes his two-book flashback. **in altum:** "into the deep," i.e. "out to sea."

35. **laeti:** "happily," as often the adjective can be translated adverbially. **spumas salis:** note the use of the *s*-sounds that perhaps evoke the sound of the sea. **aere:** the prows were covered with brass. **ruebant:** "were driving before them."

36. **aeternum…vulnus:** *vulnus* can be used of psychological "wounding" as well as of physical. For the causes of Juno's pain, cf. 19-28; for the artistic positioning of the phrase, cf. 20 n. Note the heavy metrical quality of this line.

37-8. **haec secum:** "thus to herself" (lit. "these things (she speaks) with herself"). The verb of "saying" is often omitted when the sense is clear, cf. 76, 335, 370, 559. **mene incepto:** "am I, defeated, then to desist from my purpose…?" This use of an accusative (*mene*) and infinitive (*desistere, posse*) interrogatively without a principal verb expresses strong indignation (cf. 97). The elision of *mene* and the initial vowel of *incepto* may produce a word play on the Greek word *menin* ("wrath"), the first word of the *Iliad* describing Achilles' wrath (Levitan (1993)). **Italia:** ablative of separation. **Teucrorum:** the Trojans were called *Teucri* after Teucer, their first king.

39. **quippe vetor fatis:** *quippe* gives a reason with considerable emphasis, which must be judged from the context. Here it expresses indignant scorn—"Because—a fine reason indeed!— I am forbidden by the fates." Cf. 59 and 661. Juno's subsequent actions will show that, while fate might mandate a certain outcome, she has the ability to influence the path to it, an idea echoed in her words at 7.310-16, as she decides to incite the war that will occupy the second half of the epic. **Pallasne…:** emphatically placed, suggesting Juno's rivalry with her. **exurere…submergere (40):** notice how skillfully the double horror of destruction by fire and water is suggested.

40. **Argivum:** for this genitive plural, cf. 4 n. **ipsos:** "(the Argives) themselves," i.e. men in contrast to their fleet.

unius ob noxam et furias Aiacis Oilei?
ipsa Iovis rapidum iaculata e nubibus ignem
disiecitque rates evertitque aequora ventis,
illum exspirantem transfixo pectore flammas
turbine corripuit scopuloque infixit acuto;   45
ast ego, quae divum incedo regina Iovisque
et soror et coniunx, una cum gente tot annos

---

41. **unius ob noxam…:** the second half of the line introduced with *et* explains and makes clear the first, "for one man's guilt and the frenzy of Ajax" (= "for one man's guilt, namely the frenzy of Ajax"). Cf. 27, 54. The phrase has a pointed parallel in Venus' later complaint about Juno: *unius ob iram* (1.251).

    On the night of Troy's sack, Ajax son of Oileus (so called to distinguish him from the greater Ajax son of Telamon, the subject of Sophocles' *Ajax*) dragged the Trojan priestess Cassandra from Pallas' temple (where she had taken refuge) and raped her. For this, he was punished by the goddess. See 2.403-6, and Euripides, *Trojan Women* 69-71. For the genitive *Oili* or *Oilei*, cf. 120 n.

42. **ipsa:** emphatic, "(Pallas) herself," "with her own hands." Juno accentuates Pallas' power to contrast with her own seeming weakness. **Iovis…ignem:** i.e. lightning, which set fire to the ships. **iaculata:** supply *est*. The omission of *esse*-forms from compound passives and deponents in the third person is common. Such omissions also occur in the first and second person, though much less frequently, and usually when a deponent verb is involved.

43. **disiecitque…evertitque:** the *-que…-que* construction binds the two verbs more closely than a single *et* would have, thus heightening Juno's indignation. In Euripides, *Trojan Women* 69-97 (see also 41 n.), the storm is created by Zeus and Poseidon, though Pallas is granted the use of Zeus' lightning-bolts. Virgil differs: by attributing the storm itself to Pallas (e.g. *evertitque aequora ventis*) without mention of the other gods, his version increases the goddess' power and ability to fulfill her wrath.

44. **illum:** "but him." The emphatic placement of this strong pronoun contrasts with the preceding line so forcibly that no adversative particle is needed — "she both scattered the ships and upheaved the sea with storm; *him* she seized…," cf. 184 n. **transfixo pectore:** pierced, that is, by a thunderbolt (42). A different version of Ajax's death (at the hands of Poseidon/Neptune) is given at Homer, *Odyssey* 4.499-511.

46. **ast ego:** contrasted with *ipsa* (42). *Ast* ("but") is an archaism for *at*. **divum:** cf. 4 n. **incedo:** "stride"; the verb suggests Juno's majesty as she walks among the gods (*cum aliqua dignitate ambulare*, Servius). Cf. 405, 497; 5.68, 553.

47. **soror:** Juno and Jupiter were children of Saturn, as was Neptune (cf. 130). She is thus often called *Saturnia* (cf. 23). **una cum gente tot annos:** refers to her part in the ten-year war against the Trojans.

bella gero. et quisquam numen Iunonis adorat
praeterea aut supplex aris imponet honorem?"
    Talia flammato secum dea corde volutans   50
nimborum in patriam, loca feta furentibus Austris,
Aeoliam venit. hic vasto rex Aeolus antro
luctantis ventos tempestatesque sonoras
imperio premit ac vinclis et carcere frenat.
illi indignantes magno cum murmure montis   55
circum claustra fremunt; celsa sedet Aeolus arce

48-9. **et quisquam…:** Quintilian cites this as an example of a rhetorical question* (9.2.10).
Et conveys Juno's indignation. **praeterea:** usually means "besides," but here it means
"after this," i.e. after I have appeared so helpless, cf. *Georgics* 4.502 *neque…praeterea vidit*,
"nor saw after that." **imponet:** the manuscripts are divided among this reading, *imponit*,
and *imponat*. The future *imponet*, however, seems preferable, as it best heightens Juno's
indignation. **aris:** perhaps dative after the compound verb *imponet*.

50-64. Juno asks king Aeolus to create a terrible storm by releasing the violent winds he rules.
Aeolus and his violent winds appear in *Odyssey* 10.1-79, an episode that displays the distrust
between Odysseus and his comrades. In the *Aeneid*, Aeolus plays a more central role, not
simply because he aids Juno in motivating books 1-6 (see Introduction). Aeolus is a ruler
who misuses his power (*imperium*) not to control passion (57) but to excite it. By rousing the
winds, he violates Jupiter's will (60-3). In addition, Vergil conveys the cosmic ramifications
of Aeolus' actions by incorporating images and metaphors concerning the Titans and Giants
who had fought against the gods (Hardie (1986) 90-7). Aeolus is thus perfectly allied with
Juno, the epic's representative of *furor* and of resistance to Jupiter and fate.

50. **flammato…corde:** "…this metaphorical use [of *flammato*] is not recorded earlier"
(Austin). **volutans:** describes "constant turning over" in the mind, cf. 305 *volvens*.

51. **loca…:** in apposition to *nimborum in patriam*, "a land teeming with raving (south-)
winds." *Austri* loosely describes any "violent winds." **furentibus:** on *furor*, cf. 50-64 n.

52. **Aeoliam:** also in apposition to *nimborum in patriam* (51). Vergil (8.416-17) identifies
Aeolia with Lipara, one of the volcanic islands off the northern coast of Sicily. In Homer,
Aeolus (*Od.* 10) dwells on a floating island.

53. Observe the accommodation of sound to sense in this line of only four words, arranged in
chiastic* order, whereby parallel constructions are expressed in reverse word order

54. **imperio:** a central concern of book 1. Cf. 138, 230, 270, 279, 287, and 340. See notes on
50-64 and 279.

55. **illi:** i.e. the winds. "The shift from object (*uentos*, 53) to subject is a characteristic
Virgilian device, giving variety and emphasis together" (Austin). **magno cum murmure
montis:** ablative of manner or attendant circumstance, "with a great rumbling of the
mountain." Note the alliteration*.

56. **celsa…arce:** "in his lofty citadel."

sceptra tenens mollitque animos et temperat iras;
ni faciat, maria ac terras caelumque profundum
quippe ferant rapidi secum verrantque per auras.
sed pater omnipotens speluncis abdidit atris   60
hoc metuens molemque et montis insuper altos
imposuit, regemque dedit qui foedere certo
et premere et laxas sciret dare iussus habenas.
ad quem tum Iuno supplex his vocibus usa est:
    "Aeole, namque tibi divum pater atque hominum rex   65

---

57. **mollit…temperat iras:** on the ruler's calming of violence, cf. 148-53, 291-6 with notes.
animos: "'passions,' perhaps with some play on the Greek word for wind, ênemow,
connected etymologically with *animus*" (Williams).

58. **ni faciat…ferant:** future less vivid condition, "if he should not do this…" (AG §516 b).
maria ac terras caelumque profundum: note the effective use of this tricolon* to describe
the different parts of the cosmos.

59. **quippe:** cf. 39 n. The natural order would be *quippe, ni faciat,* "for surely, otherwise";
quippe, however, is transposed to give it emphasis (cf. 4.218). **verrant:** "would sweep them
(i.e. *maria ac terras caelumque*) away"

60. **pater omnipotens:** *omnipotens* is a grand epithet for Jupiter that goes back to the early
Latin poet Ennius (and in Greek back to Homer). It occurs nine times in the *Aeneid*.

61. **hoc:** accusative, "this," referring back to 58-9. **metuens:** cf. Juno in 23. **molemque
et montis:** "massive mountains." A good instance of hendiadys*, the use of two words
or phrases put simply side by side instead of a single complex phrase in which the
words qualify each other: cf. 111 *brevia et syrtis,* "the shoals of the S.," 210, 293 *ferro et
compagibus,* "iron fastenings," 504, 648 *signis auroque.* **insuper:** adverb, "on top (of the
winds)."

62. **imposuit:** note the emphatic enjambment* of this word, followed by a strong caesura (cf.
20 n.). **regem:** i.e. Aeolus. **foedere certo:** the *foedus* represents the "terms" by which Jupiter
gave Aeolus rule over the winds. By aiding Juno, however, Aeolus will seemingly violate
this *foedus.* **qui…sciret:** relative clause of characteristic (AG §535) or of purpose (AG
§537), cf. 20, 236, 287.

63. **premere:** cf. 11.600 *pressis habenis.* **laxas…dare:** "is equivalent to *laxare*" (Williams).
iussus: i.e. by Jupiter, cf. 62 n. In this line, the winds are likened to horses through the
metaphor* of tightening and loosening the reins.

65-75. "Aeolus, destroy the Trojan fleet, and I will reward you with the nymph Deiopea as wife."

65. **Aeole, namque…:** the clause introduced by *namque* explains why Juno appeals to Aeolus
(cf. 731 *Iuppiter, hospitibus nam te dare iura loquuntur…*). **divum…rex:** an Ennian phrase
(*Annales,* fr. 207 in Warmington, fr. 203 in Skutsch) with Homeric echoes (cf. Homer,
Iliad 1.544). The monosyllabic line ending lends archaic dignity. *Divum* is genitive, cf. 4 n.

et mulcere dedit fluctus et tollere vento,
gens inimica mihi Tyrrhenum navigat aequor
Ilium in Italiam portans victosque penatis:
incute vim ventis summersasque obrue puppis,
aut age diversos et disice corpora ponto.   70
sunt mihi bis septem praestanti corpore Nymphae,
quarum quae forma pulcherrima, Deiopea,

66. **et mulcere dedit…:** the infinitives *mulcere* and *tollere* function as objects of *dedit*. The infinitive after *do* is extremely common in Vergil: 1.) sometimes it is equivalent to a verbal noun used as the direct object of the verb, as here *mulcere dedit* "gave the calming" (cf. 522-3 *condere dedit*, "granted the founding"); 2.) sometimes it seems epexegetic or added to give further "explanation," as in *dat ferre talentum*, "he gives them a talent to take away," cf. 319 n. **vento:** emphatic and goes with both infinitives. For this line, cf. Aeolus at Homer, *Odyssey* 10.22, where Zeus gave Aelous the power "both to stop and to rouse" (ἠμὲν παυέμεναι ἠδ' ὀρνύμεν) the winds.

67. **gens inimica mihi:** note the emphasis on *mihi*, which falls at the strong caesura (cf. App. A). **Tyrrhenum…aequor:** accusative of extent of space with an intransitive verb (*navigat*), a poetic construction. This sea is located between the western coast of Italy, Sicily and Sardinia.

68. **Ilium in Italiam:** *Ilium* is another name for Troy. This line refers to Aeneas' performance of his fate (cf. 1.5-7; 2.293-5); the merging of Troy and Italy may also be suggested by the presence of elision*, assonance*, and consonance*. **victos…penatis:** these are the state gods that Aeneas carried out of Troy on the night of its fall (cf. 2.747). For the etymology of *penatis*, see 703-4 n.

69. **incute…:** "hurl rage into the winds," an unusual variation on the use of *incutere* in the common phrase *incutere timorem alicui*, "to strike terror into any one"; Ennius has *Romanis incutit iram*. **summersasque obrue puppis:** *summersas* substitutes for the imperative, representing an action that must precede *obrue*, "sink and overwhelm the ships."

70. **age diversos:** "drive (the men) scattered," i.e. "so that they become scattered." For this prolepsis*, in which the adjective expresses by anticipation that which is the effect of the verb, cf. 259-60 *furentem incendat* "kindle to frenzy."

71. **bis septem…Nymphae:** Juno's bribe looks back to Hera's offer of one of the Graces to the god Sleep (Homer, *Iliad* 14.267-8). **bis septem:** a poetic fomulation for "fourteen." **praestanti corpore:** ablative of quality (AG §415).

72. **forma:** ablative of specification. **Deiopea:** what should be the accusative after *iungam* is placed in the relative clause and attracted to the nominative case of the relative. Note how the line concludes with a polysyllabic Greek name.

conubio iungam stabili propriamque dicabo,
omnis ut tecum meritis pro talibus annos
exigat et pulchra faciat te prole parentem."   75
    Aeolus haec contra: "tuus, o regina, quid optes
explorare labor; mihi iussa capessere fas est.
tu mihi quodcumque hoc regni, tu sceptra Iovemque
concilias, tu das epulis accumbere divum
nimborumque facis tempestatumque potentem."   80

---

73. **conubio...stabili:** ablative of means. *Conubium* is the Roman legal term for marriage. The quantity of the *u* is short here (as in *coniubiis* at 3.136 and *coniubio* at 4.126), though it is long in *coniubia* at 3.319; 4.213, 316, 535. In the latter instances, the *u* falls on the metrical ictus, which may explain its long quantity. **propriamque dicabo:** *proprius* is a very strong word that expresses abiding possession, while *dico* ("pronounce") is a ritual word. Juno repeats this line at 4.126, when she conspires with Venus to have Aeneas and Dido meet in a cave. Juno specially presided over marriage under the title of *Iuno Pronuba* (cf. 4.166).

74-5. **ut...exigat et...faciat:** purpose clause. **omnis...annos:** accusative of duration; note the artful enclosing structure of these words. **pulchra...prole:** ablative of means or of description (AG §409, 415).

76-80. Aeolus replies: "I will obey your commands, for I owe my kingdom to you."

76. **contra:** adverb, " in response." A verb of speaking (e.g. *dixit*) must be supplied. **tuus...:** note the emphatic and contrastive placement of *tuus* and *mihi* (77); cf. 184 n. **quid optes:** indirect question after *explorare*.

77. **fas est:** ironic, since Aeolus is supposed to follow the will of Jupiter (cf. 60-3), which Juno's actions seemingly undermine. Aeolus acts more subserviently than had Homer's Sleep in a similar circumstance (cf. 71 n.).

78. **quodcumque hoc regni:** the phrase is modestly depreciatory ("this realm such as it is"), as Aelous emphasizes his debt to Juno. **tu...:** note the emphatic repetition (anaphora*) of *tu* here and in 79 that structures an extended tricolon crescendo* describing Juno's powers in 78-80.

79. **concilias:** two different meanings must be understood — with the objects *quodcumque hoc regni* and *sceptra*, the verb means "secure for"; with *Iovem*, it means "make favorable" or "friendly." Juno's role in the acquisition of Aeolus' power over the winds is unknown before Vergil, though Servius suggests it is because she is queen of the air (Gr. *aer*). **tu das... accumbere:** supply *mihi*; *accumbere* functions as the direct object of *das* ("you grant me (the honor of) reclining"). **epulis:** dative with the compound verb *accumbere*.

80. **nimborum...potentem:** supply *me* with *potentem*. Another rare four-word line (cf. 53). This clause caps a tricolon crescendo* in which Aelous flatteringly emphasizes his indebtedness to Juno's power.

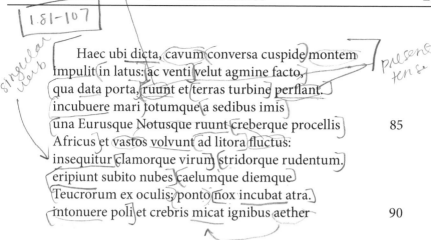

Haec ubi dicta, cavum conversa cuspide montem
impulit in latus: ac venti velut agmine facto,
qua data porta, ruunt et terras turbine perflant.
incubuere mari totumque a sedibus imis
una Eurusque Notusque ruunt creberque procellis   85
Africus et vastos volvunt ad litora fluctus:
insequitur clamorque virum stridorque rudentum.
eripiunt subito nubes caelumque diemque
Teucrorum ex oculis; ponto nox incubat atra.
intonuere poli et crebris micat ignibus aether   90

81-101. Aeolus lets loose the winds which raise a storm against Aeneas, who now wishes he had died at Troy.

81. **Haec ubi dicta:** supply *sunt* (cf. 42 n.). **conversa cuspide:** i.e. the butt end of the spear with which Aeolus strikes the mountain to release the winds. Notice the alliteration* in *cavum conversa cuspide*, which, together with the double *in* and double dactyl *impŭlĭt ĭn lătŭs* followed by a pause in the next line, suggests the ring of the blow on the hollow mountain side.

82. **impulit in latus:** cf. 81 n. **latus:** the gates or barriers (*claustra* 56) of the prison (*carcer*) are apparently in the side of the mountain. **ac:** "and (immediately)"; cf. 227 n. **velut agmine facto:** the winds are like an army in formation. Lines 81-2 resonate with 2.50-2 (*sic fatus validis ingentem viribus hastam / in latus inque feri curvam compagibus alvum/ contorsit*), where Laocoon throws a spear at the side of the wooden horse in which Greek warriors are actually hiding.

83. **qua data porta:** *qua* means "where"; with *data*, supply *est*; *porta* is nominative. Note the assonance* and the alliteration* of *t* in this line.

84. **incubuere:** the perfect of instantaneous action; "straightway they settle on the sea," cf. 90 *intonuere*. **mari:** dative with *incubuere*. **totum:** cf. 85-6 n. Note the placement of verbs at the beginning of the line/clause (also at 87, 88, 90).

85-6. **una…:** cf. Homer, *Odyssey* 5.295-6. Poets continually describe a storm as the fierce clashing of winds that are all abroad at one. Cf. Horace, *Odes* 1.9.10. **Eurus:** the East (or Southeast) wind. **Notus:** the South wind. **ruunt:** transitive with *totum (mare)* as object (84). **Africus:** the Southwest wind. The North wind (*Aquilo*) will appear at 102.

87. **insequitur:** note the emphatic placement. **clamorque virum stridorque rudentum:** note the parallel phrases that describe the storm's physical effect on the ship's cables and its emotional effect on the men. *Virum* is genitive plural (cf. 4 n.).

88-9. **eripiunt…:** cf. Homer, *Odyssey* 5.293-4. The emphatic placement of the verb (cf. 87 n.) helps convey the swiftness and violence of the winds. **ponto:** dative with *incubat*. Note the powerful image of cosmic disruption.

90. **intonuere:** cf. 84 n. **poli:** the plural occurs only here in Vergil and may be pointed — it thunders from pole to pole. **aether:** the fine fiery element which surrounds the universe is naturally spoken of as the home of the lightning.

praesentemque viris intentant omnia mortem,
extemplo Aeneae solvuntur frigore membra;
ingemit et duplicis tendens ad sidera palmas
talia voce refert: "o terque quaterque beati,
quis ante ora patrum Troiae sub moenibus altis   95
contigit oppetere! o Danaum fortissime gentis
Tydide! mene Iliacis occumbere campis
non potuisse tuaque animam hanc effundere dextra,
saevus ubi Aeacidae telo iacet Hector, ubi ingens
Sarpedon, ubi tot Simois correpta sub undis   100
scuta virum galeasque et fortia corpora volvit!"

91. **praesentem:** "imminent." **intentant omnia mortem:** cf. the phrase *ostentant omnia letum*, which Ariadne uses at Catullus 64.187 to describe her hopeless situation after Theseus has left her.

92. **solvuntur:** "are paralyzed," "numbed." **frigore:** = *timore*. The line echoes Homer, *Odyssey* 5.297 (cf. 94-101 n.).

93. **duplicis...palmas:** *duplicis* here (as often) is a more elevated word for "both" than *ambas* (cf. Lucretius 6.1145 *duplices oculi*).

94-101. Aeneas' words echo *Odyssey* 5.306-12, where Odysseus is overwhelmed by a storm sent by Poseidon. But while Odysseus says his comrades were lucky to have died at Troy because they had proper burial and received glory (Gr. *kleos*), Aeneas envies those who died at Troy in the presence of their fathers (*ante ora patrum* 95) but says nothing about burial and glory. "Where Odysseus is pragmatic and goal-oriented, Aeneas is sentimental and despairing" (Perkell (1999) 40).

94. **o terque...beati:** understand *ei erant*, "were they."

95-6. **quis:** = *quibus*, dative with the impersonal verb *contigit* ("it befell"). *Contingo* usually describes a fortunate chance; *accido* an unfortunate one, "an accident." **oppetere:** sc. *mortem*, "meet death," "die."

97-8. **Tydide:** vocative patronymic. Diomedes was the son of Tydeus and would have killed Aeneas at Troy, if not for the intervention of Aphrodite/Venus (Homer, *Iliad* 5.297-317). **mene...non potuisse...?:** "could not I have fallen?" For this construction, cf. 37-8 n. **occumbere:** just as *oppetere* (96) and *obire* are often used absolutely as "to meet (death)," "to die," so *occumbere* is often used to mean "to fall (before the attack of death)." For the full phrase, cf. 2.62 *certae occumbere morti.* **animam hanc:** "this life (of mine)," "my life."

99. **Aeacidae:** "(grand)son of Aeacus" (i.e. Achilles) in the genitive. **telo iacet:** "lies (killed) by the spear." Both *iacet* and *volvit* are graphic presents.

100-1. **Sarpedon:** the great Trojan warrior, son of Jupiter. His death at the hands of Patroclus evokes the god's great sorrow at *Iliad* 16.431-507. (Cf. also Jupiter at *Aen.* 10.467-72.) **Simois:** Trojan river. Cf. *Iliad* 12.22-3: "...Simois, where much ox-hide armour and helmets were tumbled/ in the river mud, and many of the race of the half-god mortals" (Lattimore). **ubi...:** note the expressive repetition. **tot:** construe with the tricolon* of objects *correpta scuta, galeas,* and *fortia corpora.* **virum:** cf. 87 n.

Talia iactanti stridens Aquilone procella
velum adversa ferit, fluctusque ad sidera tollit.
franguntur remi, tum prora avertit et undis
dat latus, insequitur cumulo praeruptus aquae mons.   105
hi summo in fluctu pendent; his unda dehiscens
terram inter fluctus aperit, furit aestus harenis.
tris Notus abreptas in saxa latentia torquet

102-23. The storm rages, and Aeneas sees eleven of his twenty ships sink.

102-3. **Talia iactanti:** ethical dative or dative of disadvantage; "to him," as he was "hurling
such (despairing words)," the following events occur. *Iacto* is often used of passionate
speech (cf. 2.588, 768). **stridens...procella...adversa:** this phrase describes the "whistling
gust" of wind (*stridens procella*) as it strikes the sail "full in front" (*adversa,* lit. "turned
towards"). **Aquilone:** "from the North (wind)," here an ablative explaining the origin of the
stridens procella. For the other winds at play, cf. 85-6 n. **ad sidera:** note the hypberbole* in
the description of the storm from here to 107.

104. **avertit:** used intransitively, "swings away" or "around"; Vergil uses many transitive verbs
as intransitive (cf. 402 *avertens*; 2.94 *tullisset*, 2.235 *accingunt*). The blast of wind strikes
the sail and stops the ship; the bow then swings around and "exposes the side (*latus*) to
the waves." Some reliable manuscripts give *proram,* "then it (the gust) swings the prow
around," but after *franguntur remi* the return to the nominative *procella* is too jarring.

105. **latus:** cf. 104 n. **insequitur:** note the asyndeton* (the omission of connectives between
words, phrases, or sentences) and emphatic position of the verb at the beginning of the
clause. **cumulo:** the ablative used almost adverbially, "in a heap." Cf. 157 *cursu* "in a
hurry"; 2.323 *gemitu* "with a groan," "groaning"; 5.450 *studiis* "eagerly." **aquae mons:** the
line ends with a monosyllabic word; the coincidence of verse and word accent that normally
ends Vergil's hexameter is consequently violated here; the violence of the storm may thus be
suggested.

106-7. **hi...his:** "some men...to other men..." The use of the same word in different cases is
called polyptoton*; here it is combined with anaphora*. **unda...aperit:** "the gaping sea
reveals land (i.e. the floor of the sea) between the waves." The next three words make the
point clear: "the churning waters (*aestus*) rage with sand." Cf. 102-3 n. on hyperbole* in
this passage. Note the forceful placement of the verbs *aperit, furit* next to each other and
with asyndeton*.

108. **tris...abreptas:** understand *navis* (accusative plural); *tris* = *tres*. **abreptas ...torquet:** the
participle *abreptas* stands in for another finite verb, "snatches and hurls." Cf. 69 n. **Notus:**
cf. 85-6 n.

(saxa vocant Itali mediis quae in fluctibus Aras,
dorsum immane mari summo), tris Eurus ab alto   110
in brevia et syrtis urget, miserabile visu,
inliditque vadis atque aggere cingit harenae.
unam, quae Lycios fidumque vehebat Oronten,
ipsius ante oculos ingens a vertice pontus
in puppim ferit: excutitur pronusque magister   115

109. **saxa vocant...Aras:** a parenthesis that interrupts the description of the storm's violence
and resembles a learned footnote. It is introduced by epanalepsis*, the repetition of a word
(i.e. *saxa*, 108), strictly unnecessary, from the preceding clause. **mediis quae in fluctibus:**
understand *sunt* or *latent*. **Aras:** predicate accusative, providing the name of the *saxa*.
Varro and Pliny mention a reef bearing this name between Sicily and Sardinia, though it
is unclear whether this particular reef is meant here. See the discussion in O'Hara (1996)
115-16.

110. **dorsum immane...:** "an ugly ridge" (i.e. in fine weather); in a storm (as here) it is
hidden (thus *saxa latentia*, 108). *Immane* indicates both the size and the dangerous
character of the *saxa*. **tris:** again, supply *navis* (cf. 108); note the anaphora* formed with *tris*
in 108. **Eurus:** cf. 85-6 n.

111. **in brevia et syrtis:** the substantive *brevia* ("shallows") is first used by Vergil; *syrtis* =
"sandbanks." Some read *Syrtis*, referring to sandbanks on this part of the African coast,
especially the *Syrtis Major* and *Minor*; the phrase could then be a hendiadys*, "the shallows
of the Syrtes". **mirabile visu:** "terrible to see" (lit. "with respect to seeing"). *Visu* is the
ablative of respect of the verbal noun or supine of *video*, and limits the meaning of the
neuter adjective *mirabile*. This construction "marks a dramatic way of drawing attention to
the wonderful or the horrible" (Austin). Cf. *mirabile dictu* 2.174, *horrendum dictu* 4.454,
visu mirabile monstrum 10.637.

112. **vadis:** dative with the compound verb *inlidit*, "dashes (the three ships) against the shoals
(*vadis*)."

113. **unam:** with *in puppim* (115), which is set against the massive wave in 114. **Lycios:** Lycia
was in the south of Asia Minor; its people fought for Troy. **Oronten:** the ship's captain,
who will appear in the underworld at 6.334.

114. **ipsius:** i.e. of Aeneas. **ingens a vertice pontus:** cf. Homer, *Odyssey* 5.313. The phrase *a
vertice* "from the height" expresses the fall of something sheer downwards with nothing to
check or impede its fall.

115. **in puppim ferit:** notice the emphatic enjambment* of this phrase, the violent pause after
ferit, and the two dactyls *volvitur in caput* (116) followed by a similar pause – these features
combine to suggest the shock of the falling wave.

volvitur in caput; ast illam ter fluctus ibidem
torquet agens circum et rapidus vorat aequore vertex.
apparent rari nantes in gurgite vasto,
arma virum tabulaeque et Troia gaza per undas.
iam validam Ilionei navem, iam fortis Achatae,   120
et qua vectus Abas, et qua grandaevus Aletes,
vicit hiems; laxis laterum compagibus omnes
accipiunt inimicum imbrem rimisque fatiscunt.

116-17. **in caput:** "headlong" (lit. "on his head"). Note the descriptive details provided about the helmsman; see also 115 n. **ast illam…:** i.e. *puppim* (115); for *ast*, cf. 46 n. For *rapidus*, cf. 59. **ibidem / torquet agens circum:** this phrase expands the idea in *torquet*, "spins the ship (*torquet*), turning it round and round" (lit. "round in the same spot"). **et rapidus vorat aequore vertex:** this dactylic phrase with its soundplays perhaps represents the fierce whirl of the eddy.

118. **rari:** "scattered," in artistic contrast to *vasto*. The heavily spondaic nature of the line perhaps conveys sympathy for the men's plight.

119. **arma virum:** *virum* here is genitive. The phrase recalls the epic's opening. Here, however, the words (and line) convey the Trojans' near-annihilation instead of heralding their ultimate triumph (cf. 1-7). **Troia:** here a dactyl. **gaza:** a Persian word (Servius), pointing to the Eastern heritage of Troy.

120. **iam…iam…et qua…et qua:** the anaphora* of *iam* and of *et qua* conveys the emotion excited by each fresh disaster. Cf. 220-2 n. **Ilionei…Achatae:** genitives. Vergil forms the genitive of Greek nouns variously: those ending in *–eus* have their Latin genitive in *–eos* (as in Greek), *–ei* or *–i* (e.g. *Achilli* in 30 and *Oilei* in 41); those ending in *–es*, have their Latin genitive in *–is*, *–i* (e.g. *Oronti* in 220) or *–ae* (as *Achatae* here; cf. AG §44). Ilioneus and Achates will play roles later in book 1: Achates will accompany Aeneas to Carthage (see, e.g., 579-85), while Ilioneus will represent the Trojans to Dido at 520-60 (and to Latinus at 7.212-48).

121. **et qua vectus…:** = *et (eam navem,* object of *vicit) qua vectus (est) Abas…et qua (vectus est) grandaevus Aletes.* Note how Vergil has varied the phrases describing the ships between these two lines. **Abas…Aletes:** Aletes will play a prominent role in the Trojan council's decision to send Nisus and Euryalus on their night mission (9.224-313); Abas is not mentioned again.

122. **vicit hiems:** the emphatic enjambment* of this terse phrase contrasts with the elaborate two-line description of the ships and warriors that "the storm conquered." **omnes:** i.e. the ships. **laxis…compagibus:** ablative absolute, "with" or "through their (i.e. the ships') loosened joints."

123. **rimisque fatiscunt:** "and gape at their seams," as a result of the splitting of the ships' wood. Note the effective use of assonance* and consonance* in this line, which is enclosed by two verbs. Such features help bring this passage (102-23) to its conclusion.

Interea magno misceri murmure pontum
emissamque hiemem sensit Neptunus et imis   125
stagna refusa vadis, graviter commotus; et alto
prospiciens summa placidum caput extulit unda.
disiectam Aeneae toto videt aequore classem,
fluctibus oppressos Troas caelique ruina.
nec latuere doli fratrem Iunonis et irae.   130
Eurum ad se Zephyrumque vocat, dehinc talia fatur:
   "Tantane vos generis tenuit fiducia vestri?
iam caelum terramque meo sine numine, venti,
miscere et tantas audetis tollere moles?

124-31. Neptune observes the storm and gathers the wind gods to stop it.

124-6. **Interea:** the perspective switches to that of Neptune. **magno misceri murmure:** a favorite alliteration* in describing any uproar (cf. 55). The line is very close to 4.160 (of the storm devised by Juno to drive Dido and Aeneas into a cave, where they consummate their relationship). **emissam...refusa:** supply *esse*; the resulting forms are infinitives in an accusative (*pontum, hiemem, stagna*) and infinitive construction governed by *sensit*. **stagna:** the waters at the bottom of the sea, which are ordinarily undisturbed. **graviter commotus:** "grievously troubled"; the phrase describes the anger of the sea-god but also suggests the disturbance of the sea (which Neptune personified). **alto:** "over the deep," ablative of place; construe with *prospiciens* (127).

127. **summa...unda:** ablative of separation or place from which; the preposition is omitted (AG §426). **placidum:** contrasts with the angry storm and the raging Juno, and also expresses Neptune's dignified self-control in spite of his anger (cf. 126 *graviter commotus*).

128. **toto...aequore:** ablative of place where.

129. **Troas:** Greek accusative, modified by *oppressos*. **caeli...ruina:** "the downfall of the sky" (hypberbole*) Cf. Horace, *Odes* 1.16.11-12 *tremendo / Iuppiter ipse ruens tumultu*. The phrase is here opposed to *fluctibus:* sea and sky conspire to destroy the Trojans.

130. **nec latuere...:** an example of litotes* (the description of something by negating its opposite). *Latuere* is here transitive, "did (not) escape notice of." **fratrem:** "her brother" (i.e. Neptune), cf. 47 n.

131. **dehinc:** "then," scans as a long syllable by synizesis cf. 98 n., 726-7. (AG §642).

132-141. Neptune insultingly upbraids the wind gods.

132. **generis...fiducia vestri:** "trust in your birth," spoken contemptuously, since the winds were minor deities, the offspring of the Titan Astraeus and Aurora.

133. **iam:** emphatic; disorderly before, the winds now encroach on Neptune's authority over his realm. **numine:** "approval" or "authorization." Cf. also 62-3 (with notes).

134. **tantas...moles:** "such great masses" of water (i.e. waves).

quos ego—! sed motos praestat componere fluctus. 135
post mihi non simili poena commissa luetis.
maturate fugam regique haec dicite vestro:
non illi imperium pelagi saevumque tridentem,
sed mihi sorte datum. tenet ille immania saxa,
vestras, Eure, domos; illa se iactet in aula 140
Aeolus et clauso ventorum carcere regnet."
　　Sic ait et dicto citius tumida aequora placat
collectasque fugat nubes solemque reducit.

---

135. **quos ego—! sed…:** a famous instance of aposiopesis* (the abrupt stopping of a sentence or thought for rhetorical effect); here it conveys Neptune's anger. **praestat componere:** "it is better to put in order." Once again, note Neptune's connection with creating calm and order.

136. **post:** "in the future" (adverb), i.e. if the same thing occurs again. **non simili poena:** "not by a similar (= "by a very different," i.e. heavier) punishment." A good instance of litotes*. **commissa luetis:** "will you pay" or "atone for your offences" (neuter plural).

137. **maturate:** transitive imperative. **regi…vestro:** Aelous.

138-9. **illi…ille:** i.e. Aeolus. The repetition of *ille* (cf. also *illa* 140) and the adjective *immania* help convey the disdain Neptune feels for Aeolus. *Illi* is dative (indirect object after *datum*) and emphatically placed both in its own line and when contrasted with *mihi* (139). **imperium…tridentem…datum (esse):** indirect discourse after *dicite* (137). The trident symbolized Neptune's *imperium* over the sea. **sorte:** the three sons of Saturn—Jupiter, Neptune, and Pluto—were said to have divided his empire "by lot," receiving respectively the heavens, the sea, and the underworld. **immania saxa:** "savage rocks," a derogatory description of Aeolus' realm, since *immania* here denotes roughness as well as size.

140. **vestras, Eure, domos:** i.e. "your home, Eurus, and those of your kin." Neptune in addressing Eurus is really addressing all the winds; thus *vestras* (cf. 375). **illa…aula:** again (cf. 138-9 n.) the demonstrative indicates scorn. **se iactet:** "let him boast," jussive subjunctive.

141. **Aeolus:** only now does Neptune utter this name. **clauso:** emphatic; Aeolus may give what orders he likes to the winds, as long as he keeps them imprisoned. **carcere:** the *immania saxa* of 139. **regnet:** jussive subjunctive.

142-156. Neptune immediately calms the water and rescues the ships.

142-3. **dicto citius:** *dicto* is ablative of comparison, "more swiftly than his word" (i.e. before he had finished speaking). **placat:** again note Neptune's calming function (cf. *placidum* 127; *componere* 135). **collectas…fugat:** for the construction, cf. 108 *(navis) abreptas…torquet* (with note). Note how quickly Neptune undoes the specific violence committed by the winds at 84-9, and that the actions he takes are described in a tricolon* of verbs (*placat, fugat, reducit*).

Cymothoe simul et Triton adnixus acuto
detrudunt navis scopulo; levat ipse tridenti   145
et vastas aperit syrtis et temperat aequor
atque rotis summas levibus perlabitur undas.
ac veluti magno in populo cum saepe coorta est
seditio saevitque animis ignobile vulgus;
iamque faces et saxa volant, furor arma ministrat;   150
tum, pietate gravem ac meritis si forte virum quem

144-5. Cymothoe: a Nereid. **Triton:** sea god who attends Neptune. **acuto...scopulo:** ablative of separation with *detrudunt.* **navis:** the three ships mentioned at 108. **ipse:** "Neptune himself." In contrast to his underlings Cymothoe and Triton, Neptune just has to raise his trident to achieve his will.

146. aperit syrtis: "opens" or "makes a way through the sandbanks," in which some of the ships were embedded, cf. 112. **temperat aequor:** repeats the idea in *tumida aequora placat* (142) but creates a tricolon* (with *levat* and *aperit,* joined by *et...et*) of Neptune's quick actions in calming the storm, capped by the majestic description of him gliding over the now tamed water (147).

147. rotis: synecdoche* for "chariot." **summas...undas:** cf. 127.

148-53. Perhaps the most famous simile of the *Aeneid,* one that programmatically presents the defeat of *furor* by a politician characterized by *pietas* (cf. 34-222 n.). It startlingly uses a human event (a man's quelling of civil unrest) to describe both the natural world (the calming of the sea), though Homeric similes usually do the reverse, and the action of a god. The guiding words *veluti* and *sic, cum* and *tum* should be carefully noticed.

     The civil strife in the simile naturally resonates with the discord that preceded Augustus' rise to power and reign, though references to Hesiod, *Works and Days* 81-93 and an actual event involving Cato the younger in 54 BCE (cf. Plutarch, *Cato Minor* 44) have also been suggested as influences. See Conway (1935) *ad loc.* and S. J. Harrison (1988).

148. magno in populo: surely the Roman nation is implied; note the emphatic placement of the phrase at the simile's opening. **cum saepe:** "when often" = "when, as often happens"; cf. 5.273 *qualis saepe.*

149. ignobile vulgus: set in contrast to the *pietate gravem...virum* (151).

150. furor: the *furor* of the masses recalls the fury of the stormy sea (*furit aestus,* 107) and thus also the fury of Juno. The comparison of Neptune to a man of *pietas* who quells *furor* here will thus also connect Neptune to Augustus, who will be described as subduing *Furor impius* (294).

151. virum quem: *quem* is the indefinite adjective modifying *virum.* **pietate gravem ac meritis:** "honored for *pietas* and noble deeds," modifies *virum quem.* Note that Aeneas is *insignem pietate* at 10. *Gravem* (cf. *gravitas*) expresses the possession of all those qualities which made a Roman great. **meritis:** actual good deeds, as opposed to character defined by *pietas.* This *virum* represents the idealized Roman leader.

conspexere, silent arrectisque auribus astant;
ille regit dictis animos et pectora mulcet:
sic cunctus pelagi cecidit fragor, aequora postquam
prospiciens genitor caeloque invectus aperto   155
flectit equos curruque volans dat lora secundo.
    Defessi Aeneadae quae proxima litora cursu

152. **conspexere, silent:** note the effective placement of these verbs conveying the immediate reaction of the mob to this calming figure of *pietas*. **astant:** the subject is the *impius plebs*, construed as a collective noun, "the masses."

153. **ille regit:** *ille* is emphatic (cf. 44 n.) and directs our attention from the crowd's reaction upon seeing the *pietate gravem...virum* (151) to the man himself; the phrase *ille regit*, coming at the start of the sentence, underscores his control, as opposed to the fury of the mob. Cf. also the use of *regi* (137) and *regnet* (141) in Neptune's rebuke of Aeolus and the winds. **pectora mulcet:** the simile thus ends by recalling *aequora placat* (142) of Neptune calming the seas, thus returning to the description of the sea-god's actions.

154. **aequora:** accusative after *prospiciens* (155).

155. **genitor:** also used of Neptune at 5.817 (cf. 5.14 *pater Neptune*). **caeloque invectus aperto:** *invectus* does not govern *caelo* but means "borne upon (a chariot)," or "driving": he was driving not "in" or "through" the sky, but along the top of the waves (147). *Caelo aperto* is an ablative of attendant circumstance.

156. **flectit equos…:** the exact opposite of *Georgics* 1.514, describing the violence of civil war—*fertur equis auriga, neque audit currus habenas*. **curru...dat lora secundo:** *curru... secundo* is dative. *Secundus*, from *sequor*, here is almost equivalent to *qui obsequitur*.

157-79. With seven ships, Aeneas finds and lands in a harbor. They prepare a meal.

The beauty and calm of the natural harbor in which the Trojans find refuge contrasts with the confusion and fury of the storm that shipwrecked them. Vergil's description of the harbor echoes Homer's *Odyssey* 9.116, 136-41; 10.87-96; and 13.96-106. See Nelis (2001) 73-5 for the background of this passage in Homer as well as in Apollonius. For more on Vergil's visual artistry here, see Leach (1988) 27-42.

157. **Defessi:** emphatically placed, as the focus now moves from Neptune to the Trojans. **Aeneadae:** the patronymic form usually referred the origin of a race to some distinguished chief or prince from whom it was supposed to be descended (cf. *Dardanidae*, "Trojans"; Lucretius 1.1 *Aeneadum*, "Romans"), but the actual living leader or king also came to be regarded as the "father" of his followers, who are spoken of as his "children." **litora:** placed in the relative clause instead of as accusative after *petere*, cf. 72 n. Supply *sunt* in the relative clause. **cursu:** ablative used adverbially, lit. "with running," and thus also "hurriedly," cf. 105 n.

> contendunt petere, et Libyae vertuntur ad oras.
> est in secessu longo locus: insula portum
> efficit obiectu laterum, quibus omnis ab alto   160
> frangitur inque sinus scindit sese unda reductos.
> hinc atque hinc vastae rupes geminique minantur
> in caelum scopuli, quorum sub vertice late
> aequora tuta silent; tum silvis scaena coruscis
> desuper, horrentique atrum nemus imminet umbra;   165
> fronte sub adversa scopulis pendentibus antrum,
> intus aquae dulces vivoque sedilia saxo,

158. **contendunt petere:** *contendunt* takes an infinitive as if it were a verb expressing a "wish" or "desire," and here means "are eager to," "strive emulously to." The infinitive is often so employed, where it would be impermissible in prose to extend, complete, or fully explain the meaning of a verb. See also 11 n. **vertuntur:** passive with middle sense, "turn toward," "make for."

159. **est...locus:** "there is a place..." begins the ecphrasis (cf. 418-93 n.) of the harbor, on which cf. 157-79 n.

160-1. **obiectu laterum…:** "with the barrier of its sides, by which every wave (*omnis...unda*) from the sea is broken…." The island forms a natural breakwater "by throwing its sides across" the mouth of the bay, and thus creates a harbor (*portum efficit*). **inque sinus... reductos:** *sinus* can be taken either as 1) "curves of the shore," "bays"; or 2) "ripples" of the water (cf. 11.624; *Georgics* 3.237). In either case, the *sinus* are "receding" (*reductos*). The same phrase is used at *Georgics* 4.420.

162-3. **rupes...scopuli:** the *rupes* are the long ridges of rock which form the sides of the harbor; the *gemini scopuli* are the two tower-like crags in which these ridges terminate. **minantur in caelum:** means "tower threateningly towards the sky."

164-5. **tum silvis scaena…:** *tum* introduces a fresh feature in the view; "there is also a background of bristling trees above (*desuper*), and a grove overhangs, black with dreadful shade." For *scaena* as "background," cf. *Georgics* 3.24. Originally rustic plays seem to have been acted in some convenient spot where trees, shrubs or boughs formed a natural background, a custom to which Vergil may refer here (cf. Servius). **coruscis:** refers to the movement of the tree tops which are "bristling" as they wave back and forth. **horrenti umbra:** "dreadful shade," perhaps better than "shivering shade," which would repeat the idea in *coruscis*.

166. **fronte sub adversa:** i.e. under the front of the crags facing the Trojans. *Adversa* thus suggests the perspective of the Trojans as they approach. **scopulis pendentibus:** ablative of material, explaining how and of what the *antrum* (cave) is made.

167. **vivo:** "natural"; the rock forms seats without being artificially cut. *Vivo...saxo* is ablative of material.

nympharum domus. hic fessas non vincula navis
ulla tenent, unco non alligat ancora morsu.
huc septem Aeneas collectis navibus omni   170
ex numero subit; ac magno telluris amore
egressi optata potiuntur Troes harena
et sale tabentis artus in litore ponunt.
ac primum silici scintillam excudit Achates
suscepitque ignem foliis atque arida circum   175
nutrimenta dedit rapuitque in fomite flammam.
tum Cererem corruptam undis Cerealiaque arma
expediunt fessi rerum, frugesque receptas
et torrere parant flammis et frangere saxo.

168-9. **nympharum domus:** nymphs were often associated with grottoes and most frequently with springs of fresh water. **hic fessas…:** The passage recalls Homer, *Odyssey* 9.136. Vergil's use of *ancora*, however, is an anachronism (as are the *biremis* in 182), since anchors as such were unknown in Homeric times.

170-1. **huc:** returns us to the Trojans' plight. **septem…collectis navibus:** ablative absolute. **omni ex numero:** Aeneas had twenty ships when he left Troy, cf. 381 n. **subit:** here means "seeks shelter." **telluris amore:** "longing for the land."

172. A golden line. **optata…harena:** ablative with *potiuntur*.

173. **sale tabentis:** "dripping with sea water" "or "brine."

174. **silici:** ablative. **Achates:** there may be paranomasia* here, for in Greek *achates* is a kind of stone (agate). See Servius (*ad loc.*) and O'Hara (1996).

175. **suscepit…ignem foliis:** "caught the fire in the leaves." *Suscepit* is originally a ritualistic word that resonates well with Vergil's detailed care in describing the lighting of this fire (cf. 176 n.).

176. **nutrimenta:** "fuel," i.e. the branches, etc. used to feed the fire. **rapuitque in fomite flammam:** "and quickly caught the flame on tinder." Servius says that *fomes* means "chips" (*assulae*) and derives it from *foveo*—*quod ignem fovent*.

177. **Cererem corruptam undis:** "corn damaged by the waves." Note the metonymy*. **Cerealia…arma:** "the implements of Ceres," a dignified phrase for the tools used in preparing corn for food.

178. **rerum:** genitive of specification governed by *fessi* (AG §349d).

179. **et torrere…:** for making grain into meal (*farina*), it was commonly pounded (*pinso*, cf. *pistor*) in a mortar with a pestle, for which Vergil uses the phrase *frangere saxo*. Before this was done, however, it was usual to roast or dry it (*torrere*). **et…et:** join the two infinitives dependent on *parant*.

1.180-209

Aeneas scopulum interea conscendit, et omnem   180
prospectum late pelago petit, Anthea si quem
iactatum vento videat Phrygiasque biremis
aut Capyn aut celsis in puppibus arma Caici.
navem in conspectu nullam, tris litore cervos
prospicit errantis; hos tota armenta sequuntur   185
a tergo et longum per vallis pascitur agmen.
constitit hic arcumque manu celerisque sagittas
corripuit, fidus quae tela gerebat Achates,
ductoresque ipsos primum capita alta ferentis
cornibus arboreis sternit, tum vulgus et omnem   190
miscet agens telis nemora inter frondea turbam;

180-207. *Aeneas reconnoiters, kills seven deer, divides them among his people, and offers words of encouragement.*

180-94. Aeneas' hunting of the deer recalls recalls Odysseus' actions on Circe's island, where he also climbs a cliff and kills a stag for his men (*Odyssey* 10.144-84). See Johnson (1976) 32-6, who analyzes the characteristic differences bewteen the Homeric passage, which is based more in realism and the needs of the plot, and the Vergilian, which is impressionistic and more prone to describe the emotions. See also Staley (1990) and Ross (2007) 8-9.

180-1. **prospectum...pelago:** *prospectus* ("prospect," "view") is a verbal noun qualified by the adverb *late* (cf. 21 n.); it retains a verbal construction with *pelago*, which means "over the deep" (cf. 126 *alto prospiciens*, describing Neptune). Because *scopulum* is derived from a Greek word that originally meant "a look-out place," there may be a wordplay in Vergil's use of both words here (cf. O'Hara (1996) 119).

181-3. **Anthea si quem...videat:** "in hopes (lit. "to see if") he may catch sight of an Antheus (lit. "any Antheus")...or Capys...or Caicus." Antheus will appear at 1.510 and 12.443. *Anthea* is a Greek accusative form. **Phrygias:** "Trojan." **biremis:** "biremes," a ship with two banks of rowers, anachronistic in the Trojan war era (cf. 168-9 n.). **puppibus arma:** as captain, Caicus hung his weaponry (presumably his shield) on the ship for display.

184. **navem...nullam, tris...cervos:** the two clauses contrast by their asyndetonic* placement, "no ship within sight, but three stags..." Cf. 76-7, 209, 467, 468.

185. **hos:** i.e. the *cervos...errantis.* **tota armenta:** probably plural for singular, "an entire herd," as implied by *longum...agmen* (186).

187. **constitit:** note the emphatic placement of this verb and *corripuit* in 188, both describing Aeneas' decisive actions. **hic:** adverb, "here," "at this point."

188. **fidus:** Achates' defining epithet throughout the poem.

189-91. **capita alta ferentis cornibus arboreis:** describing *ductores ipsos* (the *cervos* of 184). **primum...tum...:** "first...then." **vulgus et...:** "the common herd and general mob he routs (by) pursuing them with his weapons..." Note the contrast between *vulgus* and *ductores.*

nec prius absistit quam septem ingentia victor
corpora fundat humi et numerum cum navibus aequet.
hinc portum petit et socios partitur in omnis.
vina bonus quae deinde cadis onerarat Acestes   195
litore Trinacrio dederatque abeuntibus heros
dividit, et dictis maerentia pectora mulcet:
   "O socii (neque enim ignari sumus ante malorum),
o passi graviora, dabit deus his quoque finem.
vos et Scyllaeam rabiem penitusque sonantis   200

---

193. **fundat...aequet:** subjunctives after *priusquam* ("before") indicating purpose or anticipation (cf. AG §551b). **humi:** "to the ground," locative used adverbially. **numerum cum navibus:** Aeneas entered the harbor with seven ships (170).

194. **partitur:** supply *cervos*.

195. **vina:** object of *dividit* (197). **deinde:** modifies *dividit*. **cadis onerare:** here means "to put wine in jars so that it forms their *onus* or burden." The more usual construction is *onerare cados vino*, cf. 362-3 *navis...onerant auro*. **Acestes:** a Trojan, now king of a city in Sicily, where the Trojans land in book 3 (and later in Book 5). Aeneas had just left this city when Juno sends her storm at the opening of Book 1.

196. **Trinacrio:** "Sicilian," *Trinacria* being a Greek name for Sicily because it had three corners (i.e. was triangular). **abeuntibus:** describing Aeneas and his people. **heros:** i.e. Acestes. Giving generous gifts to departing guests (*abeuntibus*) was a standard practice in the heroic age.

197. **mulcet:** the verb used of the political figure in the simile at 153. The idea in this verb may also echo Odysseus' "honeyed words" to his crew at *Odyssey* 10.173.

198-207. This is Aeneas' second speech in the poem. Like the first (cf. 94-101 n.), it has an important Homeric model — Odysseus' outburst to his men as they are about to confront the twin threats of Scylla and Charybdis at *Odyssey* 12.208-12. The contrast between the two passages, however, is particularly revealing of Aeneas. While Odysseus displays supreme confidence in his resourceful leadership, when confronted by danger, Aeneas feels (though masks) despair; to cheer his men, he relies for hope not on his ability as a leader but on their past experiences and the promises of fate.

198. **neque enim...:** *enim* ("since") helps explain *dabit...finem* (199); *neque* here = *non*; *ante* probably should be taken with *sumus* instead of *malorum*. This parenthetical comment explains the claim *dabit...finem* made in the next line. For the sense, cf. Homer, *Odyssey* 12.208-12.

200. **vos et...vos et:** notice the strong anaphora* of the pronoun and connective. **penitus sonantis:** "deep-echoing," i.e. from their caverns (referring to the rage of Scylla's hounds, *Scyllaeam rabiem*). The Trojan seer Helenus had warned Aeneas to avoid the twin threats of Scylla and Charybdis (a whirlpool) at 3.420-32, threats Homer's Odysseus had learned about and encountered at *Odyssey* 12.73-126, 222-59, 426-46.

accestis scopulos, vos et Cyclopia saxa
experti: revocate animos maestumque timorem
mittite; forsan et haec olim meminisse iuvabit.
per varios casus, per tot discrimina rerum
tendimus in Latium, sedes ubi fata quietas   205
ostendunt; illic fas regna resurgere Troiae.
durate, et vosmet rebus servate secundis."
    Talia voce refert curisque ingentibus aeger
spem vultu simulat, premit altum corde dolorem.
    illi se praedae accingunt dapibusque futuris: 210
tergora diripiunt costis et viscera nudant;

201. **accestis:** syncopated form of *accessistis.* Cf. also 26 *repostum* with n. and 249 *compostus.*
Cyclopia saxa: "the rocks of the Cyclops," a reference to the Trojans' encounter with
the Cyclops in 3.655-81, a "rewriting" of Odysseus' encounter that is narrated by him
at *Odyssey* 9.106-542 and that, in the *Aeneid,* is described to the Trojans by the Greek
suppliant Achaemenides at 3.613-54.

202. **experti:** sc. *estis,* an uncommon omission, cf. 42 n.

203. **forsan et haec…:** "perhaps even these things it will one day be a joy to recall." This
famous thought echoes Homer, *Odyssey* 12.212: "perhaps even these things I think we will
remember" (i.e. with satisfaction).

204. **per tot discrimina rerum:** "through so many crises" (lit. dangerous situations of our
affairs). *Tot* is often used in reference to any number that is well known. Cf. 10, 232, 240,
642. Note the rhetorical repetition of the *per* clauses with asyndeton*.

205. **tendimus:** "head toward," cf. 554 n. **Latium:** this region of Italy had not technically
been revealed to Aeneas in books 2 and 3 (which describe events that occurred before the
opening of book 1). *Latium* is mentioned in the prologue (6).

206. **fas:** sc. *est,* "it is granted" (i.e. by fate and the gods). *Fas* denotes divine law, as opposed
to *ius,* human law.

207. **vosmet:** object of *servate*; the *-met* adds emphasis to the pronoun. **rebus…secundis:**
dative.

*208-22. Aeneas, concealing his own fears, encourages his followers. They feast and discuss the fate
of their comrades.*

208. **curis:** ablative of specification.

209. **spem vultu…:** notice how the strong antithesis between the contrasted clauses (cf. 184
n.) is brought out by the elaborately inverted order of the antithetical words (i.e. chiasmus*)
— spem *vultu* **simulat, premit** altum *corde* dolorem.

210. **praedae…dapibusque futuris:** datives of purpose. The seven stags killed by Aeneas
(192-3) are the *praeda.*

211. **viscera:** this passage shows the meaning of *viscera* to be "the carcase," that which is left
when the hide is stripped off.

pars in frusta secant veribusque trementia figunt,
litore aëna locant alii flammasque ministrant.
tum victu revocant viris, fusique per herbam
implentur veteris Bacchi pinguisque ferinae.   215
postquam exempta fames epulis mensaeque remotae,
amissos longo socios sermone requirunt,
spemque metumque inter dubii, seu vivere credant
sive extrema pati nec iam exaudire vocatos.

212-13. **pars…secant…locant alii:** *pars* takes a plural verb because it is equivalent to "some" (cf. 4.405). **frusta:** "scraps of food" or "morsels." **secant:** object is the *viscera* from 211. **aëna:** bronze cauldrons are used presumably for boiling meat, though meat was not eaten in this way in the Homeric age. Austin notes: "but if Vergil could swallow a non-Homeric anchor, cf. 169, he could presumably digest non-Homeric boiled meat."

214. **viris:** "strength." This is the accusative plural of *vis, vis, f.* (not *vir, viri,* m., "man," "hero"). **fusi:** *fusus* describes the attitude of one who lies down without any care or fear of being disturbed.

215. **implentur:** a good instance of the close connection between the middle and passive forms of verbs, for this word is either "they fill themselves" or "they are filled," cf. 713 *expleri mentem.* **Bacchi:** = "wine" by metonymy*, as *Cererem* = "corn" at 177. Like *ferinae,* *Bacchi* is a genitive after a word implying "want" and "fullness" (cf. AG §349, 356), though this construction with *implere* seems a Vergilian innovation.

216. **exempta:** supply *est.* **mensaeque remotae:** supply *sunt,* They clearly had no "tables," but, as ancient tables were small so that the food was often brought in on the tables and the tables taken away with the food, *mensae* can be put for the food itself (cf. the common phrase *mensa secunda* to mean "dessert").

217. **amissos longo socios sermone:** note the interlocking word order or synchysis*. **requirunt:** from the sense of "seek to recover" *requiro* acquires the sense of "feel the want of"; here it means "regretfully recall." The discussion of lost comrades recalls the Homeric scene at *Odyssey* 12.309.

218-19. **spemque metumque inter:** *inter* follows its objects (anastrophe*), and the entire phrase (like the indirect questions that follow, *seu…seu…*) follows *dubii,* "doubtful." **extrema pati:** a circumlocution to describe the possibility that their comrades have died, but note the effect of the present infinitive (*pati*) instead of the perfect. **vocatos:** there may be a special reference to the practice of calling on the dead three times at funerals.

praecipue pius Aeneas nunc acris Oronti,   220
nunc Amyci casum gemit et crudelia secum
fata Lyci fortemque Gyan fortemque Cloanthum.

220-2. **pius Aeneas:** the epithet underscores his defining concern for his people. See
Introduction. **nunc...nunc...fortemque...fortemque:** pathetic repetition, cf. 120 n.
Oronti: genitive (cf. 120 n.). Orontes died at 113. **secum:** "in his heart" (lit. "to himself").
He does not express his grief in words, cf. 208-9. Lycus and Amycus survive the storm
but both fall victim to Turnus in book 9 (lines 545-62 and 771-3 respectively). Gyas and
Cloanthus also survive and take part in the boat race at 5.114-267.

223-304: Venus and Jupiter

Having just witnessed Aeneas' shipwreck, Venus complains to Jupiter about Aeneas' continued suffering. Jupiter comforts her by revealing the mandates of Fate: not only will Aeneas succeed in his journey to his new land, but his descendants will ultimately found Rome, a city that will experience boundless empire (*imperium sine fine* 279) and will reach its height of greatness under Augustus.

This divine exchange has important Homeric models in *Iliad* 1.493-530 (Thetis complains to Zeus about the suffering of her son Achilles) and *Odyssey* 5.1-58 (Athena complains to Zeus about Odysseus' confinement on Calypso's island). The latter, however, is especially relevant here, because *Odyssey* 5 is so central to the storm passage that had opened the *Aeneid* (cf. 34-222 n.). Once again, however, the contrast between the two epics and their heroes is instructive. While the Homeric passage focuses on the personal aspect of Odysseus' suffering, the Vergilian passage places Aeneas and his travails in a broader context that is historical and nationalistic. By doing so, the poet firmly connects the distant mythological world of the Trojan Aeneas to the historical world of Vergil's Rome, offering a conception of history that presents Augustus as the telos or goal of long historical processes, sanctioned by fate and the king of the gods.

The scene also brings to a culmination a complex of ideas about moral leadership woven throughout the opening scenes of the epic. We have witnessed figures of *ira* and *furor* (such as Juno, Aeolus, the maddened rabble in the poem's first simile) who are subdued by figures associated with control and especially *pietas* (Neptune, the political figure in the first simile). Jupiter's speech adds Augustus and his subjugation of *Furor impius* (294) to this list. The passage's significance for our interpretation of Aeneas is great, for the epic in an important sense poses the following question: will Aeneas succeed in overcoming (Juno's) *furor* and establishing political control as had these "models'? His perceived success or failure in this has generated a wide variety of interpretation of Aeneas and of the poem's politics (i.e. Augustan, anti-Augustan, or somewhere in between). For the intertextual background, see Nelis (2001) 73-6. For interpretation, see Otis (1964), G. W. Williams (1983) 138-42, O'Hara (1990) 128-63, Feeney (1991) 137-42, and Ross (2007) 22, 107-9.

Et iam finis erat, cum Iuppiter aethere summo
despiciens mare velivolum terrasque iacentis
litoraque et latos populos, sic vertice caeli   225
constitit et Libyae defixit lumina regnis.
atque illum talis iactantem pectore curas
tristior et lacrimis oculos suffusa nitentis
adloquitur Venus: "o qui res hominumque deumque
aeternis regis imperiis et fulmine terres,   230

223-53. Venus asks Jupiter why Aeneas and the Trojans are being kept from Italy.

223-6. Vergil emphatically shifts focus to the divine realm (e.g. *aethere summo* 223), by describing Jupiter's physical perspective on Aeneas and mortal suffering. Vergil thus sets the stage for Jupiter's important meeting with Venus.

223. **iam finis erat:** signals a transition to a new scene, though the phrasing does not make clear what specifically has just ended — the storm, the mourning of lost comrades, or something else? **aethere summo:** understand *ab* or *ex*.

224. **mare velivolum:** "the sea studded with sails" (lit. "the sea of speeding sails"). The adjective, which goes back to Ennius (*Annales,* fr. 376 in Warmington, fr. 380 in Skutsch), pictorially represents the sea as it appeared to Jupiter looking down from heaven, cf. *iacentis* "outstretched" (beneath his view).

225. **latos:** "wide-extended," i.e. occupying wide territories. **sic:** summing up *aethere... populos*; "thus (i.e. gazing down...), Jupiter stood (*constitit*)." **vertice caeli:** understand *in* with *vertice*. At *Iliad* 5.754, Jupiter sits "on the highest peak of many-ridged Olympus."

226. **lumina:** "eyes."

227. **atque illum...:** *illum* (i.e. Jupiter), object of *adloquitur* (229). *Atque* is a strong connecting particle that introduces an event that is closely connected (here in time) with the preceding sentence. **talis...curas:** apparently the concerns aroused by his observation of the world below (225-6).

228. **tristior:** "rather sad" or perhaps "sadder than usual," modifying *Venus* (229), who is usually described as happy (cf. her Homeric epithet "laughter loving," Gr. *philommeides*). **lacrimis oculos suffusa nitentis:** *oculos nitentis* is the object of *suffusa* (a middle participle), lit. "having suffused her shining eyes with tears."

229. **qui...:** understand *tu* as antecedent.

230. **aeternis regis imperiis:** *regis* is not the genitive of *rēx*; rather it has a short *e* and is from *rĕgere* ("rule"). The theme of *imperium* is important in Jupiter's speech (cf. 279).

quid meus Aeneas in te committere tantum,
quid Troes potuere, quibus tot funera passis
cunctus ob Italiam terrarum clauditur orbis?
certe hinc Romanos olim volventibus annis,
hinc fore ductores, revocato a sanguine Teucri,   235
qui mare, qui terras omnis dicione tenerent,
pollicitus. quae te, genitor, sententia vertit?
hoc equidem occasum Troiae tristisque ruinas
solabar fatis contraria fata rependens;
nunc eadem fortuna viros tot casibus actos   240

231-3. **quid meus…:** the singular of *potuere* (i.e. *potuit*) should be understood with *meus Aeneas* (a phrase revealing Venus' loving concern for her son). **quid…quid:** the repetition helps convey Venus' frustration. **tantum:** modifies *quid* ("What (crime) so great…") and should strictly be followed by the relative clause of result with subjunctive *quibus claudatur* = *ut eis claudatur*, "so great that all the world is barred to them," but the indicative (*clauditur*) is more vivid and definite. **quibus…passis:** dative, with Aeneas and the Trojans (*Aeneas…Troes*) as antecedent. **ob Italiam:** an unusual phrase that must mean "because of (their fate in) Italy."

234. **certe:** construe closely with *pollicitus (es)* in 237. **hinc:** "from them," i.e. from Aeneas and the Trojans, emphasized by *a sanguine Teucri* in 235 (see note). **Romanos:** accusative in indirect statement after *pollicitus* (237, see n.); *fore* from 235 should also be understood here. **olim:** "one day." **volventibus annis:** "as the years roll on."

235. **hinc:** the repetition of *hinc* here from 234 emphasizes the promises Jupiter had made to Venus, which now seem broken. **revocato a sanguine Teucri:** "from Teucer's restored family line." Teucer was an early king of Troy.

236. **qui…tenerent:** relative clause of purpose (cf. 62 n.). For *dicione tenere* cf. 622; 7.737 *dicione premebat*. The repetition of *qui* helps convey the encompassing nature of Roman dominion that Jupiter had promised. **omnis:** many manuscripts read *omni* and take it with *dicione* to mean "with every sort of dominion," i.e. "with complete dominion." The authority of *omnis*, however, is somewhat stronger and better fits the sense of the passage, since with *terras* it suggests the geographical range of Rome's power.

237. **pollicitus:** the omission of *es* is not common (cf 42 n.). **quae te…sententia vertit?:** perhaps an inversion for *cur sententiam vertisti?*

238-9. **hoc:** i.e. your promise; ablative of means. **occasum…solabar:** "I sought solace for the fall of Troy" (lit. "I solaced the fall of Troy"), a somewhat uncommon instance of *solor*, taking as its object not the person solaced but the thing that provides the need for solace. **fatis…rependens:** "with fates (i.e. happier fates) compensating opposite (i.e. unhappy) fates." For *rependo* cf. Ovid, *Heroides* 15.32 *ingenio formae damna rependo meae.*

240. **eadem fortuna:** the proverbial evil fortune of Troy (cf. *Troiana fortuna* 6.62).

insequitur. quem das finem, rex magne, laborum?
Antenor potuit mediis elapsus Achivis
Illyricos penetrare sinus atque intima tutus
regna Liburnorum et fontem superare Timavi,
unde per ora novem vasto cum murmure montis   245
it mare proruptum et pelago premit arva sonanti.
hic tamen ille urbem Patavi sedesque locavit
Teucrorum et genti nomen dedit armaque fixit

241. **quem das finem…laborum:** this question attributes to Jupiter the ultimate control of Aeneas' destiny, while simultaneously emphasizing Juno's suspicion that Jupiter has changed his mind (*quae te…sententia vertit* 237) and broken his promise (*pollicitus* 237).

242-50. **Antenor (242)…nos (250):** observe the antithesis marked by the position of the words — "Antenor could…(but) we cannot"; cf. 184 n.

242-4. **mediis…Achivis:** ablative of separation with *elapsus*. **mediis…penetrare…intima… superare:** these words and the description of the river Timavus, 244-6, all emphasize the difficulties Antenor was able to overcome and in spite of which (*tamen* 247) he was successful. Antenor was a prominent Trojan warrior who, after the war, founded the city *Patavium* in the region of Venice (cf. 247 n.). See Livy 1.1 for his story. For the tradition of Antenor as a Trojan turncoat, see Austin *ad loc.* **Illyricos sinus:** "Illyrian gulfs" means the Adriatic gulf along the shores of Illyria. Having passed them, Antenor would come to the "inmost (i.e. lying farthest up the gulf) realms of the Liburni (i.e. a people of Illyria)." **tutus:** adjective describing Antenor that can be translated adverbially, "safely." **superare:** "sail by," a nautical idiom (Servius). **fontem…Timavi:** the Timavus river (modern Timavo) flows from the Alps into the Gulf of Trieste, and has part of its course underground (cf. *montis* in 245).

245-6. **unde…:** "from which (i.e. from the *fons*, cf. 242-4 n.) through nine mouths the flood comes bursting and buries the fields beneath a sounding sea." The *ora* are the "springs" from which the river emerges; the *arva* are the marshy meadows on either side of the river. **vasto cum murmure montis:** probably describes the sound made as the river emerges from under the mountains. **mare…pelago:** by using these words, Venus exaggerates the power of the river Timavus, which Antenor still sails by (cf. *superare* in 244), to contrast it with Aeneas' seemingly insurmountable troubles.

247. **hic:** referring to the general area just described. However, Patavium (modern Padua), the city founded by Antenor (*ille*), is actually more to the southwest of this area. **urbem Patavi:** "the city of Patavium," though Latin more usually will keep *urbs* and the city's name in the same case, e.g. *urbs Patavium* or *urbs Roma*. The genitive *-i* of nouns in *-ium* is regular in Vergil, cf. 258 *Lavini*.

248. **genti nomen dedit:** Livy (1.1.3) says that the place they first landed was called *Troia*, though the general body of colonists was called *Veneti*. Cf. 242-4 n. **armaque fixit/ Troïa (249):** "hung up the arms of Troy," i.e. in the temples as a sign of peace. It was customary on retiring from any calling to dedicate the instruments of it. So a retired soldier dedicates his arms as a sign that his wars are over (as here), and a poet his lyre (Horace, *Odes* 3.26.3-4).

Troia, nunc placida compostus pace quiescit:
nos, tua progenies, caeli quibus adnuis arcem,   250
navibus (infandum!) amissis unius ob iram
prodimur atque Italis longe disiungimur oris.
hic pietatis honos? sic nos in sceptra reponis?"
      Olli subridens hominum sator atque deorum
vultu, quo caelum tempestatesque serenat,   255
oscula libavit natae, dehinc talia fatur:
"parce metu, Cytherea, manent immota tuorum
fata tibi; cernes urbem et promissa Lavini
moenia sublimemque feres ad sidera caeli

---

249. **placida...:** probably refers not to Antenor's death, but to the fact that he (in contrast to Aeneas) has finished his wanderings and founded a city. **compostus:** shortened form of *compositus* by syncope (cf. 26 n.).

250. **nos:** contrasts with Antenor (242); Venus identifies herself with Aeneas and his fortunes. **tua progenies:** in apposition to *nos.* **caeli...arcem:** Aeneas was said not to have died but to have been taken up to heaven, where he became one of the *Di Indigetes* "native gods"— benefactors of the human race like Hercules and Romulus who were deified for their good deeds. **adnuis:** "nod assent to," "promise," with special reference to the famous "nod" of Jupiter by which he expresses his will (as Zeus does at *Iliad* 1.528-30).

251. **navibus...amissis:** ablative absolute. **infandum!:** accusative of exclamation. **unius ob iram:** *unius* = Juno. Note how Venus does not mention Juno by name.

253. **hic pietatis honos?:** this question (like the next) contains a rebuke of Jupiter. **sceptra:** by metonymy* means "empire."

254-96. *Jupiter reassures his daughter Venus and reveals the fates of Aeneas, his descendants, and the glory of Rome, culminating in the reign of Augustus.*

254. **Olli:** an archaic form of the dative of *ille,* sometimes used by Vergil (cf. 4.105, 5.10) for special effect; it is governed by *subridens.* **hominum sator atque deorum:** a grand phrase describing Jupiter; it echoes both Homer and Ennius.

256. **oscula...:** "lightly touched his daughter's lips." The usual meaning of *oscula* is "kisses," though "lips" is its primary meaning, as it is the diminutive of *os.* Vergil seldom uses such diminutives.

257. **parce metu:** lit. "spare your fear," i.e. "cease fearing." **metu:** contracted form of the dative, regular in Vergil, cf. 156 *curru;* 3.292 *portu,* 692 *sinu.* **Cytherea:** i.e. Venus. Cythera is an island off the southeastern coast of the Peloponnese (i.e. Laconia), and is sacred to Venus because, according to myth, she was born from the sea near it.

258. **tibi:** ethical dative which can be translated as "I assure you" (AG §380). **Lăvini:** *Lavinium* is the city Aeneas will found in Italy. Roman poets exercise latitude with regard to the quantities of proper names. Cf. 343 *Sȳchaeus,* 348 *Sȳchaeum.*

259. **sublimemque feres:** *sublimemque* is proleptic*, cf. 70 n., "and you will carry him on high."

magnanimum Aenean; neque me sententia vertit.   260
hic tibi (fabor enim, quando haec te cura remordet,
longius, et volvens fatorum arcana movebo)
bellum ingens geret Italia populosque ferocis
contundet moresque viris et moenia ponet,
tertia dum Latio regnantem viderit aestas,   265
ternaque transierint Rutulis hiberna subactis.
at puer Ascanius, cui nunc cognomen Iulo
additur (Ilus erat, dum res stetit Ilia regno),

---

260. **magnanimum Aenean:** compound epithets convey an elevated tone. **neque me sententia vertit:** responds to the phraseology of Venus' question at 237.

261. **hic:** i.e. Aeneas. **tibi:** ethical dative, cf. 258 n. **fabor:** future tense of *for, fari, fatus sum* ("speak," "tell"; cf. also 256). With *fatorum* (formed from the past participle of this verb) in the next line, Jupiter plays with the etymology of *fata* (cf. 258, 262).

262. **longius…:** "and further unrolling (them) will bring to light the secret records of fate"; *volvens = evolvens*. Because ancient books were wrapped around rollers, they had to be unrolled to be read; thus *evolvere librum* means "read a book," and *volumen*, "a roll" or "book."

263. **Italia:** ablative; *(in) Italia*.

264. **moresque…et moenia ponet:** *mores* includes laws, customs, and institutions; it contrasts with *moenia*, the outward defences of a community. *Mores ponere* is formed on the analogy of *leges ponere*, "to set up laws," which were actually "set up" on tables of wood or brass.

265. Aeneas will live only three years after the founding of Lavinium, and then become a god. Cf. 250 n. However, Anchises will later predict that Aeneas at an advanced age (*longaevo serum* 6.764) will have a son by Silvia; see Cairns (1989) 187. **Latio:** *(in) Latio*. **dum… viderit:** *viderit* and *transierint* (266) are future perfects in the *dum* ("until") clause (AG §553).

266. **terna…hiberna:** *hiberna* (neuter plural) literally means "winter encampment," but here probably is equivalent to *hiemes* ("winters"). With *terna*, it describes the passing of "three winters" and parallels *tertia…aestas* ("third summer") of the preceding line. **transierint:** cf. 265 n. **Rutulis…subactis:** probably ablative absolute, but it could also be dative of reference. Aeneas therefore dies the third year after the defeat of Turnus (i.e. the end of the *Aeneid*).

267-8. **cognomen:** strictly *cognomen* is the name added to the *nomen* (i.e. name of the *gens*) to identify the family (e.g. *Cicero, Scipio*). **Iulo:** i.e. Ascanius. *Iulo* is dative by attraction to *cui*, a traditional construction. **Ilus:** a king of Ilium. **stetit…regno:** "while Ilium's state (*res…Ilia*, i.e. Troy) stood strong in empire."

In these lines, Jupiter explains the origin of Ascanius' other name, which makes the transtion to *Iulius* (288) easy. He thus creates an ancient connection between Ascanius (Aeneas and Venus) and the Julian *gens* (i.e. the family of Julius Caesar and thus also

triginta magnos volvendis mensibus orbis
imperio explebit, regnumque ab sede Lavini   270
transferet, et Longam multa vi muniet Albam.
hic iam ter centum totos regnabitur annos
gente sub Hectorea, donec regina sacerdos
Marte gravis geminam partu dabit Ilia prolem.
inde lupae fulvo nutricis tegmine laetus   275
Romulus excipiet gentem et Mavortia condet
moenia Romanosque suo de nomine dicet.

---

of Augustus; see Introduction). Iulus, as an alternate name for Ascanius, was probably invented in the late Republic to associate Ascanius with the Julians, though there is some controversy over the dating of the name (cf. Austin on 2.563).

269. **triginta…:** "with his empire he will fulfil thirty mighty circles with their rolling months." Thus Aeneas will rule for three years (265-6), Ascanius for thirty (*triginta magnos orbis*), and their descendants for three hundred (*ter centum* 272). **volvendis:** "rolling"; Latin sometimes uses the gerundive as a present intransitive participle. Cf. 9.7 *volvenda dies* and Ennius, *Annales* fr. 421 in Warmington, fr. 545 in Skutsch *clamor ad caelum volvendus*.

270. **ab sede Lavini:** for the genitive, cf. 247 n.

271. **Longam…Albam:** Alba Longa in Latium. Cf. Livy 1.3: *Ascanius…aliam* (*urbem*) *sub Albano monte condidit, quae ab situ porrectae in dorso urbis Longa Alba appellata.*

272. **hic:** "here" (i.e. at Alba Longa). **iam:** marks a fresh stage in the history, "when this point is reached," "then." **totos…annos:** accusative of duration. *Totos* ("whole" or "complete," cf. *magnos* 269) emphasizes the fullness of the time. **regnabitur:** an impersonal use of the passive, "empire shall be held" (lit. "it will be ruled").

273. **gente sub Hectorea:** note that though Hector died at Troy, he still lives on through his Trojan descendants and their successes.

274. **Marte gravis:** "pregnant by Mars," modifying Ilia. **partu dabit:** "will give in birth" (i.e. "will give birth to"; cf. *pariet*). **Ilia:** usually called Rhea Silvia; she was the daughter of King Amulius, a vestal virgin (*sacerdos*), and mother of Romulus and Remus. Her story is told in Livy 1.3-4.

275. **lupae fulvo nutricis tegmine:** The wolf-skin, seemingly part of Romulus' traditional attire (cf. Propertius 4.10.20), refers to the she-wolf who found and suckled the abandoned babies Romulus and Remus. The image of the wolf nursing these twins was a famous one. Cf. 8.630-4 (on Aeneas' shield) and Livy 1.4.

276. **excipiet:** "will take under his care." **Mavortia:** an adjectival form of *Mars* (cf. *Martia*). Romulus was Mars' son, though the adjective must also suggest the importance of Mars (and thus of war) for the Roman state.

277. **Romanos:** predicate accusative, "he will call (his people) Romans."

his ego nec metas rerum nec tempora pono:
imperium sine fine dedi. quin aspera Iuno,
quae mare nunc terrasque metu caelumque fatigat,   280
consilia in melius referet, mecumque fovebit
Romanos, rerum dominos gentemque togatam.
sic placitum. veniet lustris labentibus aetas
cum domus Assaraci Phthiam clarasque Mycenas
servitio premet ac victis dominabitur Argis.   285
nascetur pulchra Troianus origine Caesar,

---

278. **his:** i.e. the Romans (dative). **nec metas…:** *metas* describes limits in extent, *tempora* in duration. *Rerum* is a very general word that means "fortunes"; here "great fortunes," (though in 178, 462 the reverse).

279. **imperium sine fine dedi:** a line of great significance, for it ties the limitless empire of the Romans to Jupiter's will and the necessities of fate. **quin:** "moreover."

280. **metu:** the force of this word is unclear — is it Juno's own fear, or the fear she instills in others? The former is probably better ("in her fears"; cf. 23). **mare…terras…caelum:** note that Juno's resistance to fate involves actions in the three main spheres of the cosmos. **fatigat:** "harasses."

281. **in melius referet:** "will change for the better."

282. **rerum dominos:** *rerum* here means "of the world." **gentemque togatam:** "and the nation of the toga." *Rerum dominos* and *gentem togatam* are both in apposition to *Romanos*. The *toga* was the traditional dress of the Romans when engaged in civic (as opposed to martial) duties. Augustus, who liked old habits, is said to have been accustomed to quote this line ironically (Suetonius, *Augustus* 40).

283. **sic placitum:** "such is my pleasure," "so it is decreed" (lit. "so it has pleased me"), a formal phrase expressing a divine resolution that allows no change or question. **lustris labentibus:** "as the sacred seasons glide along." The *lustrum* is a religious period, so the use of *lustris* here gives the phrase a solemn sound.

284. **domus Assaraci:** Assaracus was Anchises' grandfather; the phrase thus means "Troy" or the "Trojans" (i.e. through wars of their descendants, the Romans). **Phthiam:** Achilles came from Phthia, Agamemnon from Mycenae, Diomedes from Argos. These cities of the Trojan war era are used in the description of Rome's domination of Greece, which culminates in the taking of Corinth by Mummius (146 BCE). Rome will thus avenge the Greeks' destruction of Troy.

285. **victis…Argis:** ablative of place where.

286-96. The end of Jupiter's speech brings the revelation of fate down to Vergil's own day. Lines 292-6 are generally taken as referring to Augustus (see notes below), who thus represents the goal or *telos* of fate toward which Aeneas strives. The identity of the person mentioned at 286-91, however, is greatly disputed. He is called *Caesar…Iulius* (286-8), but whether the Dictator or Augustus is meant is uncertain (see 286-8 n.). Strong arguments are put forth for both identifications, but neither side can claim absolute certainty. Given

imperium Oceano, famam qui terminet astris,
Iulius, a magno demissum nomen Iulo.
hunc tu olim caelo spoliis Orientis onustum
accipies secura; vocabitur hic quoque votis.   290

---

this ambiguity, we must therefore ask, in the words of O'Hara (1990) 160, "Why has Vergil not been clear on such an important point?" For the arguments concerning the identity of this figure, see Austin *ad* 286 ff. (leans toward the Dictator), G. W. Williams (1981: 140-2, Augustus), O'Hara (1990: 155-63; 1994, ambiguity), Kraggerud (1994, Augustus), Harrison (1996, Augustus), and Ross (2007: 107-8, Dictator).

286-8. **pulchra...origine:** ablative of origin after *nascetur.* **Caesar...Iulius (288):** either the Dictator or the emperor Augustus (see 286-96 n.). The emperor, whose original name was *G. Octavius,* became *G. Iulius Caesar Octavianus* upon his testamentary adoption by the dictator Julius Caesar in 44 BCE. (He later took the name *Augustus* in 27 BCE.) As a result, Augustus could be the man here referred to as *Iulius Caesar,* and he certainly is the passage's focus by line 292 (cf. notes below). However, *Iulius Caesar* would more naturally indicate the Dictator, and the details in 286-91 have also been so interpreted.

287. **imperium...:** relative clause of purpose. In Homer, *Oceanus* is the stream that flows round the whole earth. Jupiter thus foretells that *Iulius Caesar* (cf. 286-8 n.) will reign over the entire earth and his glory will reach heaven. Cf. 6.782.

288. **Iulius...Iulo:** the name *Iulius* is emphatically placed and emphazies the connection between Aeneas' son *Iulus* (cf. 267) and the Caesar here indicated (cf. 286-8 n.). **a magno demissum nomen Iulo:** stands in apposition to *Iulius.*

289. **olim:** "one day," "in days to come," "at that time." It becomes a topos for poets to allude to the day when the emperor will enter heaven as indefinitely distant, cf. Horace, *Odes.* 1.2.45 *serus in caelum redeas.* **caelo:** i.e. *in caelo.* **spoliis Orientis onustum:** modifies *hunc;* this phrase could refer to the Dictator (though with some difficulty), but it more convincingly refers to Augustus (cf. Vergil, *Georgics* 2.171 *extremis Asiae iam victor in oris*). After the battle of Actium (31 BCE) Octavian reduced Egypt, and eventually celebrated a triple triumph at Rome in 29 BCE (described on Aeneas' shield, 8.714-28). At that time he dedicated a temple to Julius Caesar (*Divus Iulius,* cf. Ovid, *ex Ponto* 2.2.83-4), and began to accept divine honors in Asia from "non-Romans who knew themselves as Hellenes" (Purcell (2005) 102). The temple of Janus was also closed as a sign of universal peace (cf. 294-6).

290. **secura:** "free from care," describing Venus (*tu* in 289), who at the moment is full of concerns for Aeneas and the future Romans. Lines 289-90 describe an anticipated apotheosis, but whose is debated: Caesar's, who was in fact declared a god in 42 BCE? Augustus', who had limited worship as a god during Vergil's lifetime (cf. 289 n.)? Or perhaps Augustus' expected deification? **hic quoque:** "he also" (i.e. as well as Aeneas); *hic* refers back to *hunc* (289). Cf. 250 n.

aspera tum positis mitescent saecula bellis;
cana Fides et Vesta, Remo cum fratre Quirinus
iura dabunt; dirae ferro et compagibus artis
claudentur Belli portae; Furor impius intus
saeva sedens super arma et centum vinctus aënis   295
post tergum nodis fremet horridus ore cruento."
Haec ait et Maia genitum demittit ab alto,

---

291. **aspera…:** i.e. the golden age shall return; cf. 6.792-3. This is a variation on a golden line*, which Vergil at times uses to mark the commencement or close of highly rhetorical passages (e.g. *Georgics* 1.468 *impiaque aeternam timuerunt saecula noctem*). This line cannot apply to the Dictator easily, since his assassination plunged Rome into more civil war. It could, however, refer to the relative peace under Octavian/Augustus after he had ended the civil wars or to the hope for the peace he would ultimately bring about.

292. **Fides:** this virtue is assumed to be characteristic of early Rome and is therefore called *cana* ("grey-haired"). **Vesta:** the goddess of the hearth is introduced perhaps to represent the nation as one family. **Remo cum fratre Quirinus:** cf. *Georgics* 2.533. *Quirinus* = Romulus; the phrase symbolizes the brotherly love which had succeeded the civil wars and the strife of brother against brother. Yet the two brothers did not so rule, and the murder of Remus by Romulus was often figured as a type of civil discord (cf. Horace, *Epodes* 7.19). We must therefore ask why Jupiter is made to include a detail that was not in some sense true.

293. **dirae…:** "the gates of war grim with iron and close-fastened bars," or by hendiadys* "close-fastened bars of iron." The temple of Janus was closed when there was peace throughout the Roman state: tradition (Livy 1.19) relates that it was only so closed three times—by Numa (Rome's second king), by T. Manlius after the first Punic war, and by Augustus 29 BCE (cf. 289 n.). The gates are described in 7.607-14, where they are opened at the start of the Italian war. There may be a recall here of Ennius, who imagines the god of war confined as a prisoner within the temple: *postquam Discordia taetra / belli ferratos postes portasque refregit* (*Annales* fr. 258-9 in Warmington, fr. 225-6 in Skutsch).

294-6. **Furor impius:** the adjective *impius* describes something monstrous, and is especially used by the Roman poets when speaking of civil war, because it is a violation of the laws of nature. Combined with *Furor* here, it represents an emphatic counterpart to the ideals seemingly embodied in Augustus' reign, which will subjugate *Furor impius*. We are told that Augustus placed a painting of Bellum and Furor in the Augustan Forum. See Servius *auctus* (i.e. the Servian commentary as expanded probably in the seventh/eighth century CE) on this line and Pliny, *Natural History* 35.27. **impius intus / saeva sedens super:** note the alliteration*. For the importance of *furor* in the poem, see e.g. 34-222 n. **horridus:** modifies *Furor* but can be construed adverbially, "horribly," "grimly."

297-304. Jupiter sends Mercury to induce the Carthaginians to welcome Aeneas.

297. **Maia genitum:** Mercury, the messenger of the gods, was the son of *Maia* (ablative of origin).

ut terrae utque novae pateant Karthaginis arces
hospitio Teucris, ne fati nescia Dido
finibus arceret. volat ille per aëra magnum   300
remigio alarum ac Libyae citus astitit oris.
et iam iussa facit, ponuntque ferocia Poeni
corda volente deo; in primis regina quietum
accipit in Teucros animum mentemque benignam.

298. **novae…Karthaginis:** there may be a wordplay (paronomasia)* here, since the city's name *Karthago* means *nova civitas* in Punic (see 12 n.).

299-300. **hospitio Teucris:** double dative construction, cf. 21-2 n. **ne…arceret:** note the switch from present (*pateant* 298) to imperfect subjunctive (here *arcerent*) in this purpose clause. The main verb *dimittit* is an historic present and thus might take either a primary or secondary sequence subjunctive in dependent clauses. But the tense switch might also be explained by the implied flow of thought, as Austin notes: "there is a virtual ellipse ('he did all this in order that…')." **fati nescia:** the phrase is effective as long as these words are left vague, since Dido would surely have driven Aeneas away, if she had actually known about fate. See Farron (1989) on the thematic development of this phrase.

301. **remigio alarum:** lit. "with rowing of wings." This nautical metaphor* for flying goes back to Aeschylus, *Agamemnon* 52, and is used of Daedalus at 6.19.

302. **facit, ponuntque…:** parataxis* showing that the effect follows the cause at once. Parataxis* is the sequential ordering of independent clauses (as opposed to hypotaxis*, the subordination of one clause to another).

303-4. **quietum…animum mentemque:** "a gentle spirit and kind intent." *Animus* is often the seat of the emotions, *mens* of the intellect, but the distinction cannot always be strictly maintained.

305-417: Aeneas meets his mother Venus

Aeneas (with his comrade Achates) encounters his mother Venus, who is disguised as a huntress named Harpalyce. She says that they have landed in Carthage and explains the story of Dido, the city's queen. Like the preceding episodes, this one continues to transform Odysseus' experiences in *Odyssey* 5-8. In this context, Aeneas' encounter can be read against Odysseus' entreaty of Nausicaa in *Odyssey* 6.145-97 and Athena's disguised encounter with Odysseus in *Odyssey* 7.14-77, as he is about to enter the palace of Nausicaa's father, King Alcinous. But again there are important differences. For example, while Odysseus acts with great poise in his encounters, Aeneas seems thoroughly exhausted by his troubles and even complains to Venus about his suffering. Aeneas' human frailties are more numerous than Odysseus' and will be tested throughout the epic. Apart from its interaction with the *Odyssey*, this scene plays another important function: it introduces the story of Dido, and we quickly see that her life parallels Aeneas' in many ways: both are exiles, who have lost their spouses, and travel west to found a new city (cf. also 561-78 n.). Dido's Carthage thus stands as an example of what Aeneas might attain. On this scene, see E. L. Harrison (1972-73, 1992), Greenwood (1989), O'Hara (1990) 9-14, Reckford (1995-96), Nelis (2001) 75-9, and Khan (2003).

> At pius Aeneas per noctem plurima volvens,   305
> ut primum lux alma data est, exire locosque

305-324. Aeneas and Achates explore the country and meet Venus, disguised as a huntress looking for her sisters.

305. **at pius Aeneas:** *at* returns us from the divine realm (cf. 223-6 n.) to the human, where we immediately see Aeneas' *pietas* in action, as he tends to his people. **volvens:** equivalent to a relative clause with an imperfect, "who was pondering."

306. **ut primum:** "as soon as." **lux alma:** *lux* is "kindly" or "nuturing," because light is essential to life. (In 3.311 *lux alma* is the "light of life" as opposed to the night of death.) **exire...:** infinitive dependent on *constituit* (309) — as are *explorare* (307), *quaerere* and *referre* (309). *Exire* and *explorare* are linked by *-que*, as are *quaerere* and *referre* in 309, though the two pairs lack a connective (i.e. asyndeton*).

explorare novos, quas vento accesserit oras,
qui teneant (nam inculta videt), hominesne feraene,
quaerere constituit sociisque exacta referre.
classem in convexo nemorum sub rupe cavata   310
arboribus clausam circum atque horrentibus umbris
occulit; ipse uno graditur comitatus Achate
bina manu lato crispans hastilia ferro.
cui mater media sese tulit obvia silva
virginis os habitumque gerens et virginis arma   315

307-8. **quas...feraene (308):** indirect questions after *quaerere*. Cf. 309 n. **quas...oras:** accusative of place to which without preposition, as often in poetry, "to what shores..." **vento:** ablative of means. **teneant:** understand *oras* (307) as object. **hominesne feraene:** the question of *qui teneant* is resolved into two parts — he wishes to see "who occupy the land," i.e. whether men or beasts do so. *-Ne...-ne* is used instead of the more usual *utrum... an*. **inculta:** "desert wastes." **videt:** the final syllable is long; cf. 651 *peterēt*. Like other poets, Vergil sometimes lengthens a final short syllable when it coincides with the *ictus*, the metrical stress that falls on the first long syllable of each foot (see Appendix A).

309. **quaerere:** governs the indirect questions in 307-8, though the questions could also be construed after *explorare* ("to find out what..."). Cf. 306 n. **exacta:** here "the results of his enquiries."

310. **in convexo nemorum:** "beneath overarching woods," lit. "in a vaulted" or "overarched place of woods." Vergil seems to be describing a stream over which the trees form an arch or vault. *Convexo* is a noun formed from the neuter of the adjective *conversus*. The neuter of many adjectives is thus used substantivally. Cf. 111 *in brevia*, 219 *extrema*, 281 *in melius* "for the better."

311. **circum:** adverb; construe with *clausam*. **horrentibus umbris:** *horrentibus* really describes the "bristling" trees but here is used of their "shadows" (cf. enallage*).

312. **uno...comitatus Achate:** the use of the ablative without *ab* after *comitatus* is usual. *Uno* here means "alone."

313. **bina:** poetic for "two" (cf. *duo*). Cf. 381 *bis denis*, 393 *bis senos*. **lato...ferro:** ablative of quality or description (AG §415), "of broad iron head." **crispans:** here, "holding" or "balancing." This line is repeated at 12.165.

314. **mater...sese tulit obvia:** "his mother went to meet," lit. "brought herself" or "advanced opposite." The dative *cui* is a connecting relative pronoun and refers to Aeneas. The adjective *obvia* is in the nominative and governs the dative *cui*. We might have more naturally expected the accusative *obviam*.

315. **gerens:** here "displaying," or perhaps "having"; this word is used in Latin not only of things that can be carried or put on such as *arma*, but also of the eyes, face, forehead, etc. Cf. the description of Hector at 2.278: *vulneraque illa gerens*.

Spartanae, vel qualis equos Threissa fatigat
Harpalyce volucremque fuga praevertitur Hebrum.
namque umeris de more habilem suspenderat arcum
venatrix dederatque comam diffundere ventis,
nuda genu nodoque sinus collecta fluentis.   320
ac prior 'heus,' inquit, 'iuvenes, monstrate, mearum
vidistis si quam hic errantem forte sororum
succinctam pharetra et maculosae tegmine lyncis,
aut spumantis apri cursum clamore prementem."

316-17. **Spartanae:** modifying *virginis* (315). **qualis...:** similes* are often condensed; here the fuller expression would be something like *talis fuit qualis est Harpalyce cum equos fatigat* (Austin). **equos...fatigat:** "wearies horses," i.e. tires them out by the speed of her running. **Threissa...Harpalyce:** "Thracian Harpalyce." This is the earliest mention of Harpalyce, a Thracian princess who was forced to live in the woods after her father was driven from power (Servius). She functions as a kind of prototype for Camilla in book 11. **volucremque fuga praevertitur Hebrum:** "and outstrips (*praevertitur*) in flight the swift Hebrus." The river *Hebrus* in Thrace, however, was not renowned to be a rapid river, according to Servius.

318. **de more:** i.e. she is dressed as a *venatrix* (cf. 319). **habilem:** "handy," i.e. easy both to wear and to use.

319. **venatrix:** in apposition to Venus, the subject of *suspenderat* and *dederat*. Note how this word essentially summarizes the description contained in 315-18. **dederatque comam diffundere ventis:** "and had given her hair to the winds to scatter." The infinitive seems epexegetic, further "explaining" the phrase *dederat ventis*.

320. **nuda genu...:** *genu* is accusative of respect; *sinus* is probably accusative after *collecta* taken in a middle sense. Throughout this description of Venus, one should probably think of Diana the huntress (cf. 337 n.).

321-2. **prior:** here "first." Venus addresses them before (thus *prior*) they address her. **monstrate...vidistis si quam:** "point (her) out, if you have seen any...," not "tell me whether you have seen," which would be an indirect question and require the subjunctive *videritis*.

323. **succinctam pharetra...tegmine:** *succingere* means "hold one's clothes up with a belt." Here *succinctam pharetra* means that the quiver hangs from the belt which holds the robe up. With *tegmine* the participle is perhaps used more loosely as "girded" or "equipped."

324. **aut:** joins *errantem* (322) and *prementem*, the two main actions involved in hunting.

Sic Venus; et Veneris contra sic filius orsus: 325
"nulla tuarum audita mihi neque visa sororum,
o quam te memorem, virgo? namque haud tibi vultus
mortalis, nec vox hominem sonat; o, dea certe
(an Phoebi soror? an Nympharum sanguinis una?),
sis felix nostrumque leves, quaecumque, laborem   330
et quo sub caelo tandem, quibus orbis in oris
iactemur doceas; ignari hominumque locorumque
erramus vento huc vastis et fluctibus acti:

325-34. Aeneas prays to the huntress (his disguised mother) for help.

Aeneas' response to Venus echoes Odysseus' words to Nausicaa (*Odyssey* 6.149-85).

325. **Sic Venus:** a verb of speaking (e.g. *fata est*) is omitted, as often in poetry. Note the responsion between (disguised) mother and son, achieved with *contra* and by the repetition both of *sic* and of the name *Venus* (*Venus...Veneris...filius*). **orsus:** from *ordior* ("begin"), not *orior* ("rise").

326. **mihi:** the dative of the agent is used here after the perfect passives, *audita (est)* and *visa (est)*, though it is more common after the passive periphrastic. Note that Aeneas' initial response (*audita...visa*) answers Venus' specific questions involving what Aeneas and Achates have seen (*vidistis* 322) and heard (*clamore* 324).

327. **o quam te memorem, virgo:** "Oh, how am I to address you, maiden?" The potential subjunctive conveys Aeneas' hesitation. In the words *o, dea certe* (328) he resumes his address, using the general term "goddess"; then line 329 *an Phoebi soror?...una?* is a parenthesis in which he hesitantly asks if she is Diana or a nymph (cf. 329 n.). **namque... mortalis (328):** supply *est*.

328. **nec vox hominem sonat:** "nor does your voice sound human"; *hominem* is a cognate or internal accusative. Cf. *Satyrum movetur* (Horace, *Epistulae* 2.2.125).

329. **an...una?:** the verb *es* must be supplied to complete the questions. **Phoebi soror:** i.e. Diana. Odysseus asks the same question of Nausicaa, who is compared to Artemis (*Odyssey* 6.151). Cf. 327 n.

330. **sis...leves:** optative subjunctives (cf. *Eclogue* 5.65 *sis bonus o felixque tuis*). **felix:** "propitious" or "gracious." **quaecumque:** an ellipsis* for "whoever you are"; supply *es*.

331. **quo sub caelo tandem:** "beneath what sky indeed." Understand *iactemur* (332) in this indirect question. *Tandem* is commonly used in questions to add emphasis, cf. *quousque tandem abutere, Catilina, patientia nostra?* (Cicero, *in Catilinam* 1.1).

332. **iactemur:** cf. 331 n. **doceas:** optative subjunctive (cf. *sis* and *leves* in 330). **hominumque locorumque:** genitives after *ignari*. *Locorumque* creates a hypermetric line: its *-que* is elided before the vowel that begins the next line (cf. *nexaeque* 448).

333. **vastis et fluctibus:** the postponement of *et* is a stylistic device providing metrical flexibility that the neoteric poets of the mid-first century BCE (e.g. Catullus) took over from the Hellenistic poets (e.g. Callimachus and Theocritus, third century BCE).

multa tibi ante aras nostra cadet hostia dextra."

Tum Venus: "haud equidem tali me dignor honore;   335
virginibus Tyriis mos est gestare pharetram
purpureoque alte suras vincire coturno.
Punica regna vides, Tyrios et Agenoris urbem;
sed fines Libyci, genus intractabile bello.
imperium Dido Tyria regit urbe profecta,   340
germanum fugiens. longa est iniuria, longae

---

334. **multa...hostia:** "many sacrifices" (i.e. many a sacrifice); understand a protasis such as "if you grant our request." **tibi:** "in your honor."

335-71. Venus tells the story of Dido, her flight from Tyre and her founding of Carthage.

335. **tali me dignor honore:** like the adjective *dignus*, the verb *dignor* can take the ablative of the thing of which a person is deemed worthy (here *tali honore*, cf. 334).

336. **virginibus Tyriis:** dative and emphatic by position.

337. **purpureoque...:** purple boots bound high upon the leg are clearly the regular mark of Diana (Vergil describes her statue as *puniceo suras evincta coturno* at *Eclogue* 7.32). Venus is thus explaining Aeneas' mistake in calling her Diana (*Phoebi soror*) at 329. Because purple dye came chiefly from Tyre, it is natural that a Tyrian-looking huntress would wear purple boots. With *Punica* in 338, there may be an etymological play on *puniceus*, which can mean both "Punic" and "purple" (O'Hara (1996) 124-5).

338. **Punica:** cf. 337 n. **regna:** plural for singular, common in Vergil and poetry more generally. **Agenoris urbem:** Agenor was a Phoenician king and forefather of Dido. *Agenoris urbem* is an erudite way of saying "Carthage."

339. **fines Libyci:** supply *sunt*. *Fines* (lit. "neighboring lands") here means "neighbors." **genus intractabile bello:** in loose apposition to *fines Libyci*. Cf. 4.40 *Gaetulae urbes, genus insuperabile bello.*

340. **imperium...regit:** "holds sway." *Imperium* is the act or office of commanding, not the country or "empire" over which the command is exercised, though it often approximates this sense (cf. 287). It is here cognate accusative after *regit*. **Dido:** her name, according to Servius *auctus* (cf. 294-6 n.), was initially *Elissa*, but after she committed suicide instead of marrying an African prince in violation of her love for her deceased husband (cf. 494-642 n.), she was called *Dido*, which is Phoenician for *virago*, "heroic woman" (cf. Hexter (1992) 348-50). The name *Dido* is preferred in Vergil, though *Elissa* appears at 4.335, 610; 5.3.

341. **germanum:** Dido's brother Pygmalion, whose crimes are described at 346-56. The succinct participial phrase *germanum fugiens* is emphatically placed and punctuated by a caesura; it introduces the impious story of Pygmalion very effectively. **iniuria:** here a "tale of injustice."

ambages; sed summa sequar fastigia rerum.
huic coniunx Sychaeus erat, ditissimus agri
Phoenicum, et magno miserae dilectus amore,
cui pater intactam dederat primisque iugarat   345
ominibus. sed regna Tyri germanus habebat
Pygmalion, scelere ante alios immanior omnis.
quos inter medius venit furor. ille Sychaeum
impius ante aras atque auri caecus amore
clam ferro incautum superat, securus amorum   350

---

342. **ambages:** "complicated story." *Ambages* is used literally (i.e. "roundabout path") at 6.29 for the "windings" of a labyrinth, but its metaphorical sense is common, cf. *Georgics* 2.46 *per ambages et longa exorsa tenebo,* and such phrases as *mitte ambages* ("come to the point"), *positis ambagibus.* **fastigia:** here means "main points" (i.e. high points), an unusual usage of this word.

343. **huic:** dative of possessor. **Sychaeus:** note that the first syllable is long here, but short at 348 (cf. 258 n.). **ditissimus agri:** cf. 14 n. (Some editors, including Austin and Mynors, accept the emendation *auri* for the *agri* attested in the manuscripts, on the ground that Tyre was a purely commercial city entirely unconcerned in agriculture and dependent on imported corn for food.)

344. **miserae:** dative of agent after *dilectus* (cf. 326 n.).

345-6. **cui:** *Sychaeo.* **intactam.** i.e. a "virgin." **primisque...ominibus:** i.e. "in earliest marriage." *Ominibus* refers to taking the auspices, without which the Romans never entered on any solemn or important business. It was especially necessary that marriage should be celebrated at certain lucky seasons and on lucky days. **iugarat:** = *iugaverat.* **regna:** cf. 338 n.

347. **Pygmalion:** this Pygmalion is not to be confused with the artist who falls in love with his own sculpture (cf. Ovid, *Metamorphoses* 10). **scelere ante...:** *scelere* is ablative of respect; the comparative *immanior* with *ante alios omnis* expresses an intense degree of cruelty (cf. 4.141 *ante alios pulcherrimus omnis*).

348. **quos inter:** the preposition follows its object (*quos,* i.e. Pygmalion and Sychaeus), an example of anastrophe*. Note the destructive role of *furor* here. Cf. 34-222 n.

349. **impius ante aras...:** Pygmalion's greed made him blind to the monstrous nature of his crime, the treacherous murder of a relative (cf. *clam, incautum*) at the altar (*aras*) of the household gods (4.20-1). **auri...amore:** *amore* is ablative of cause explaining *caecus* and governs the objective genitive *auri.*

350. **securus amorum...:** *securus* ("without care") is formed from *sine + cura* and followed by an objective genitive (cf. 349 n.); *amorum* is plural for singular: "without care for (his sister's) love."

germanae; factumque diu celavit et aegram
multa malus simulans vana spe lusit amantem.
ipsa sed in somnis inhumati venit imago
coniugis ora modis attollens pallida miris;
crudelis aras traiectaque pectora ferro   355
nudavit, caecumque domus scelus omne retexit.
tum celerare fugam patriaque excedere suadet
auxiliumque viae veteres tellure recludit
thesauros, ignotum argenti pondus et auri.
his commota fugam Dido sociosque parabat.   360

351-2. **et aegram…amantem:** "and making up many things (i.e. excuses) cruelly deceived the heart-sick lover (Dido) with empty hope." Note the emphatic placement of *aegram… amantem* at their line-ends. **malus:** describes Pygmalion but can be translated adverbially, "wickedly." Note how the use of *m* and *s* provides a fluidity reflecting the ease and success with which Pygmalion deceives his sister.

353. **in somnis:** though *somnus* generally means "sleep," it can be used in such constructions as *per somnum* and *in somnis* to mean "in one's dreams." **inhumati:** emphasizes the cruelty of Pygmalion's slaying of Sychaeus. We learn in 6.327-30 that unburied souls must wander for one hundred years before Charon can transport them across the river Acheron into the underworld.

354. **ora modis attollens pallida miris:** the phrase echoes Lucretius 1.123 *simulacra modis pallentia miris,* which Vergil uses verbatim at *Georgics* 1.477. The alliteration* of *modis miris* gives a mystical character to the words. Note that this apparition will be echoed by that of Hector in book 2, who urges Aeneas to flee his homeland to found a new city (2.270-95).

355. **crudelis aras:** *aras* is plural for singular (as is *pectora*); *crudelis,* while grammatically modifying *aras,* really describes Pygmalion because of his heinous crime.

356. **nudavit:** "laid bare"; take metaphorically with *aras,* literally with *pectora* (an example of zeugma*). **caecum:** "dark" and thus "secret," "hidden." **domus:** genitive.

357. **suadet:** sc. *Didonem.* Whereas prose would more normally use substantive clasues of result with the subjunctive (e.g. *ut celeret…*) after *suadeo* to express the action being urged, Vergil (and poets more generally) often use infinitives, here *celerare* and *excedere.* Cf. AG §563.

358. **auxiliumque viae:** describes the *veteres…thesauros,* in apposition to which stands the phrase *ignotum…auri.*

360. **his:** i.e. by Sychaeus' apparition and revelations.

conveniunt quibus aut odium crudele tyranni
aut metus acer erat; navis, quae forte paratae,
corripiunt onerantque auro. portantur avari
Pygmalionis opes pelago; dux femina facti.
devenere locos ubi nunc ingentia cernes   365
moenia surgentemque novae Karthaginis arcem,
mercatique solum, facti de nomine Byrsam,
taurino quantum possent circumdare tergo.
sed vos qui tandem? quibus aut venistis ab oris?
quove tenetis iter?" quaerenti talibus ille   370

---

361. **conveniunt quibus:** the antecedent of *quibus* is the implied subject of *conveniunt* (i.e. those who flee with Dido). **odium crudele tyranni:** this is in part an instance of enallage* (cf. 311 n.), and means "hatred of the cruel tyrant," but cruel tyranny also creates "cruel hatred of the tyrant"; so we speak not only of "cruel wrong" but also of "cruel suffering."

362. **quae forte paratae:** sc. *sunt;* "which by chance were ready," i.e. ready to set sail.

364. **Pygmalionis opes:** i.e. the buried treasure, which Pygmalion had murdered Sychaeus to gain, but which he loses nonetheless. **pelago:** ablative, "on" or "over the sea." **dux femina facti:** supply *est.* Courage (cf. also 340 n.) and leadership are important elements of Dido's characterization in Book 1.

365. **locos:** accusative of place to which without preposition (cf. 307-8 n.). **cernes:** Venus points out Carthage in the distance.

366. **novae Karthaginis:** on the paronomasia*, cf. 12 n. Dido's tale has already displayed numerous parallels with Aeneas'. In this line, Venus emphasizes Dido's success in founding her city, the very thing that Aeneas strives to accomplish.

367-8. **mercatique…:** "and purchased ground (called Byrsa from the name of the deed), as much as they could enclose with an oxhide." They purchased as much ground as an oxhide (*byrsa*) would enclose, whereupon they cut the hide into narrow strips, connected them, and spread them out to cover a wide area. This story probably arose from a false etymology: the Phoenicians called the citadel of Carthage *Bosra*, which the Greeks associated with *byrsa*, their own word for "oxhide." **quantum:** = *tantum quantum*, "as much as…" **possent:** subjunctive because the line seemingly reports the terms of the agreement.

369. **vos qui:** = *qui vos estis*? **quibus aut venistis ab oris:** the *aut* is delayed in Hellenistic fashion, cf. 333 n.

370. **quo:** "(to) where…?". **talibus…:** supply *verbis*. This phrase can refer either back to Venus' speech or forward to Aeneas' response, for which a verb such as *respondit* must be understood.

suspirans imoque trahens a pectore vocem:
    "O dea, si prima repetens ab origine pergam
et vacet annalis nostrorum audire laborum,
ante diem clauso componet Vesper Olympo.
nos Troia antiqua, si vestras forte per auris   375
Troiae nomen iit, diversa per aequora vectos
forte sua Libycis tempestas appulit oris.

372-386. *Aeneas identifies himself and begins lamenting his suffering but is interrupted by the huntress.*

372-3. **O dea:** note that Venus had essentially denied she was a goddess at 335-7. **si...vacet:** impersonal usage of the verb, "if there were time (for you) to..." **repetens ab:** lit. "tracing back the record from," "beginning from"; *prima*, modifying *origine*, is pleonastic*. **annalis:** "record," "history"; originally "the yearly register" of events kept by the *pontifices* but later used for an "historical work" (e.g. the *Annals* of Tacitus). Note the stress that Aeneas lays on his tribulations.

374. **ante:** adverbial, "first" (i.e. before the tale is ended). **componet:** this reading has much better manuscript authority than *componat*. The construction *si...pergam* (present subjunctive)...*componet* (future indicative) is a mixed condition; the future marks much greater certainty than the subjunctive. **clauso...Olympo:** the sky (the sense of *Olympo*) is "closed" at night as a house is closed, and similarly it is "opened" in the morning, cf. 10.1 *Panditur interea domus omnipotentis Olympi.* **Vesper:** the evening star. This line further underscores Aeneas' sufferings (cf. 372-3 n.) by considering them in a cosmic context.

375. **Troia antiqua:** ablative of place from which, dependent on *appulit* (377), which in turn governs the accusative *nos* and has *tempestas* as its subject. Note the emphatic placement of *nos* and *Troia.* **si...forte...:** "if by chance"; with the indicative this phrase often expresses no doubt whatever as to the fact, but merely puts it hypothetically. Aeneas thus brings up his heroic past with modesty. (Interestingly, the liar Sinon uses similar language at 2.81-2.) **vestras:** i.e. of you and your countrymen, cf. 140 n.

376. **per aequora vectos:** modifying *nos* (375), this phrase also appears at 6.335, 692; 7.228, *Georgics* 1.206, and echoes Catullus' description of his difficult journey to perform last rites for his brother (*multa per aequora vectus* 101.1).

377. **forte sua:** "by its own chance" or "whim," an unusual phrase, but with it Aeneas emphasizes that he and his people did not choose to land where they did and are not enemies. **Libycis...oris:** dative after the compound verb *appulit*.

sum pius Aeneas, raptos qui ex hoste penatis
classe veho mecum, fama super aethera notus.
Italiam quaero patriam et genus ab Iove summo.   380
bis denis Phrygium conscendi navibus aequor,
matre dea monstrante viam data fata secutus;
vix septem convulsae undis Euroque supersunt.
ipse ignotus, egens, Libyae deserta peragro,
Europa atque Asia pulsus." nec plura querentem   385
passa Venus medio sic interfata dolore est:

378. **sum pius…:** Aeneas finally answers Venus' question *sed vos qui tandem?* (369), and identifies himself with his defining virtue, *pietas*. The line and scene echo *Odyssey* 9.19-20 where Ulysses says to Alcinous: "I am Odysseus, great Laertes' son,/ Known for my cunning throughout the world,/ And my fame reaches even to heaven" (Lombardo). Like Aeneas, Odysseus had also singled out his defining trait, his cunning. **qui…:** the relative clause provides evidence of his self-proclaimed *pietas*. **raptos…penatis:** the flashback narrative of Troy's fall in book two closes with the image of Aeneas fleeing Troy with his father Anchises on his shoulders holding the Penates, and with his son Ascanius holding his hand (cf. 2.717-24).

379. **fama:** ablative.

380. **Italiam…:** Aeneas can make these claims because Dardanus the son of Jupiter (28 n.) and ancestor of the Trojans was said originally to have come from Italy (3.167).

381. **bis denis…vix septem…(383):** contrasted clauses put side by side, and marked by emphatic words, cf. 184 n. **denis:** "ten," cf. 313 n. Aeneas had twenty ships before Juno's storm. He landed at Carthage with seven (383), and had himself witnessed the sinking of Orontes' ship (cf. 112-17 and 584-5). As a result there are still twelve ships unaccounted for. **conscendi…aequor:** "I climbed the Phrygian sea," i.e. I put out to sea from Troy. This phrase seems an unusual development of *conscendi navem*, "board a ship" or "embark."

382. **matre dea monstrante:** emphasizes both his divine parentage and his *pietas*, though it is Apollo and his priests (not Venus) who provide much of the guidance during his travels from Troy to Carthage. **data fata secutus:** *fata* here probably means "oracles" (referring especially to that given by Apollo at Delos, 3.94-8) and not Aeneas' larger destiny.

383. **vix septem…:** not "scarcely seven" but "scarcely (i.e. with difficulty) do seven shattered by waves and (the East) wind survive." Cf. 381 n. On the seven ships, cf. 170.

384. **ignotus, egens:** the asyndeton* helps emphasize Aeneas' sufferings, though *ignotus* seemingly contradicts Aeneas' claim that he is *fama super aethera notus* (379). **Libyae deserta:** again in bitter contrast to *Europa atque Asia* (385).

385. **querentem:** "the word *querentem* summarises the content of his speech. He is far from being the perfect Stoic" (Williams).

"Quisquis es, haud, credo, invisus caelestibus auras
vitalis carpis, Tyriam qui adveneris urbem.
perge modo atque hinc te reginae ad limina perfer.
namque tibi reduces socios classemque relatam   390
nuntio et in tutum versis Aquilonibus actam,
ni frustra augurium vani docuere parentes.
aspice bis senos laetantis agmine cycnos,
aetheria quos lapsa plaga Iovis ales aperto
turbabat caelo; nunc terras ordine longo   395
aut capere aut captas iam despectare videntur:

387-401. The huntress (Venus) directs them to Carthage and reveals that their comrades are safe.

387-8. **Quisquis es:** Harpalyce/Venus pretends she has not recognized Aeneas' name (378).
haud: construe with *invisus. **auras** / **vitalis carpis:** "you breathe the breath of life,"
cf. Lucretius 3.405 *vivit et aetherias vitalis suscipit auras.* **qui adveneris:** relative clause
expressing cause (cf. AG §534e).

390-1. **namque...:** *reduces* and *relatam/actam* are predicate, describing *socios* and *classem*
respectively; *esse* must therefore be understood for each clause (e.g. *nuntio socios reduces
esse...*). **in tutum:** "to safety," "to a safe (place)," cf. 310 n. **versis Aquilonibus:** "when the
north winds had (been) turned" or "changed."

392. **ni frustra...:** note the playful irony* of this line as Venus continues her charade as
a Tyrian huntress (cf. 336). *Vani* should be translated adverbially ("falsely," not "false
parents"). The combination of *frustra* and *vani* is pleonastic*.

393-400. Venus points to and describes an omen of twelve swans, which, though chased by
an eagle, escape and reach land (393-6). She interprets it to mean that Aeneas' twelve ships,
though beset by the terrible storm (= eagle), have reached safe harbor (397-400). O'Hara
(1990) 9-14 notes the omen's deceptive quality because it omits reference to a thirteenth
ship, that of Orontes, which had sunk (cf. 381 n.). Vergil uses another swan omen at
12.244-56.

393. **bis senos...cycnos:** the swans represent the twelve missing Trojan ships. Swans were
sacred to Venus. **agmine:** emphatic, their "orderly array" is opposed to the "rout" described
in *turbabat* (395).

394. **aetheria...plaga:** this ablative phrase describes the supreme height (*aetheria*) and
unbounded range (*plaga*) of the domain from which the eagle (*Iovis ales*) swoops down.

396. **aut capere...:** this line should be taken closely with Venus' interpretation of the swans
at 400. Venus makes this clear not only with *haud aliter* (399) but also with the parallel
aut...aut constrctions in 396 and 400. As a result, *terras...capere* (395-6) is parallel to
portum tenet (400), *captas despectare* to *pleno subit ostia velo* (400). And just as *portum tenet*
describes those ships which have reached their goal and are no longer sailing, as opposed
to those which are only near their goal and still have their sails spread, so *terras capere*
must describe those swans which are on the ground and are no longer flying, and *captas
despectare* those swans which are still only near the ground and have their wings still

ut reduces illi ludunt stridentibus alis
et coetu cinxere polum cantusque dedere,
haud aliter puppesque tuae pubesque tuorum
aut portum tenet aut pleno subit ostia velo.   400
perge modo et, qua te ducit via, derige gressum."
    Dixit et avertens rosea cervice refulsit,
ambrosiaeque comae divinum vertice odorem
spiravere; pedes vestis defluxit ad imos;
et vera incessu patuit dea. ille ubi matrem   405
agnovit tali fugientem est voce secutus:

---

spread. Therefore it is probably best to construe *terras capere* as "occupy the ground," and *captas despectare* as "gaze down on the ground already occupied (by the others)." Still it is a difficult line, and Hardie (1987) argues for Housman's emendation of *stellas* for *terras* (395), at least in part, to make better sense of *capere* and *captas*, since the swans are not on the ground but still in the air in 398. Cf. the discussions in Austin (*ad loc.*) and Khan (2003) 267-71, who read *capere* in 396 as meaning that the swans have not yet reached land but are only approaching. By this reading, *capere* corresponds to *pleno subit ostia velo* in 400, and the *aut...aut* constructions in 396 and 400 are not parallel but chiastically related.

397. **stridentibus alis:** "with rustling wings."

398. **et coetu cinxere...:** the force of this line is marked by the change of tense from *ludunt* (397) to *cinxere* and *dedere;* its action precedes that of the previous line. Thus the swans, as they descend, "play with noisy wing" after they have first circled round the sky in triumph with songs of joy.

400. **portum tenet...:** cf. 396 n.

402-17. Venus reveals her identity and disappears, but first hides Aeneas and Achates in a cloud.

402. **avertens:** intransitive, cf. 104 n. **refulsit:** the compound verb expresses that something stands out brightly against a dark background or in comparison with something previously obscure, cf. 588.

403. **ambrosiae...comae:** *ambrosia* is either 1) the food of the gods or 2) an unguent of the gods. Here clearly the adjective is connected with its second meaning, cf. *Georgics* 4.415 *ambrosiae odorem.* "Fragrance" was regularly associated with the presence of a deity (cf. Euripides, *Hippolytus* 1391, Aeschylus, *Prometheus Bound* 115), and Zeus' locks are called ambrosial at *Iliad* 1.529. **vertice:** ablative of separation, "from her head."

404. **pedes...:** cf. 320 n. Goddesses were usually depicted wearing long, flowing robes.

405. **et vera...:** "and by her step she was revealed a true goddess"; for *incessu* cf. 46 n. **dea. ille:** Vergil has hiatus (cf. 16 n.) after a short vowel only here and *Eclogues* 2.53 *pruna* (*honos...*). In both cases there is a strong pause, and here the pause helps intensify Aeneas' astonishment.

406. **tali...voce:** i.e. with these words.

"quid natum totiens, crudelis tu quoque, falsis
ludis imaginibus? cur dextrae iungere dextram
non datur ac veras audire et reddere voces?"
talibus incusat gressumque ad moenia tendit.   410
at Venus obscuro gradientis aëre saepsit,
et multo nebulae circum dea fudit amictu,
cernere ne quis eos neu quis contingere posset
molirive moram aut veniendi poscere causas.
ipsa Paphum sublimis abit sedesque revisit   415
laeta suas, ubi templum illi, centumque Sabaeo
ture calent arae sertisque recentibus halant.

---

407. **crudelis tu quoque:** i.e. you as well as everyone/everything else.

409. **non datur:** "is it not granted" or "allowed." **veras:** i.e. without disguise (cf. *falsis imaginibus*). Reed (2007) 187 n. 20 sees an allusion in this line to the abandoned Ariadne's lament at Catullus 64.166: *nec missas audire queunt nec reddere voces?*

411. **obscuro...aëre.** the Homeric model here is *Odyssey* 7.14-17, where Athena pours a thick mist round Odysseus to make him invisible (cf. also *Iliad* 3.380-1, where Aphrodite rescues Paris by hiding him in a "thick mist"). The Greek word for mist (*aer*), the lower denser air, as opposed to the bright upper air, can have the meaning "mist," "cloud"; the Latin *aer* does not naturally have this meaning, though the epithet *obscuro* suggests it. Later the encircling cloud is called *nebula* (439) and *nubes* (516, 580, 587). **gradientis:** accusative plural describing Aeneas and Achates.

412. **dea:** strictly in apposition with *Venus,* but really, as its position shows, goes with *circumfudit,* and indicates that the "enfolding" was an act of divine power. **circum...fudit:** *circumfudit* by tmesis (Gr. "cutting), the separation of elements of a compound word by interjecting a word or phrase in between.

413-14. **cernere ne quis...:** negative purpose clause. **moliri...moram:** "contrive delay." "*Moliri* has here the idea of creating an obstacle as well as making with effort (424)" (Williams).

415. **Paphum:** Paphos in Cyprus was one of the central places for Venus' worship. **sublimis:** adjective that can be translated adverbially, "through the sky." Cf. *Odyssey* 8.362-3: "And Aphrodite, who loves laughter and smiles, [went] / To Paphos on Cyprus, and her precinct there/ With its smoking altar" (Lombardo). Note Vergil's amplification of Homer's single "smoking altar" here.

416. **templum illi:** supply *est. Illi* is dative and refers to Venus. **Sabaeo:** "Sabaean," "of the Sabaeans," a people in SW Arabia famous for their frankincense (*tus*).

418-93: Aeneas at Juno's temple in Carthage

Following Venus' advice (cf. 389), Aeneas and Achates, still hidden in a mist (cf. 411-12) proceed to Carthage. The sight of this growing and bustling city elicits admiration from Aeneas: *o fortunati, quorum iam moenia surgunt!* (437). The two Trojans then find a grove in which a temple is under construction, decorated with murals portraying events from the Trojan war. Vergil pauses to describe the artwork, eight murals that might be divided into pairs: the victories of the Trojans presumably under Hector (466-7) and of the Greeks under Achilles (468); the deaths of Rhesus (469-73) and Troilus (474-8); the Trojan women supplicating Pallas (479-82) and Priam supplicating Achilles (483-7); the fighting of Memnon (488-9) and of Penthesilea (490-3). Aeneas' "tour" of Carthage and the murals have important models in the *Odyssey*, where Odysseus, also hidden in a mist created by a goddess (Athena), admires Phaeacia and the royal palace (Book 7), and hears tales about Troy (Book 8). See, e.g., Knauer (1964a) and Clay (1988), who also discerns the influence of the Cyclops episode of *Odyssey* 9.

A detailed and vivid description of an object, person, or event is called an *ecphrasis* (pl. *ecphrases*), though, in a more restricted sense, the term ecphrasis was applied to a detailed description specifically of a work of art, as here. This scene presents the first of three particularly important ecphrases of art in the *Aeneid* — the other two being the doors on Apollo's temple at Cumae (6.20-33) and Aeneas' shield (8.626-728). The murals at Carthage are generally taken to reflect on the character of Aeneas and on the larger themes of the poem, but their meaning is contested. Their description, though in the poet's voice, privileges Aeneas' perspective (cf. 456 n.), and we are also given Aeneas' verbal reaction to them (459-63). To Aeneas, the paintings suggest both that the greatness of the Trojans, though defeated, is celebrated everywhere, and that their suffering elicits compassion — even among the Carthaginians (cf. also 450-2). Yet, some readers have found this understanding somehow inadequate. Despite Aeneas' words, the pictures (also) show — and thus in some way celebrate — the Greeks' victory over the Trojans, and they do so at the temple of the goddess Juno, Aeneas' greatest enemy (e.g. Horsfall (1973-74)). He does not seem aware of these facts or possibilities, and thus we are left with important interpretive questions: is Aeneas misinterpreting the murals? Is there only one way to interpret the murals, and does it have to be Aeneas'? What do Aeneas' reactions tell us about him? Finally, how do these representations shed light on the concerns of the narrative frame (and epic more generally) in which they are enclosed?

For more on Vergilian ecphrasis and Dido's murals, see R.D. Williams (1960), Horsfall (1973-74: 78-9 = 1990: 136-8) , Johnson (1976) 99-105, Thomas (1983), Clay (1988), Leach (1988) 309-19, Fowler (1991), Lowenstam (1993), Barchiesi (1997, 1999), Bartsch (1998), Putnam (1998), Lowrie (1999), and Nelis (2001) 79-82.

Corripuere viam interea, qua semita monstrat.
iamque ascendebant collem, qui plurimus urbi
imminet adversasque aspectat desuper arces.　　　　　420
miratur molem Aeneas, magalia quondam,
miratur portas strepitumque et strata viarum.
instant ardentes Tyrii: pars ducere muros
molirique arcem et manibus subvolvere saxa,
pars optare locum tecto et concludere sulco;　　　　　425
iura magistratusque legunt sanctumque senatum.

I.421-965

418-40. Achates and Aeneas climb a hill and enviously watch Carthage being built.

For this scene, cf. *Odyssey* 7.37-45, where Athena leads Odysseus through the Phaeacians' city to King Alcinous' palace.

418. **Corripuere viam…:** when people walk or run vigorously they seem to "seize" or "devour" the way; hence very often in poetry *carpere viam* (6.629), *iter, fugam,* or more strongly *corripere viam*, as here. **qua:** "where."

419. **plurimus:** "with its great size."

420. **adversas:** "opposite" or "facing," modifying *arces*.

421. **miratur…miratur (422):** anaphora*, initial placement, asyndeton*, and spondaic rhythm all contribute to the greatness of Aeneas' wonder. **molem:** the "mass" of the growing city. **magalia:** "huts"; in *Georgics* 3.340 Vergil uses *mapalia* for an "encampment" of nomad Libyans; *magalia* is a Phoenician word (Servius).

422. **miratur portas…:** for the phrase, cf. Horace, *Odes* 3.29.11-12, where Maecenas, from his palace on the Esquiline, loved to *mirari beatae / fumum et opes strepitumque Romae.* **strata viarum:** roughly means *stratas vias* "paved roads" but with more stress on the adjective which functions something like a substantive ("the paving of the roads"). The phrase is used at Lucretius 1.315, 4.415.

423. **ducere…:** the five infinitives in 423-5 can be construed as historic infinitives or as governed by *instant*. **ducere muros:** this phrase describes "building" a wall not in respect of its height but of its length; it is "to draw out a line of wall."

424. **moliri…subvolvere:** cf. 423 n. *Moliri* means "build"; *subvolvere* "roll up" (i.e. to where the rocks would be used in construction).

425. **tecto:** dative, "for a house" or "building." **concludere sulco:** "to enclose with a trench." Vergil may allude here to the regular practice in founding a city of demarcating its walls with "a furrow" (*sulcus*). For syntax, cf. 423 n.

426. **legunt:** zeugma*; the verb means "choose" with *magistratus* and *senatum*, but "make" or "adopt" with *iura*. There was an actual senate at Carthage called the *Gerousia* from about 400 BCE. However, the words *magistratus* and *senatum* describe the city in particularly Roman terms. This line has strong manuscript authority but disrupts the balance of the clause *pars…pars* (423, 425) followed by *hic…alii…, hic…alii* (427-8). Many therefore omit it, or place it elsewhere (Goold, e.g., places it after 368).

hic portus alii effodiunt; hic alta theatris
fundamenta locant alii, immanisque columnas
rupibus excidunt, scaenis decora alta futuris.
qualis apes aestate nova per florea rura   430
exercet sub sole labor, cum gentis adultos
educunt fetus, aut cum liquentia mella
stipant et dulci distendunt nectare cellas,
aut onera accipiunt venientum, aut agmine facto
ignavum fucos pecus a praesepibus arcent;   435
fervet opus redolentque thymo fragrantia mella.
"o fortunati, quorum iam moenia surgunt!"
Aeneas ait et fastigia suspicit urbis.
infert se saeptus nebula (mirabile dictu)

---

427. **hic portus…:** the harbor of Carthage, called Cothon, was in fact artificial. **theatris:** an anachronism.

428. **alii:** note the change from the *pars* construction (423-35) in the continued description of the building activity.

429. **excidunt:** "quarry." **scaenis:** an anachronistic detail that looks forward to stages at Rome. Cf. also *theatris* (427).

430-6. This simile* comparing the bustling Carthaginians building their city to bees is indebted to *Georgics* 4.162-9, where industrious bees are described in terms of human society.

430-1. **qualis…labor:** "such labor," subject of *exercet*. **nova:** ablative modifying *aetate*.

431-2. **adultos…fetus:** "full-grown young." **līquentia:** from *līquor* (deponent), but elsewhere Vergil has *līquens* from *līqueo*. The quantity of the *i* seems to have been uncertain (cf. Lucretius 4.1259 *līquidis et līquida*) but ultimately became short in all words except the verb *liquor*.

433. **nectare:** here "honey."

434. **venientum:** = *venientium*.

435. **ignavum fucos pecus…:** *ignavum…pecus* stands in apposition to *fucos* (drones); for the stylized word order, cf. *Eclogues* 3.3 *infelix o semper oves pecus* and *Georgics* 4.246 *aut dirum tineae genus*.

437. **o fortunati…:** expresses Aeneas' own longing to found the city fate has ordained for him, the central theme of the *Aeneid* (cf. 5-6).

438. **suspicit:** "looks up to"; a skilful word, intimating that by now he has descended from the hill (420) and come close up to the city.

439. **mirabile dictu:** *dictu* is an ablative of respect formed from the supine. For this construction, see 111 n.

per medios, miscetque viris neque cernitur ulli.   440
   Lucus in urbe fuit media, laetissimus umbrae,
quo primum iactati undis et turbine Poeni
effodere loco signum, quod regia Iuno
monstrarat, caput acris equi; sic nam fore bello
egregiam et facilem victu per saecula gentem.   445
hic templum Iunoni ingens Sidonia Dido
condebat, donis opulentum et numine divae,
aerea cui gradibus surgebant limina nexaeque
aere trabes, foribus cardo stridebat aënis.

---

440. **miscet:** supply *se* from the preceding line. **neque cernitur ulli:** for the dative of agent, cf. 326 n.

441-93. At a magnificent temple of Juno, they find paintings of scenes from the Trojan war. For this passage, cf. *Odyssey* 7.81-132

441. **laetissimus umbrae:** "very luxuriant in shade." For the genitive, cf. 14 n.

442. **quo...loco (443):** "in which place." **iactati undis et turbine Poeni:** note again the parallels between the Carthaginians and the Trojans (cf. 3-4).

443. **effodere loco signum:** according to Servius, a priest of Juno told Dido where to found the city. When digging was started, a head of an ox was discovered, but since oxen are usually subservient, another site was chosen where the head of a horse was uncovered. The horse is a sign of war (cf. 3.540 *bello armantur equi*) and wealth (cf. 14, for these two characteristics of Carthage).

444-5. **sic nam fore...:** indirect discourse, dependent on the sense of "telling" contained in *monstrarat* (= *monstraverat*)—"for (she had told them that) so (i.e. if they found the sign, and in agreement with its significance) the race would be..." **facilem victu:** "ready of livelihood" (Austin).

446. **hic:** adverb. **Sidonia:** Sidon, like Tyre, was a town on the coast of Phoenicia. Dido is called "Sidonian," as well as Tyrian.

447. **donis...:** "wealthy in offerings and the divine power of the goddess," an instance of zeugma*.

448-9. **aerea...:** "its (*cui*, dative, antecedent is *templum*) bronze threshold rose high above steps; the cross-beams were plated in bronze (*nexaeque aere trabes*); the hinge of the bronze doors creaked." The opulence of the temple entrance is conveyed by the emphasis on bronze (*aerea...aere...aënis*). The word *limina* literally indicates the threshold but may suggest the whole doorway or entrance; the *fores* are the actual doors; *trabes*, the great cross-beams or girders above it which support the roof and are *nexae aere* not because the rivets were of bronze but because they were "joined with bronze," i.e. consisting of plates of bronze riveted together. *Trabes* as cross-beams can also be found at Horace, *Odes* 2.18.3. **nexaeque:** note the hypermetric elision of the *-que*. Cf. 332 n.

hoc primum in luco nova res oblata timorem   450
leniit, hic primum Aeneas sperare salutem
ausus et adflictis melius confidere rebus.
namque sub ingenti lustrat dum singula templo
reginam opperiens, dum quae fortuna sit urbi
artificumque manus inter se operumque laborem   455
miratur, videt Iliacas ex ordine pugnas
bellaque iam fama totum vulgata per orbem,
Atridas Priamumque et saevum ambobus Achillem.
constitit et lacrimans "quis iam locus" inquit "Achate,

---

450. **nova res oblata:** "a strange thing encountered (by him)." **timorem:** despite Venus' protection, Aeneas still feared the danger they might encounter in this new city.

451-2. **hic primum…sperare:** for the potential irony* in this reaction, see 418-93 n. **ausus:** supply *est*. **et adflictis…:** i.e. put more trust in his fortunes, though they have been bad up until now. *Confidere* governs the dative *adflictis rebus*.

453. **namque…dum:** note the delay of *dum*; cf. 333 n.

454-5. **opperiens:** "waiting for." Note that at 389 Venus told Aeneas to approach Dido at her palace. **dum quae….:** "while he marvels at the city's fortune, the hands (i.e. artwork) of various artists intermingled (*inter se*) and the work of their labors…" **quae fortuna sit urbi:** indirect question after *miratur* (456). **manus:** "work created by the hands." For this meaning, cf. 2.306 *labores*, "things produced by labor"; 5.359 *artes*, "works of art"; 6.683 *manus*, "exploits."

456. **videt:** since Aeneas is subject, the description of the murals is introduced as representing his experience of them; cf. also *miratur* 456, *videbat* 466, *conspexit* 487, and 459 n. **ex ordine:** the battles are depicted one after the other (though not quite in chronological order).

457. **fama:** ablative.

458. **Atridas:** Agamemnon and Menelaus, the leaders of the Greeks. **ambobus:** i.e. the Atridae and Priam. Achilles was naturally "wrathful" against Priam; he was angry at the Atridae because Agamemnon took the captive Briseis from him, setting in motion the events that make up the theme of the *Iliad*, the wrath of Achilles.

459. **lacrimans:** note the emphasis on Aeneas' emotional response to the paintings here, at 465, 470, 485, and see 456 n. In the Classical world, tears were consistent with heroic character: e.g. Hector's shade cries as 2.271, Aeneas at 2.279, the Trojan seer Helenus at 3.348. Odysseus also famously cries when he hears Demodocus' songs about Troy. Johnson (1976), however, suggests that Aeneas' crying is characteristically different. Odysseus' tears ultimately contribute to the plot for they are involved in the uncovering of his identity among the Phaeacians, while Aeneas' tears focus on the portrayal of his emotions. **iam:** "by this time."

quae regio in terris nostri non plena laboris?   460
en Priamus. sunt hic etiam sua praemia laudi;
sunt lacrimae rerum et mentem mortalia tangunt.
solve metus; feret haec aliquam tibi fama salutem."
sic ait atque animum pictura pascit inani
multa gemens, largoque umectat flumine vultum.   465
namque videbat uti bellantes Pergama circum
hac fugerent Grai, premeret Troiana iuventus,
hac Phryges, instaret curru cristatus Achilles.

---

461. **sunt hic…:** "here too honor has its fitting rewards" (lit. "even here there are to honor its own rewards"). For this use of *suus*, cf. 3.469 *sunt et sua dona parenti*.

462. **sunt lacrimae rerum:** *rerum* is the genitive of that which causes the tears. *Mortalia* expresses generally the troubles to which mortals are subject, and the recollection of them touches other mortals, who know they are also vulnerable.

463. **metus:** accusative plural. **feret haec…:** Aeneas suggests that the Carthaginians will show compassion to them.

464. **pictura pascit inani:** a sort of oxymoron*. Food is substantial; here Aeneas "feeds" his heart on that which is unsubstantial, unreal. In addition, as Lowenstam (1993) 49 notes, "The irony is that the scenes comforting him prefigure similar tribulations that he must soon undergo." Note that *inani* occurs in the same metrical position in the pathetic description of Troilus (476).

465. **multa gemens:** *multa* is an internal accusative that can be translated adverbially: "groaning much" or "heavily." **largoque…flumine:** note the hyperbole*, emphasizing Aeneas' emotional response.

466. **namque videbat:** cf. 418-93 n. **uti:** an older form of *ut* ("how"), initiating a string of indirect questions in 466-8. **bellantes Pergama circum:** note the position of these words which qualify all the nominatives in the next two lines. *Circum* follows its object, an example of anastrophe*. *Pergama* was the citadel of Troy but was often used as a synonym for Troy.

467-8. **hac…hac:** "here…there." **fugerent Grai, premeret Troiana iuventus:** this and the next line are excellent illustrations of the co-ordination of contrasted clauses in Latin, cf. 184 n. The actions of the Greeks and Trojans in 467 stand in chiastic* relation to their actions in 468; the contrast is emphasized by asyndeton*. The verbs *fugerent, premeret,* and *instaret* are subjunctives in indirect question (cf. 466 n.). **hac Phryges:** understand *fugerent* from 467.

nec procul hinc Rhesi niveis tentoria velis
agnoscit lacrimans, primo quae prodita somno   470
Tydides multa vastabat caede cruentus,
ardentisque avertit equos in castra prius quam
pabula gustassent Troiae Xanthumque bibissent.
parte alia fugiens amissis Troilus armis,
infelix puer atque impar congressus Achilli,   475
fertur equis curruque haeret resupinus inani,

469. **nec procul hinc:** indicates the movement to describe another picture. **Rhesi:** Rhesus was a Thracian prince who came to assist the Trojans. An oracle had declared that Troy would never be taken if his famous snow-white horses were to taste the grass or water of Troy. As a result, Ulysses and Diomedes (*Tydides*) killed him and carried off his horses just after he had arrived among the Trojans. For his story, see *Iliad* 10.433-502 and the tragedy *Rhesus* (transmitted under Euripides' name, though his authorship is greatly doubted). **tentoria:** "tents."

470. **agnoscit lacrimans:** note the emphasis on Aeneas as viewer, cf. 459 n. **primo... prodita somno:** the phrase modifies *tentoria*, which stands by metonymy* for the soldiers. Rhesus and his men go to sleep their first night in Troy without taking any precautions and are thus "betrayed by sleep" for it leaves them open for attack. *Primo...somno* may also suggest the idea that the earliest sleep is the deepest .

471. **Tydides:** "the son of Tydides," i.e. Diomedes.

472-3. **in castra:** i.e. to the Greeks' *castra*. **prius quam...gustassent:** the subjunctive (*gustassent*) with *prius quam* ("before") expresses Diomedes' purpose in driving the horses away, cf. 193 n. and 469 n. **Xanthum:** a Trojan river.

474-8. Troilus' death. An oracle said that Troy would not be sacked if Troilus (a son of Priam) should reach the age of twenty. Troilus' story, like Rhesus' (469-73), involves an oracle that, if it had been fulfilled, would have made Troy invincible. In this passage Vergil emphasizes Troilus' youth, his mismatch with Achilles, and the pathos of his death. (The Shakespearean tale of Troilus and Cressida is medieval in origin.)

474. **parte alia:** a formulaic phrase in ecphrases that indicates the movement to another section of the artwork being described. Cf. 469 *nec procul hinc*. **amissis...armis:** note the extreme vulnerability of Troilus' situation.

475. **puer:** cf. Horace *Odes* 2.9.15-16 *impubem...Troilon*. **impar congressus Achilli:** *Achilli* is dative after *congressus*, "ill-matched to (fight) Achilles" (lit. "having met Achilles unequally"). The theme of young warriors who die in ill-suited combat is prominent in the second half of the epic — e.g. Euryalus, Pallas, and Lausus.

476. **fertur equis:** cf. *Georgics* 1.514 *fertur equis auriga neque audit currus habenas*. **curruque haeret...inani:** "clings to the empty car." The phrase *curru...inani* is dative with *haeret*, cf. 156.

lora tenens tamen; huic cervixque comaeque trahuntur
per terram, et versa pulvis inscribitur hasta.
interea ad templum non aequae Palladis ibant
crinibus Iliades passis peplumque ferebant   480
suppliciter, tristes et tunsae pectora palmis;
diva solo fixos oculos aversa tenebat.
ter circum Iliacos raptaverat Hectora muros
exanimumque auro corpus vendebat Achilles.
tum vero ingentem gemitum dat pectore ab imo,   485

477. **huic:** "his" (i.e. Troilus'). *Huic* is dative of reference, whereas English would use a possessive adjective.

478. **versa...hasta:** "by his (i.e. Troilus') inverted spear." **pulvis:** the *-is* is probably lengthened because it falls on the metrical ictus (cf. 307-8 n.), though some argue that the final syllable may have at one time been long. Cf. Enn. *Ann.* fr. 264 in Skutsch, 279 in Warmington *iamque fere pulvis ad caelum.*

479-82. This scene recalls the Trojan women's offering of a Gr. *peplos* (a woman's robe) to Pallas in *Iliad* 6.297-311.

479. **interea:** Aeneas now focuses on the next painting. **non aequae:** i.e. "angry" (an instance of litotes*).

480. **crinibus...passis:** "with hair dishevelled," ablative absolute. *Passis* is from *pando* (3), "spread out" (not *patior*). **Iliades:** "Trojan women." **peplumque ferebant:** the *peplos* was the special robe of Pallas.

481. **suppliciter:** "in suppliant fashion." **tunsae:** should be construed as a middle participle, here with present force — "having beaten" = "beating."

482. **diva solo...:** Pallas' reaction is similar to that at *Iliad* 6.311, where "Athena rejected their prayer." *Solo* is ablative, "on the ground."

483-7. Achilles' slaying of Hector and ransoming of the body to Priam look back to *Iliad* 22 and 24 respectively. Note that unlike the preceding descriptions, this one contains no words signaling the movement to another picture.

483-4. **raptaverat...vendebat:** the painter has seemingly conveyed the dragging of the body (pluperfect, *raptaverat*) in his portrayal of the corpse's ransoming (imperfect, *vendebat*). In Homer (*Iliad* 24.16) Hector is dragged around Patroclus' tomb, not the Trojan walls, and Apollo guards the body from disfigurement. With *vendebat*, "Vergil's tableau puts its emphasis on the crudely disembedded exchange of body for gold" (Syed (2005) 204), though see the important article on Vergilian ecphrasis by Fowler (1991) 31-3, which shows the difficulty of determing "whose points of view the pictures and the descriptions represent." **Hectora:** a Greek accusative.

485. Again, Aeneas' emotional response is ephasized, cf. 459 n.

ut spolia, ut currus, utque ipsum corpus amici
tendentemque manus Priamum conspexit inermis.
se quoque principibus permixtum agnovit Achivis,
Eoasque acies et nigri Memnonis arma.
ducit Amazonidum lunatis agmina peltis   490
Penthesilea furens mediisque in milibus ardet,
aurea subnectens exsertae cingula mammae
bellatrix, audetque viris concurrere virgo.

---

486. **ut:** "as." **currus:** Achilles' chariot. **ipsum corpus amici:** the corpse of Hector, who is an *amicus* from Aeneas' perspective. Hector's body had been tied to Achilles' chariot. See 483-7 n.

488. **se...agnovit:** Aeneas recognizes himself in the pictures.

489. **Eoasque...:** Memnon was the son of Aurora; his troops are thus *Eoas acies* ("Dawn's troops"; the Greek word for dawn is *Eos*). He brought the Aethiopians to assist Troy but was killed by Achilles. His exploits and those of the Amazons form part of the later legends which clustered around the *Iliad* and were treated by the "Cyclic poets." Memnon seems to have figured prominently in the lost epic *Aethiopis* by Arctinus, in which the Amazons are said to have been introduced.

490-3. Penthesilea, like Memnon, helped the Trojans but was killed by Achilles (cf. 489 n.). She was queen of the Amazons. The warrior Camilla is compared to her at 11.662.

490. **lunatis agmina peltis:** "troops with crescent shields." The ablative seems a poetic extension of the use of the ablative of quality. Interestingly, in the description of Penthesilea at 490-3, "the words *lunatis*, *peltis*, and *subnectens* are used here for the first time in Latin letters" (Putnam (1998) 35).

491. **furens...ardet:** note that Penthesilea's valor is emphasized.

492. **aurea...:** the girdle is fit slanting across her breast. The accusative *cingula* is plural for singular; *exsertae* ("uncovered") *mamae* is dative with the compound verb *subnectens*.

493. **audetque...:** "and she, a warrior maiden, dares to combat men." Notice the alliteration*, assonance*, and wordplay in *viris...virgo.*

494-642: Dido and the Trojans

Up until this point, Aeneas has heard about Dido's tragic past from Venus and observed the building of her city. Now the queen herself enters: she is regal and impressive as she engages in the business of state (cf. 496-508). Though Aeneas is transfixed by Dido's grandeur and success, Dido's impressive introduction will contrast with her tragic fall by the end of book 4. Ultimately, her career will be the antithesis of Aeneas', largely because Jupiter, history, and fate are not on her side or that of her city Carthage.

The presence of Dido in Aeneas' story is anachronistic, since Carthage itself was founded nearly four hundred years after the Trojan war. It was a feature, however, that may have entered the tradition as early as Naevius' *Bellum Punicum* (third century BCE). There, we are told that Aeneas goes to Carthage, but the loss of nearly all of the epic leaves Dido's role unclear. An older version of Dido's death, in fact, does not even involve Aeneas: she committed suicide on a pyre, not because of her impossible passion for Aeneas, but so that she would not have to marry a neighboring chieftan and thus violate her vow to her deceased husband Sychaeus. Yet another strand of the tradition, reported by Varro, says that Anna (Dido's sister) fell in love with Aeneas and killed herself as a result.

The exact development of the Dido-Aeneas affair leading up to the *Aeneid* thus remains unclear, but it seems that Vergil has exercised great originality in his adaptation of it. Vergil's Dido is a complex intertextual figure. Again, the Phaeacian books of the *Odyssey* are at play, but with many twists. Dido enters the scene much like Nausicaa at *Odyssey* 6.102-9, and offers help to Aeneas, much as Nausicaa had to Odysseus. But throughout the Carthaginian books, Dido also takes on characteristics of Alcinous and Arete, Nausicaa's parents, and includes echoes of Apollonius' Medea, herself modeled on Homer's Nausicaa. More generally, the entreaties to Dido, the entrance of Aeneas, and his interaction with Dido echo *Odyssey* 7.133-347, where Odysseus entreats king Alcinous and queen Arete.

Vergil thus elevates the Dido legend to a central place in his epic, making the Carthaginian affair a major challenge for Aeneas, testing his resolve to follow fate and thus his ability to control his passions. At the same time, Dido's story will raise important and difficult questions about the nature and morality of the gods, who incite a woman to violate solemn vows to her deceased husband, only to bring about her death as a result.

For discussion of the many models for Dido, see Pease (1935) 11-30, Hexter (1992), Gordon (1998) 198-200, and Nelis (2001) 82-93. Cairns (1989) 29-57 uses ancient conceptions of the monarch to show that both Dido and Aeneas are presented as essentially good monarchs in Book 1, though Dido's virtues will deteriorate in Book 4.

> Haec dum Dardanio Aeneae miranda videntur,
> dum stupet obtutuque haeret defixus in uno,   495
> regina ad templum, forma pulcherrima Dido,
> incessit magna iuvenum stipante caterva.
> qualis in Eurotae ripis aut per iuga Cynthi
> exercet Diana choros, quam mille secutae
> hinc atque hinc glomerantur Oreades; illa pharetram   500

494-519. Dido advances to the temple with her retinue, when Aeneas, still hidden in mist, sees a group of his lost comrades approach the queen.

494. **Dardanio Aeneae:** dative of agent after *videntur*, cf. 326 n., 440. Dardanus was an ancestor of the Trojans. *Dardanio* (= "Trojan") therefore connects Aeneas emphatically with the images of the war just described.

495. Note how the asyndeton* of *dum* clauses and the tricolon* of verbs (*videntur, stupet, haeret*) convey Aeneas' passive gazing in contrast to Dido's regal and active introduction at 496-508.

496. **regina ad templum…:** the spondaic nature of this line adds grandeur to Dido's entrance. Probably because of Aeneas' ensuing passion for her, we learn from the start that she is *forma pulcherrima* (*forma* is ablative of respect explaining the nominative *pulcherrima*).

497. **incessit:** Dido's majesty is also suggested by this word, which is used of Juno (46) and Venus (405), cf. 46 n. **magna iuvenum stipante caterva:** the retinue indicates her importance. She is described similarly at 4.136 (so too Laocoon at 2.40).

498-502. This simile is adapted from Homer *Odyssey* 6.102-8, where it is applied to Nausicaa among her attendants: "as lithe as Artemis with her arrows striding down/ from a high peak – Taygetus' towering ridge or Erymanthus — / thrilled to race with the wild boar or bounding deer/ and nymphs of the hills race with her/ daughters of Zeus whose shield is storm and thunder,/ ranging the hills in sport, and Leto's heart exults/ as head and shoulders above the rest her daughter rises,/ unmistakable – she outshines them all, though all are lovely" (Fagles). (Apollonius adapted this same Homeric simile in his description of Medea at *Argonautica* 3.876-884.)

  In his transformation of the Homeric simile, Vergil focuses on Diana's happiness and grandeur (not her beauty and playfulness, as in Homer). In addition, the Diana as huntress simile connects Dido and the huntress Penthesilea just portrayed (cf. 490-3 n.), and forms a companion with the simile comparing Aeneas to Diana's brother Apollo at 4.143-9. (Cf. also Venus as Diana at 329.) It is an interesting example of how Vergil transforms his "sources" to achieve multiple effects. (It should be noted, however, that the Roman grammarian Probus found Vergil's version inappropriate to the context and lacking in Homer's details, cf. Aulus Gellius, *Attic Nights* 9.9.12-17.)

498. **Eurotae:** a river in Sparta, known for its temple of Diana. **Cynthi:** Cynthus was a hill in Delos, on which Latona gave birth to her twins, Diana and Apollo.

500. **Oreades:** mountain-nymphs, a Greek nominative plural with short *–es*.

fert umero gradiensque deas supereminet omnis
(Latonae tacitum pertemptant gaudia pectus):
talis erat Dido, talem se laeta ferebat
per medios instans operi regnisque futuris.
tum foribus divae, media testudine templi,   505
saepta armis solioque alte subnixa resedit.
iura dabat legesque viris, operumque laborem
partibus aequabat iustis aut sorte trahebat:
cum subito Aeneas concursu accedere magno
Anthea Sergestumque videt fortemque Cloanthum   510
Teucrorumque alios, ater quos aequore turbo
dispulerat penitusque alias avexerat oras.

501. **deas:** i.e. *Oreades* (500).

502. **Latonae…:** conveys Latona's joy as she contemplates her daughter (cf. 498 n.).
pertemptant: describes intense emotion, "overwhelm." Note the elaborate word order of
this parenthetic comment that comes close to being a golden line*.

503. **laeta:** note the emphasis on Dido's happiness and grandeur as she enters, qualities in
stark contrast to her imminent downfall.

504. **per medios:** "through the midst of her people." **instans:** "urging on," governs the
datives *operi* and *regnis…futuris*; the phrase is an instance of hendiadys* (cf. 61 n.). Dido is
engaged in the very activities of city-building that Aeneas aspires to.

505. **foribus…media testudine:** ablatives of place where (AG §421). The *fores* are the doors
of the shrine (*cella*) at the back of the main hall, which has an arched or vaulted roof
(*testudine*). At Rome it was common for the senate to convene in the hall of a temple, and
Dido's activities here may resonate with this practice.

506. **armis:** by metonymy* *armis* equals *armatis* ("armed guards"); probably the *caterva*
mentioned at 497.

507-8. **iura…leges:** *ius* is often used for the whole body of the law, whereas *lex* is a single
definite law, but here there is no distinction (cf. Horace, *Epistules* 1.16.41 *qui leges iuraque
servat*). **viris:** "…probably no more than 'people'; but there may be emphasis on Dido
as a woman, a lawgiver among men" (Austin). **partibus…iustis:** "with just division" or
"apportionment"; *aequabat* and *iustis* emphasize the queen's judicious and fair character.
trahebat: usually a name or lot is drawn; here it is a job (*laborem*). Note that Vergil focuses
especially on Dido's *iustitia* and *pietas* (as displayed by her building of the temple).

510. **Anthea Sergestumque....Cloanthum:** Aeneas had displayed special concern about the
whereabouts of Antheus and Cloanthus at 181 and 222 (see notes). This is Sergestus' first
mention; he (along with Cloanthus) will take part in the boat race at 5.114-267. **Anthea:**
Greek accusative.

511. **aequore:** "over the sea," not "in the sea."

512. **penitusque…:** here "far off," cf. 536; 6.59 *penitusque repostas / Massylum gentis*. **alias…
oras:** accusative of motion toward without *ad*.

obstipuit simul ipse, simul percussus Achates
laetitiaque metuque; avidi coniungere dextras
ardebant; sed res animos incognita turbat.   515
dissimulant et nube cava speculantur amicti
quae fortuna viris, classem quo litore linquant,
quid veniant; cunctis nam lecti navibus ibant
orantes veniam et templum clamore petebant.
    Postquam introgressi et coram data copia fandi,   520
maximus Ilioneus placido sic pectore coepit:
"o regina, novam cui condere Iuppiter urbem
iustitiaque dedit gentis frenare superbas,

---

513. **obstipuit:** gaping seems to be Aeneas' (*ipse*) dominant reaction at Carthage thus far, cf.
495 n. **simul...simul...:** = *et...et...* ("both....and..."). *Obstipuit* and *percussus* are singular but
describe both Aeneas and Achates.

514-15. **avidi:** take closely with *ardebant* and translate adverbially. **coniungere:** for the
infinitive after *ardebant*, cf. 11 n. **res...incognita:** "the uncertain circumstance," i.e.
Aeneas and Achates do not know how their comrades survived the storm, how they made it
to Dido's court, or how the Carthaginians will treat them.

516. **dissimulant:** "they conceal (their eagerness)" (cf. 208-9). **nube cava:** they are still
concealed by Venus' *obscuro aëre* (411).

517-18. **quae...veniant:** a series of three indirect questions dependant on *speculantur* (516).
With *quae foruna viris*, supply *sit*. **quid:** "why." **cunctis...navibus:** understand *ex*.

520-60. *Ilioneus asks Dido for help to repair their ships either for their further voyages to Italy or
for settling in Sicily.*

Ilioneus carefully states that the shipwrecked Trojans pose no threat to Dido's new city, and
makes clear their admiration for their leader Aeneas. His speech is filled with tricolon*
constructions (cf. 540-1, 544-5, 546-7, 549-50, 551-2, 555-6, 557-8), which add to its
solemnity and thus also to the weight of his stated opinion of Aeneas.

520. **introgressi...data:** *sunt* and *est* (respectively) are omitted.

521. **maximus:** sc. *natu,* "eldest" (cf. 654); so *minores* 532 = "a younger generation,"
"descendants," and commonly *maiores* = "ancestors." Ilioneus plays a similar role in Book 7,
when he addresses King Latinus (7.213-48).

522-3. **condere...dedit:** "permitted (you) to found," cf. 66 n. For the potential wordplay*
in *novam...urbem,* cf. 12 n. **iustitia:** Ilioneus accords Dido great respect (cf. *o regina*), and
here focuses on the justice of her rule that looks back to the scene at 507-8. **gentis frenare
superbas:** the *gentis* are the neighboring Libyan tribes. Dido seems to be a civilizing force,
in contrast to the *furor* and danger to the Trojans (and Rome) she will soon represent. Cf.
Anchises' famous words about Roman ideals to Aeneas in the underworld: *parcere subiectis
et debellare superbos* (6.853).

Troes te miseri, ventis maria omnia vecti,
oramus: prohibe infandos a navibus ignis,   525
parce pio generi et propius res aspice nostras.
non nos aut ferro Libycos populare penatis
venimus, aut raptas ad litora vertere praedas;
non ea vis animo nec tanta superbia victis.
est locus, Hesperiam Grai cognomine dicunt,   530
terra antiqua, potens armis atque ubere glaebae;
Oenotri coluere viri; nunc fama minores
Italiam dixisse ducis de nomine gentem.

---

524. **maria...vecti**: an extension of the use of the cognate accusative; cf. *ire iter, ire viam* "go a road," and *vehi maria* "carried over the seas" (cf. 3.191 *currimus aequor*).

525. **oramus:** note the effective enjambment* of this word, made still more emphatic by the strong caesura that follows it.

526. **parce pio generi:** Ilioneus emphasizes the Trojans' quintessential virtue *pietas*. At the same time, Dido's ensuing willingness to "spare" the Trojans may again look forward to Anchises' *parcere subiectis* (6.853); see 522-3 n. **propius...aspice:** "look more closely (i.e. and thus kindly) upon..."

527-8. **non...populare...venimus:** the *non* is emphatic. The use of the infinitive after verbs of motion to express purpose is an archaic construction, found especially in the early comic poets (e.g. Plautus), but one that Lucretius and the Augustan poets took up. Cf. 3.5 *quaerere... agimur* "are driven to seek." **penatis:** here "hearths" or "homes." **raptas... vertere praedas:** *raptas* has the sense of an infinitive, "to seize and drive away." Cf. 69 n. **praedas:** "plunder," referring especially to cattle.

529. **non...animo:** our spirit has no such violence. **animo...victis:** datives of possessor. **superbia:** cf. 522-3 n.

530-3. This passage is repeated at 3.163-6.

530. **Hesperiam...dicunt:** explanatory parenthesis, cf. 12; understand *eum* ("it," i.e. *locum*) and take *Hesperiam* as a predicate accusative. The word *Hesperia* (lit. "Western land") is of Greek formation (Gr. *hesperia ge*) that Roman poets often use to indicate Italy (cf. 3.185; Ennius, *Annales* fr. 20 in Skutsch, 24 in Warmington *est locus Hesperiam quam mortales perhibebant*).

531. **terra...:** this description of Italy echoes that of Carthage at 12-14, further suggesting a similarity between Aeneas' fated land and Dido's burgeoning city. For *antiqua*, cf. 12 n. *Terra* and *ubere* are ablatives of respect with *potens*.

532-3. **nunc fama minores...dixisse:** an accusative and infinitive construction governed by *fama (est)*; for *minores*, see 521 n. **Italiam dixisse...gentem:** "called the people Italian." **ducis de nomine:** Italus is said to have been king or chief (cf. *ducis*) of the Oenotrians, a people of southern Italy.

hic cursus fuit,
cum subito adsurgens fluctu nimbosus Orion   535
in vada caeca tulit penitusque procacibus Austris
perque undas superante salo perque invia saxa
dispulit; huc pauci vestris adnavimus oris.
quod genus hoc hominum? quaeve hunc tam barbara morem
permittit patria? hospitio prohibemur harenae;   540
bella cient primaque vetant consistere terra.
si genus humanum et mortalia temnitis arma,
at sperate deos memores fandi atque nefandi.
rex erat Aeneas nobis, quo iustior alter
nec pietate fuit, nec bello maior et armis.   545

---

534. **hic cursus fuit:** "this was our course," i.e. we were seeking Italy, not Carthage. This line
was left incomplete at the time of Vergil's death. Donatus, in his *Life of Vergil*, says that on
his deathbed Vergil asked that the *Aeneid* be burnt, but he ultimately left it in the hands of
Varius and Tucca to edit *ea conditione, ne quid adderent quod a se editum non esset, et versus
etiam imperfectos, si qui erant, relinquerent.* There are roughly 58 such verses in the entire
Aeneid (the number is disputed because some original "half lines" may have been completed
by scribes). There are two other incomplete verses in book 1 (560, 636).

535. **adsurgens...nimbosus Orion:** *adsurgens* is confusing here, since stormy weather is
usually associated not with the rising of Orion in the summer (when this episode seems to
take place, cf. 756) but with its setting in November. It would seem as if Orion is simply to
be associated with storms.

536. **tulit:** supply *nos*. **penitus:** cf. 512 n. The heavily dactylic character of this line (with its
use of the sounds *c*/*q*, and *p*) helps convey the violence of the storm being described.

537. **perque...perque:** rhetorical repetition to emphasize strongly the dangers they had passed
through. Note how these prepositional phrases enclose the line with the alliterative* and
perhaps onomatopoetic* *superante salo* in the center.

538. **dispulit:** supply *nos*. **pauci:** "a few of us."

539-40. **quod genus...quaeve...patria?:** these pointed questions play against Ilioneus'
praise of Carthage as a civilizing force (523). **hunc...morem:** refers to the treatment of the
Trojans described in 540-1. Note the use of *p* and *r* in 540.

541. **prima...terra:** ablative, "on the very border of the land."

543. **at sperate...:** i.e. yet expect (*sperate*, here not "hope") that the gods will reward you
according to your deeds. For this usage of *at* following the protasis, cf. also 557. *Fandi* and
nefandi are used here as the genitives of *fas* and *nefas,* which are indeclinable.

544-5. **quo:** ablative of comparison. Note how the mention of the gods and moral behavior
in 542-3 leads into this description of Aeneas. From the start, he is characterized by his
pietas, iustitia, and *virtus* (*bello...armis*). Cf. 603-5 and 507-8 n. on Dido.

quem si fata virum servant, si vescitur aura
aetheria neque adhuc crudelibus occubat umbris,
non metus, officio nec te certasse priorem
paeniteat: sunt et Siculis regionibus urbes
armaque, Troianoque a sanguine clarus Acestes.   550
quassatam ventis liceat subducere classem
et silvis aptare trabes et stringere remos,
si datur Italiam sociis et rege recepto
tendere, ut Italiam laeti Latiumque petamus;
sin absumpta salus, et te, pater optime Teucrum,   555
pontus habet Libyae nec spes iam restat Iuli,

546-7. **quem...virum:** "this man" or "hero." **vescitur aura/ aetheria:** Aeneas is subject; *aura aetheria* is ablative with *pascitur* ("feeds on," here means "breathes"). *Aetheria* ("heavenly") contrasts with *umbris*. *Vescitur aura* is a Lucretian phrase (cf. 5.587 *vesci vitalibus auris*). **crudelibus...umbris:** ablative of place where (i.e. in the underworld).

548. **non metus:** sc. *nobis est*, a dative of possession construction (cf. AG §373) **officio... paeniteat:** "nor would you regret to contend in kindness first" (lit. "nor would it cause you regret to contend..."). *Paeniteat* is a potential subjunctive.

549. **et:** "also." If Aeneas is dead, they still have friends in Sicily who can protect them and pay Dido back for her help.

550. **Acestes:** cf. 195 n.

551. Ilioneus finally asks Dido for help. **subducere:** "draw in to shore," "beach."

552. **silvis aptare trabes:** "to shape planks in the forests," i.e. for repairing their ships. **stringere remos:** means "strip (trees for) oars." It "is a compression for *stringere frondibus ramos remorum in usum*" (Austin).

553. **si datur...:** i.e. by the gods and/or fate; supply *nobis*. See also 554 n. **Italiam:** cf. 2 n. **sociis et rege recepto:** *recepto* modifies both *sociis* and *rege* but grammatically matches the word it stands next to.

554. **tendere:** this verb can mean not only to stretch but also to aim (e.g. a weapon or a glance). Here the latter meaning is used in an intransitive sense "aim for" or "head toward." Cf. 204-5 *per tot discrimina rerum / tendimus in Latium*. **ut...petamus:** purpose clause connected closely in thought to 551-2; it should therefore be translated directly after 552 (and thus before the *si datur* clause of 553).

555. **sin absumpta salus...:** supply *est*; *sin* provides a protasis alternative to 553. Ilioneus here voices his preferred course of action if the first (i.e. reaching Italy with Aeneas and his other comrades, 553-4) is now lost. Note that Iloneus suddenly and emotionally apostrophizes* Aeneas (*pater optime Teucrum*), though he (Ilioneus) is actually addressing Dido.

556. **pontus habet:** death at sea (i.e. without burial) was a particularly horrible death for the Romans. **spes...Iuli:** "hope in Iulus"; *Iuli* is objective genitive. Iulus represents their hope for the future.

at freta Sicaniae saltem sedesque paratas,
unde huc advecti, regemque petamus Acesten."
talibus Ilioneus; cuncti simul ore fremebant
Dardanidae.   560
    Tum breviter Dido vultum demissa profatur:
"solvite corde metum, Teucri, secludite curas.
res dura et regni novitas me talia cogunt
moliri et late finis custode tueri.
quis genus Aeneadum, quis Troiae nesciat urbem,   565
virtutesque virosque aut tanti incendia belli?

557. **at:** "yet" or "at any rate." For *at* introducing the apodosis after *si, sin, quamvis,* cf. 543.
sedesque paratas: i.e. the city Acestes has already founded (cf. 195 n.)

558. **unde huc advecti:** sc. *sumus.* **regem...Acesten:** "Acestes as (our) king"; *regem* is predicate accusative.

559. **talibus Ilioneus:** supply *dixit*; with *talibus* understand *verbis.* **fremebant:** "shouted (in agreement)."

560. An unfinished line. Cf. 534 n.

561-78. *Dido offers her help as well as a portion of her kingdom to the Trojans.*
Dido's first speech shows that she is not only an admirable ruler but also as a magnanimous one, who goes so far as to invite the Trojans to settle in Carthage (572-3). The irony, of course, is that, despite her kindness, Aeneas will bring about her undoing. See Reed (2007) 89-95 for the complex ways that Dido aligns herself here with Aeneas.

561. **vultum demissa:** construe *demissa* as a middle, lit. "having cast down her face" (i.e. with downcast face).

562. **solvite corde metum:** a variation for *solvite corda metu.* The alliteration* of *s* and *c* in the imperative phrases *solvite corde...secludite curas* and asyndeton* add compassionate force to Dido's request that the Trojans set their minds at ease.

563-4. **res dura:** "hard fortune"; Dido was surrounded by hostile peoples (cf. 4.40-3). **talia cogunt moliri:** "drive me to undertake such actions." *Molior,* from *moles,* always denotes doing something with difficulty (cf. 414, 424) or, as here, something burdensome or repugnant to the feelings. **custode:** the singular used collectively to mean "guards," as *miles* is constantly used to mean "troops." Note the spondaic nature of this line, as Dido explains her people's initial treatment of the Trojans, about which Ilioneus had indignantly complained (539-41).

565. **quis...quis:** note the anaphora*, as well as another (cf. 562 n.) use of asyndeton*. **Aeneadum:** cf. 157 n. Dido thus acknowledges the preeminence of Aeneas among the Trojans (cf. 544-5). **nesciat:** potential subjunctive.

566. **virtutes:** here the abstract idea is given a concrete meaning, "courageous deeds," perhaps with a wordplay with the word *viros,* directly following. **incendia:** "conflagration"; so we speak of both a war and a fire "breaking out." Note the tricolon* of direct objects, all governed by *nesciat* (565).

non obtunsa adeo gestamus pectora Poeni,
nec tam aversus equos Tyria Sol iungit ab urbe.
seu vos Hesperiam magnam Saturniaque arva
sive Erycis finis regemque optatis Acesten,   570
auxilio tutos dimittam opibusque iuvabo.
vultis et his mecum pariter considere regnis?
urbem quam statuo, vestra est; subducite navis;
Tros Tyriusque mihi nullo discrimine agetur.
atque utinam rex ipse noto compulsus eodem   575
adforet Aeneas! equidem per litora certos

567-8. **obtunsa:** "unfeeling" or "dulled." **pectora:** here either "hearts" or "minds" (or perhaps both). **nec tam…:** "nor does the Sun yoke his horses so turned away (i.e. "distant") from our Tyrian city." The meaning of these lines is that "we are not so uncivilized," but it is expressed first in emotional or intellectual (567) and then in geographical terms (568).

569. **Hesperiam:** cf. 530 n. **Saturniaque arva:** an expansion of *Hesperiam*; cf. also *Eclogues* 4.6 *Saturnia regna*. After he had been expelled from heaven by his son Jupiter, Saturn sought refuge in Italy, where he brought about a golden age. Vergil briefly tells this story at 8.319-25.

570. **Erycis:** Eryx was a Sicilian mountain named after another son of Venus. He challenged Hercules to wrestle, was defeated, and was buried there. **regemque…Acesten:** cf. 558 n. Thus lines 569-70 refer to the two places (Italy and Sicily) that Ilioneus had explained the Trojans were interested in reaching (551-8). Dido will help them reach either destination.

571. **tutos:** sc. *vos*, object of both *dimittam* and *iuvabo*. Dido thus fulfils Jupiter's plan (cf. 298-300, 303-4).

572. **vultis et…:** Venus offers a third (cf. 569-70) alternative — settling in Carthage, an option Iloneus had not suggested.

573. **urbem quam statuo, vestra est:** a well-known instance of the antecedent being expressed in the relative clause instead of in the main sentence, or, as it is more usually called, the attraction of the antecedent to the case of the relative (see AG §306a). Note the resulting emphasis on the first three words. The line also contains irony. Reed (2007) 91 notes: "here in hindsight Dido's identification of Carthaginians and Trojans becomes a sinister foreshadowing of the Roman conquest and destruction of the city in 146 BCE."

574. **mihi:** dative of agent. **agetur:** "will be treated," an uncommon meaning of *ago*. The equality with which Dido will regard the two peoples is perhaps further suggested by the consonance* in *Tros* and *Tyrius*, as well as by her use of the enclitic *–que* and of the singular verb *agetur* for the compound subject *Tros Tyriusque*.

575-6. **utinam…adforet:** an unfulfillable wish; *adforet* = *adesset*. **rex ipse:** i.e. Aeneas. **noto… eodem:** "by the same wind," i.e. as that which brought you here. **Aeneas!:** the name falls emphatically at a strong caesura. **certos:** "dependable men."

dimittam et Libyae lustrare extrema iubebo,
si quibus eiectus silvis aut urbibus errat."
    His animum arrecti dictis et fortis Achates
et pater Aeneas iamdudum erumpere nubem   580
ardebant. prior Aenean compellat Achates:
"nate dea, quae nunc animo sententia surgit?
omnia tuta vides, classem sociosque receptos.
unus abest, medio in fluctu quem vidimus ipsi
summersum; dictis respondent cetera matris."   585
vix ea fatus erat cum circumfusa repente
scindit se nubes et in aethera purgat apertum.
restitit Aeneas claraque in luce refulsit

---

577. **iubebo:** sc. *eos* (the *certos* in 576) as object.

578. **si...errat:** "in case he is wandering shipwrecked (*eiectus*) in some woods or city."

579-612. While Dido speaks, Achates and Aeneas burst forth from the cloud in which Venus had enclosed them. Aeneas thanks Dido for her aid.

Aeneas's speech displays a confidence and control that his lament at the sight of the storm (94-101) and his earlier speech to Venus (372-85) had lacked. He lives up to Ilioneus' estimation of him (544-9).

579-80. **animum arrecti:** *animum* is an accusative of respect. **et...et...:** "both...and..." **erumpere:** *erumpere* here is transitive, "burst forth from." Many intransitive verbs thus acquire a secondary meaning and become transitive, cf. 2.31 *stupet*, "is amazed at" and 5.438 *tela exit*, "avoids the blows."

581. **ardebant:** cf. 514-15 n. **prior Aenean compellat Achates:** note that Achates urges on Aeneas, not the reverse, as might be expected.

582. **nate dea:** *dea* is ablative of origin or source; *nate* is the vocative of the participle *natus*. Note the respect with which Achates addresses Aeneas, cf. 585 n.

584. **unus abest...:** i.e. Orontes, whose death was witnessed at 113-17.

585. **dictis respondent cetera matris:** cf. 390-1, 399-400, though Venus (*matris*) did not mention the death of Orontes (584). Just as Achates' address started with reference to Aeneas' goddess mother (582 *nate dea*), so it ends (*matris*).

587. **se:** construe with both *scindit* and *purgat* ("parts and disperses"). For *aether* as opposed to *aer*, cf. 411 n.

588. **restitit...refulsit:** for the force of the compounds, cf. 402 n. As the cloud rolled back, the figure of Aeneas "stood clear against it" (*restitit*), i.e. he "stood out" impressively. **in luce refulsit:** this phrase is used of Venus at 2.590, where she appears to Aeneas; *refulsit* is also used of Venus as she reveals her identity to Aeneas at 402.

os umerosque deo similis; namque ipsa decoram
caesariem nato genetrix lumenque iuventae   590
purpureum et laetos oculis adflarat honores:
quale manus addunt ebori decus, aut ubi flavo
argentum Pariusve lapis circumdatur auro.
tum sic reginam adloquitur cunctisque repente
improvisus ait: "coram, quem quaeritis, adsum,   595
Troius Aeneas, Libycis ereptus ab undis.
o sola infandos Troiae miserata labores,
quae nos, reliquias Danaum, terraeque marisque
omnibus exhaustos iam casibus, omnium egenos,
urbe, domo socias, grates persolvere dignas   600

589-93. This passage echoes *Odyssey* 6.229-38 (cf. also *Odyssey* 23.156-65), where Athena enhances Odysseus' stature and appearance.

589-91. **os umerosque:** accusatives of respect; cf. *nuda genu* (320). **namque ipsa…:** the subject is *ipsa genetrix* (i.e. Venus); the verb *adflarat* (a syncopated pluperfect of *adflaverat*; cf. 26 n.) takes three accusatives (*decoram caesariem, lumen iuventae purpureum, laetos honores*). **purpureum:** "radiant." The adjective here probably refers more to Aeneas' glow or radiance than to color (i.e. "rosy").

592. **quale…:** "such grace (*decus*) as…" This simile* is based on *Odyssey* 6.232-5 (roughly = *Odyssey* 23.159-63). **manus:** i.e. a craftsman's hands; nominative plural. Cf. 455.

593. **Pariusve lapis:** i.e. Parian marble, known especially for its beautiful whiteness.

594. **cunctis:** with *improvisus* in 595. His sudden appearance was "unexpected by all."

595. **coram, quem quaeritis, adsum:** understand *ego* as antecedent of *quem*. The adverb *coram* means "face to face," "in your presence." Note that Dido had just wished *utinam rex ipse…adforet Aeneas* (575-6).

596. **Troius Aeneas:** emphatic enjambment*; note that *Trōius* is trisyllabic.

597. **o sola…:** Aeneas' claim is somewhat of an exaggeration, since the Trojan Acestes has helped Aeneas (cf. 195; in book 3 we will also learn of Helenus' aid). Dido, however, is the first non-Trojan to do so.

598. **quae:** antecedent is Dido. **nos:** object of the verb *socias* (600); it is modifed by *exhaustos….egenos* (599). **reliquias Danaum:** in apposition to *nos*. For the phrase, cf. 30.

599-600. **omnium:** the harsh elision involving *omnium* (Vergil's only use of this form) is made easier by the emphasis which repetition (*omnibus…omnium*) throws very strongly on the first syllable. **urbe, domo socias:** "you grant us, lacking all things (*omnium egenos*), a share in your city, your home." Note the asyndeton* in *urbe, domo* that helps add emphasis to Dido's generosity.

non opis est nostrae, Dido, nec quidquid ubique est
gentis Dardaniae, magnum quae sparsa per orbem.
di tibi, si qua pios respectant numina, si quid
usquam iustitia est et mens sibi conscia recti,
praemia digna ferant. quae te tam laeta tulerunt   605
saecula? qui tanti talem genuere parentes?
in freta dum fluvii current, dum montibus umbrae
lustrabunt convexa, polus dum sidera pascet,
semper honos nomenque tuum laudesque manebunt,
quae me cumque vocant terrae." sic fatus amicum   610
Ilionea petit dextra laevaque Serestum,

---

601. **non opis est…:** "is not in (lit. "of") our power nor (in the power of) whatever anywhere
exists of the Trojan race." *Opis* is a predicate genitive (cf. AG §343c); the clause *quidquid…
est* stands in for a second predicate genitive.

602. **gentis Dardaniae:** partitive genitive after *quidquid*. **quae sparsa:** sc. *est*; *gentis* is the
antecedent of *quae*.

603-4. **di:** subject of *ferant* (605), an optative subjunctive (AG §441). **pios:** because of the
kindness she has just shown, Aeneas attributes to Dido the very quality (*pietas*) that defines
him throughout the epic. **si quid/ usquam iustitia est:** "if justice is (i.e. means) anything
anywhere." **sibi:** dative of reference. Aeneas cannot repay Dido, but he can pray that she
may receive the favor of heaven. For the meaning of this use of *si quis* with indicative, cf.
also 375 n.

605-6. **te…tulerunt:** "gave you birth." **qui tanti…parentes:** *tantus* here means "great" or
"glorious." In his address to Nausicaa in *Odyssey* 6.154-7, Odysseus expresses these ideas
much more elaborately.

607. **montibus:** ablative of place where (AG §421). Note that Aeneas brings his speech to an
elaborate close with two tricolon* structures (*dum…dum…dum*, 607-8; *honos nomenque…
laudes*, 609). For the prevalence of tricola in Ilioneus' speech, cf. 520-60 n.

608. **polus dum sidera pascet:** *polus* here means "sky." The phrase seems to compare the stars
to a countless flock whose pasture-ground is the sky. It is reminiscent of Lucretius 1.231
unde aether sidera pascit?, where the *aether* which surrounds the universe and keeps the stars
alive and burning is said to "feed" them.

609. **tuum:** modifies *nomen* but should also be construed with *honos* and *laudes*. This line
appears verbatim at *Eclogues* 5.78, where the fame of Daphnis is described. Aeneas, of
course, turns out to be wrong: his affair with Dido will in fact destroy her fame.

610. **quae…cumque:** tmesis (cf. 412 n.).

611. **Ilonēa:** Greek accusative. **dextra laevaque:** understand *manu* with both adjectives. Note
the chiastic* arrangement of *Ilionea…dextra laevaque Serestum*.

post alios, fortemque Gyan fortemque Cloanthum.
Obstipuit primo aspectu Sidonia Dido,
casu deinde viri tanto, et sic ore locuta est:
"quis te, nate dea, per tanta pericula casus   615
insequitur? quae vis immanibus applicat oris?
tune ille Aeneas quem Dardanio Anchisae
alma Venus Phrygii genuit Simoentis ad undam?
atque equidem Teucrum memini Sidona venire
finibus expulsum patriis, nova regna petentem   620

612. **post:** "afterwards" (adverb). **fortemque Gyan fortemque Cloanthum:** the chaistic arrangment in 611 gives way to parallel adjective-accusative phrases, joined by *-que...-que* and the repetition of *fortem*. These stylistic features provide effective closure to the presentation of Aeneas' speech.

613-30. In amazement Dido welcomes Aeneas and compares herself to him in misfortune.

613-14. **Obstipuit:** note the emphatic placement. **primo aspectu:** "at the first sight of the man" (supply *viri* from 614). **deinde:** "then," following the temporal idea in *primo aspectu*. Dido is struck with amazement, first at the appearance of Aeneas (cf. 589-91) and then at the thought of his misfortunes.

615. **quis...casus:** subject of *insequitur* (616).

616. **immanibus...oris:** dative after *applicat*. *Immanibus* ("cruel") suggests the dangerous nature of the coast and the savage character of the inhabitants. **applicat:** sc. *te* (i.e. Aeneas), "brings" or "drives you to."

617. **tune ille Aeneas...?:** understand *es*. This question further conveys Dido's surprise (perhaps enhanced by the double elision) at Aeneas' sudden and unexpected appearance. **Dardanio Anchisae:** also at 9.647. Note the hiatus* and spondee in the fifth foot; this combinations happens rarely in Vergil, and only with noun-epithet pairings (e.g. 3.74 *Neptuno Aegaeo*).

618. **alma Venus:** *alma* is the regular and recurring epithet of Venus (cf. Lucretius 1.2) as the giver of life, but is of course especially applicable to her in her relation to Aeneas (cf. 306 n.). **Simoentis:** cf. 100 n.

619. **Teucrum memini:** the present infinitive (*venire*) with *memini* is the standard construction, where the perfect might have been expected, "I remember that Teucer came..." Ajax, the brother of Teucer, slew himself in anger at being refused the arms of Achilles by the Greek leaders. When Teucer returned home to his father Telamon in Salamis, he was driven away (hence *expulsum* 620) by him for not having avenged his brother, and founded a second Salamis in Cyprus. (This Teucer is not the Teucer mentioned in 235.) **Sidona:** cf. 446 n.; it is a Greek accusative form, and here indicates motion toward (no preposition needed, because it is the name of a city; cf. AG §427).

620. **finibus expulsum patriis:** "expelled from his native land"; cf. 619 n.

auxilio Beli; genitor tum Belus opimam
vastabat Cyprum et victor dicione tenebat.
tempore iam ex illo casus mihi cognitus urbis
Troianae nomenque tuum regesque Pelasgi.
ipse hostis Teucros insigni laude ferebat 625
seque ortum antiqua Teucrorum a stirpe volebat.
quare agite, o tectis, iuvenes, succedite nostris.
me quoque per multos similis fortuna labores
iactatam hac demum voluit consistere terra.
non ignara mali miseris succurrere disco." 630
sic memorat; simul Aenean in regia ducit
tecta, simul divum templis indicit honorem.
nec minus interea sociis ad litora mittit

---

621. **Beli:** Dido's father; the name is probably a Greek form of the Phoenician word Baal that seems to mean "ruler" (cf. 729-30 n.; Reed (2007) 78).

623-4. **casus...cognitus urbis/ Troianae:** supply *est*, "the fall of the Trojan city has been known to me." **regesque Pelasgi:** "and the Greek kings," i.e. Agamemnon and Menelaus. The *Pelasgi* (from the North Aegean) were thought to be among the oldest inhabitants of Greece; their name was often used as a synonym for "Greeks."

625. **ipse hostis:** has the sense "even though he was an enemy" and refers to the Greek Teucer. **Teucros:** "Trojans," cf. 626 n.

626. **volebat:** "claimed." Teucer was the first king of Troy (cf. 235), from whom the Trojans were called *Teucri*. The Greek Teucer (cf. 619 n.) was the son of Telamon by Hesione, a daughter of Laomedon king of Troy, and so, as his name implies, really of Trojan origin.

627. **agite:** "come now," the imperative of *ago* is often found with this meaning, especially in comedy.

628-9. **similis fortuna:** Dido explicitly draws the parallel between herself and Aeneas, a similarity that had been suggested earlier. **iactatam:** cf. 3 *iactatus*.

630. **non ignara:** "not ignorant of," i.e. "well schooled in" (an example of litotes*). **disco:** "I learn" or "am learning"; the present is more modest than the perfect.

631-42. Dido prepares a public sacrifice and sends provisions to Aeneas' ships.

631-2. **simul...simul:** here adverbial, "at once...at once" (cf. 513 n.); note the anaphora* and asyndeton*. **templis:** ablative of place where without preposition. **indicit honorem:** "proclaim a sacrifice." *Indicit* is a technical word for the "proclamation" by the pontifices of a special festival or one the exact date of which was not fixed.

633. **nec minus:** "also," "likewise." **sociis:** dative; i.e. Aeneas' comrades.

viginti tauros, magnorum horrentia centum
terga suum, pinguis centum cum matribus agnos,   635
munera laetitiamque dii.
at domus interior regali splendida luxu
instruitur, mediisque parant convivia tectis:
arte laboratae vestes ostroque superbo,
ingens argentum mensis, caelataque in auro   640
fortia facta patrum, series longissima rerum
per tot ducta viros antiqua ab origine gentis.

634-5. **viginti...centum...centum:** note the emphasis on the number of animals (and thus munificence) involved in Dido's action. **magnorum horrentia...terga suum:** *suum* is genitive plural of *sus* ("swine," "boar"); "the phrase acts for a noun with a compound epithet ('bristly-backed swine')" (Austin). Note also that Vergil writes *magnorum terga suum*, though we might have expected the cases of *terga* and *suum* to be reversed (i.e. *magnorum tergorum sues*).

636. **munera laetitiamque dii:** a half line (cf. 534 n.), "(she sends) gifts and the joy of the day." The reading *dii*, however, is disputed. The manuscripts have *dei*, but Aulus Gellius (*Attic Nights* 9.15.8) explains that *dii* here is an archaic genitive of *dies*.

637. **at domus interior:** used later in the description of Priam's palace at 2.486, just before it is sacked. Dido's palace is also luxurious and about to suffer a great catastrophe.

638. **instruitur:** "is adorned," "prepared."

639-42. Understand a form of *esse* in each of the clauses describing the decorations on the tables: e.g. *laboratae vestes...*, "there are (*sunt*) coverlets embroidered with...."

639. **laboratae vestes:** the *vestes* are *vestes stragulae* used for covering the couches on which they reclined. The Phoenicians were not only celebrated for their purple-dyed robes but also for their skill in embroidery, cf. 337 n.

640. **argentum:** here "silver plate"; supply *est* ("there is"). **mensis:** ablative of place where. **caelata:** "engraved." Drinking-vessels of gold and silver carved in relief, often with figures representing historical or legendary events, were much valued at Rome and are continually referred to.

641-2. **fortia facta patrum:** Dido's noble ancestry is emphasized. Her apparent reverence for her ancestors seems very Roman. **series...gentis:** take in apposition to the *caelata facta*. **per tot ducta viros:** the participle *ducta* modifies *series longissima*; *per* governs *tot viros* ("heroes").

643-756: Venus, Cupid, and the Banquet

Venus intervenes to ensure Aeneas' safe reception at Carthage, even though Jupiter has already taken steps to achieve this (cf. 297-304). She elicits the help of Cupid, another son, to assume the appearance of Ascanius (her grandson) and to infect Dido with an irresistible passion for the Trojan hero. Her decision to promote this passion is unclear and ultimately problematic, because of the troubles it will cause Aeneas and the tragic end it helps bring about for Dido.

The scene clearly develops from Hellenistic literature and has special resonance with the opening of book 3 of Apollonius' *Argonautica*. There Aphrodite, at the urging of Hera and Athena, has Eros inflame Medea with love for Jason. Vergil has transformed this model to create a scene that makes clear the impossibility of Dido's situation. She is devoted to her deceased husband Sychaeus and determined never to marry again, but Venus and Cupid drive her mad with passion for Aeneas, a love that can only be temporary since Aeneas must eventually leave her because of fate. Dido's downfall is virtually unavoidable. Venus' lack of concern about Dido here resonates with Aphrodite's about Medea in Apollonius.

This scene marks a shift in focus in the narrative, whereby Dido's perspective will become the dominant one through which we will view her affair with Aeneas. See, e.g., Otis (1964) 61-96 (his important discussion of Vergil's "subjective style" in the Dido episode). For the Apollonian background, see Nelis (2001) 93-6. For the contrasting and characteristic ways that Homer, Apollonius and Vergil deal with the onset of love, see Johnson (1976) 36-45. For further interpretation, see Frangoulidis (1992), Reckford (1995-96) 22-9, and Khan (2002).

Aeneas (neque enim patrius consistere mentem
passus amor) rapidum ad navis praemittit Achaten,
Ascanio ferat haec ipsumque ad moenia ducat;   645
omnis in Ascanio cari stat cura parentis.

643-56. Aeneas sends Achates to the ships for Ascanius, telling him to bring gifts for Dido.

643-4. **patrius...amor:** i.e. "a father's love" for his son. Aeneas' thoughts turn to Ascanius; cf. 646 n. **consistere:** "to rest." **rapidum:** adjective that can be construed adverbially, "hurriedly."

645. **ferat...ducat:** subjunctives in indirect command (with *ut* omitted), after the idea of "bidding" contained in the preceding line. **ipsum:** Ascanius.

646. **cari:** "loving," not "dear," since here the adjective describes the subject (Aeneas) not the object (Ascanius) of the emotion. **stat:** stronger than *est*, perhaps reinforcing the powerful bond between father and son that is such an important part of Aeneas' *pietas*.

munera praeterea Iliacis erepta ruinis
ferre iubet, pallam signis auroque rigentem
et circumtextum croceo velamen acantho,
ornatus Argivae Helenae, quos illa Mycenis,   650
Pergama cum peteret inconcessosque hymenaeos,
extulerat, matris Ledae mirabile donum;
praeterea sceptrum, Ilione quod gesserat olim,
maxima natarum Priami, colloque monile
bacatum, et duplicem gemmis auroque coronam.   655
haec celerans iter ad navis tendebat Achates.

---

647. **Iliacis...ruinis:** ablative of separation. Note the interlocking adjective/noun phrases (or synchysis*).

648. **iubet:** understand *eum* (Achates, cf. 656) as object. **signis auroque:** hendiadys*, "with figures made of gold," i.e. in gold thread. The *palla* was a cloak worn by Roman women. Here the elaborate golden decorations make it *rigentem*.

649. **croceo...acantho:** the edge of the veil was decorated with a "yellow acanthus" leaf design, a popular motif. **velamen:** "veil." Again, note the interlocking word order (cf. 647 n.).

650. **ornatus:** accusative plural, in apposition to *pallam* (648) and *velamen* (649). **Argivae Helenae:** Helen's husband Menelaus was king of Sparta, from where Paris carried her to Troy. The epithet *Argivae* (here = "Greek") is Homeric (e.g. *Iliad* 2.161). **quos illa Mycenis:** *illa* is the subject of *extulerat* (652). *Mycenis* is ablative. Though Helen was from Sparta, *Mycenae* is used as a synonym for Greece.

651. **Pergama:** cf. 466 n. **cum peteret:** a circumstantial clause (cf. AG §546). Note that the final syllable of *peterēt* is long, though it is short by nature (see 307-8 n.). **inconcessosque hymenaeos:** i.e. Paris' abduction of Helen. Ironically, like Helen, Dido will "betray" her husband by having an affair with a Trojan. Note the uncommon quadrisyllabic line ending in *hymenaeos*.

652. **matris Ledae:** Helen's mother was Leda, whom Jupiter, in the shape of a swan, had raped.

653. **Ilione:** a daughter of Priam who married Polymestor, the Thracian king (who in turn killed Ilione's brother Polydorus, as explained at 3.49-56).

654-5. **collo...monile:** "a circlet for the neck," i.e. a "necklace." **bacatum:** the necklace has jewels shaped like berries (*bacae*), which are probably pearls. We might simply translate as a "beaded" or "pearl necklace." **duplicem...:** "a double crown of gems and gold"; the crown seemingly had two circlets, one of gold, the other of jewels. *Gemmis auroque*, however, could also be a hendiadys* for "jewels set in gold" (Austin).

656. **haec celerans:** "rushing (to carry out) these orders."

At Cytherea novas artis, nova pectore versat
consilia, ut faciem mutatus et ora Cupido
pro dulci Ascanio veniat, donisque furentem
incendat reginam atque ossibus implicet ignem.   660
quippe domum timet ambiguam Tyriosque bilinguis,
urit atrox Iuno et sub noctem cura recursat.
ergo his aligerum dictis adfatur Amorem:
"nate, meae vires, mea magna potentia, solus,
nate, patris summi qui tela Typhoëa temnis,   665

657-94. *Venus asks Cupid to take on the appearance of Ascanius and infect Dido with passion for Aeneas. The real Ascanius is taken away to Idalia.*

657. **At Cytherea:** *At* indicates a change of scene, here bringing us to the divine realm. *Cytherea* = Venus, cf. 257 n. At last sighting, Venus had left Aeneas and gone to Paphos (415-17). **versat:** "keeps turning over," "ponders"; cf 2.62 *versare dolos*, "to practice tricks," describing Sinon. Note the asyndeton* and the repetition of the adjective *novus*.

658-60. **ut...veniat...incendat...implicet:** an object clause of result governed by the idea in *versat consilia*.

658. **faciem...et ora:** objects of the middle participle *mutatus*. *Facies* here = "shape"; *ora* = "face."

659. **veniat:** cf. 658-60 n. **furentem:** proleptic*, "kindle (*incendat* 660) to madness," cf. 70 n. Note the metaphors* of madness (*furentem*), fire (*incendat, ignem* 660; 688), and poison (*veneno* 688) to describe Dido's goddess-inspired passion for Aeneas. Venus here functions as a force of *furor*. She will later act in conjunction with Juno (4.90-128) and, as a result, further orchestrate Dido's downfall.

660. **incendat...implicet:** cf. 658-60 n. **ossibus...:** the fire enwraps her bones so as to consume them. The bones (and especially the marrow of the bones) were considered the seat of feeling, and love is a fire that feeds on them, cf. 4.66 *est mollis flamma medullas*.

661. **quippe:** cf. 39 n. **timet:** the subject is Venus. **ambiguam:** "unreliable" or "untrustworthy," i.e. seemed friendly but might prove the opposite (cf. 671). **bilinguis:** though more usually referring to the forked tongue of a serpent, *bilinguis* could also mean "double-tongued" (i.e. saying one thing and meaning another). To the Romans, the Carthaginians were stereotypically treacherous because of the Punic wars (cf. Livy 21.4.9 *perfidia plus quam Punica*; Horace, *Odes* 4.4.49 *perfidus Hannibal*).

662. **urit...Iuno:** "Juno burns (i.e. vexes) her." **sub noctem:** "just before night." **cura:** Venus' concern for her son.

663. **aligerum:** "winged" (lit. "wing-bearing"), an elevated compound adjective first appearing in the *Aeneid*.

664-5. **solus:** construe with the relative clause *patris...temnis* (665), "you who alone scorn..." **tela Typhoëa:** "the bolts which killed Typhoeus," one of the Giants who tried to overthrow Jupiter. In ancient works of art Love was frequently represented breaking a thunderbolt.

ad te confugio et supplex tua numina posco.
frater ut Aeneas pelago tuus omnia circum
litora iactetur odiis Iunonis acerbae,
nota tibi, et nostro doluisti saepe dolore.
nunc Phoenissa tenet Dido blandisque moratur   670
vocibus, et vereor quo se Iunonia vertant
hospitia: haud tanto cessabit cardine rerum.
quocirca capere ante dolis et cingere flamma
reginam meditor, ne quo se numine mutet,
sed magno Aeneae mecum teneatur amore.   675

666. **ad te confugio et supplex…:** Venus flatteringly plays on the idea that all the gods (cf. Jupiter in 665) are subordinate to Cupid's powers.

667-8. **frater ut…acerbae:** indirect question governed by the impersonal construction *nota (sunt)* in 669 (see n.). **iactetur:** the *u* is long. Other instances of this lengthening of *-ur* in verbs before a vowel where the ictus is on the lengthened syllable are 2.411 *obruimur*; 4.222 *adloquitur*; 5.284 *datur*. Most manuscripts read *iacteturque*; the *-que* would lengthen the *-ur* but would be difficult to construe. **odiis:** perhaps not simply singular for plural, but a plural indicating the repeated troubles caused Aeneas by Juno's hate.

669. **nota:** the plural for the singular in such phrases (where we use the idiom "it is well known that…," "it is impossible to…," and the like) is fairly common in Greek but rare in Latin. **doluisti…dolore:** "grieved because of my grief." The repetition emphasizes the idea of sympathy.

670. **blandisque moratur / vocibus (671):** perhaps referring to Dido's offer of part of her realm to the Trojans (572-4). This claim would seem an exaggeration (Aeneas has just arrived), but the phrase rhetorically heightens Venus' sense of urgency.

671-2. **quo se Iunonia vertant / hospitia:** *quo* = "where." Carthage was Juno's favorite city (15-16), and Venus assumes she is behind Dido's actions. Ironically Jupiter has already made Dido kindly receive the Trojans (297-304) in response to Venus' own complaints. **haud…rerum:** "she (Juno) will not rest at such a turning-point of fortune." The metaphor in *cardo* is that of a hinge that could either open or close a door.

673. **capere…cingere flamma:** metaphors* from attacking a town; *flamma* is ablative of means. **dolis:** note how Venus describes her plan. Interestingly, in book 2 *dolus* is used by the narrator Aeneas as a problematic aspect of Ulysses, Sinon, and the Greeks more generally (cf. 2.44, 62, 152, 196, 252, 264). Readers may thus view Venus' emphasis on her trickery (cf. also *dolos* in 682, and *dolo* in 684) with some ambivalence, particularly given the tragic end Dido will ultimately experience.

674-5. **ne…:** negative purpose clause. **quo…numine:** "because of some divine power." The ablative *quo…numine* suggests that Juno might try to change Dido's love for Aeneas to hatred (thus *se…mutet* with Dido as subject). **Aeneae:** objective genitive after *amore*. **mecum teneatur:** "'be kept on my side,' continuing the military metaphor of 673" (Williams).

qua facere id possis nostram nunc accipe mentem:
regius accitu cari genitoris ad urbem
Sidoniam puer ire parat, mea maxima cura,
dona ferens pelago et flammis restantia Troiae;
hunc ego sopitum somno super alta Cythera   680
aut super Idalium sacrata sede recondam,
ne qua scire dolos mediusve occurrere possit.
tu faciem illius noctem non amplius unam
falle dolo et notos pueri puer indue vultus,
ut, cum te gremio accipiet laetissima Dido   685

676. **qua:** relative pronoun that precedes its "antecedent" *mentem* (here "plan"). The relative clause is one of purpose and thus has the subjunctive *possis*.

677. **accitu:** "at the summons of."

678. **Sidoniam:** cf. 446 n. The *o* here is short, though elsewhere it is long, as in 446.

679. **dona ferens:** in book 2 the priest Laocoon, in considering what to do about the "Trojan" horse, will famously express his distrust of the Greeks with a similar phrase: *timeo Danaos et dona ferentis* (2.49). Venus' act of deception (her use of Ascanius/Cupid) will have as disastrous consequences for Dido, as the trick of the wooden horse does for the Trojans. Cf. 673 n. **pelago et flammis:** construe as ablatives of separation after *restantia* ("surviving from").

680. **sopitum somno:** *sopio* is practically the same word as *somnus*, but the combination of *somnus* with *sopor* and *sopio* is common, the alliteration* conveying the idea of rest. **super alta Cythera:** "on Cythera's heights," neuter plural (though *Cythera* also appears in the feminine singular). Cf. 257 n.

681. **Idalium:** a grove and city in Cyprus sacred to Venus. **sacrata sede:** supply *in*. The phrase presumably refers to a sanctuary or temple, and can be construed with both *super alta Cythera* and *super Idalium*. Note the continued use of the alliteration* of *s* (cf. 680 n.).

682. **ne qua:** "lest in any way." **mediusve occurrere:** *occurrere* has the sense here of "happen upon" or "get involved accidentally"; *medius* has an adverbial force, "in the way," "in between."

683. **tu:** contrasts with *ego* (680). **illius:** i.e. Ascanius. **noctem...:** accusative of duration construction, "for not more (than) one night." With numerals *quam* is often omitted after comparatives, especially *plus* and *amplius* (e.g. *neque enim plus septima ducitur aestas, Georgics* 4.207).

684. **falle:** "imitate," "impersonate," a remarkable use of this verb, which more usually would mean "deceive," "escape (the notice of)." **pueri puer:** this juxtaposition (expressed with polyptoton*) rhetorically conveys the similarity of appearance Cupid will assume. **notos... vultus:** "familiar features" (Austin).

685. **ut:** begins a purpose clause that encloses two *cum*-clauses (685-7) and is completed in 688 (see n.). **laetissima:** note Venus' malevolent irony*. Dido is imagined rejoicing at the very moment that Cupid infects her with a destructive passion for Aeneas.

regalis inter mensas laticemque Lyaeum,
cum dabit amplexus atque oscula dulcia figet,
occultum inspires ignem fallasque veneno."
paret Amor dictis carae genetricis, et alas
exuit et gressu gaudens incedit Iuli.   690
at Venus Ascanio placidam per membra quietem
inrigat, et fotum gremio dea tollit in altos
Idaliae lucos, ubi mollis amaracus illum
floribus et dulci aspirans complectitur umbra.

686. **regalis inter mensas:** "amid the royal tables (i.e. feast)." **laticemque Lyaeum:** *Lyaeus* is the Latin translation for the Greek cult name used of Bacchus that means "liberator." Thus *laticem Lyaeum* is an elevated phrase that means "Bacchus' water" (i.e. wine). Poets for convenience often use proper names as adjectives (cf. 4.552 *cineri Sychaeo*). Venus would seem to emphasize the inability of Dido's regal position and wealth to protect her from the power of love.

687. **dabit amplexus...oscula dulcia figet:** note the chiastic* construction (*amplexus* is accusative plural), as well as the repetition of *cum* (cf. 685). Again, note how Venus emphasizes the irony of Dido's anticipated reaction to Ascanius/Cupid (cf. 685 n.).

688. **fallasque veneno:** "and cheat her with poison," "poison her unawares"; for other destructive metaphors*, cf. 659 n. Indeed Dido's affair with Aeneas will result in her suicide. *Inspires* and *fallas* are subjunctives in a purpose clause (cf. *ut* 685).

690. **gressu gaudens...:** *gressu* is emphatic, marking that Cupid now walks (like Iulus/Ascanius) instead of flying. *Gaudens* expresses his boyish delight in the part he is playing, unconcerned with the pain that could (and will) result. The alliteration* in *gressu gaudens* perhaps underscores his frivolity.

691. **Ascanio:** dative of reference; note that his other name *Iulus* had been used in the previous line.

692. **inrigat:** "makes flow"; this verb can be used either of making a stream flow (as here), or of the stream itself and thus mean "flow over," "water," (e.g. 3.511 *fessos sopor inrigat artus*). The advance of sleep over the limbs is compared to the rapid and peaceful movement of water through irrigation channels onto thirsty lands. **fotum gremio:** "nestled in her bosom." Cf. the phrase *gremio accipiet*, used of Dido's expected embrace of the false Ascanius (i.e. Cupid) in 685.

693. **Idaliae:** cf. 681 n. **amaracus:** "marjoram." This plant has associations with marriage and love, as we can see from Catullus 61.6-7 (a marriage hymn): *cinge tempora floribus / suave olentis amaraci.*

694. **dulci aspirans...umbra:** "with fragrance-breathing shade" (lit. "breathing on him with fragrant shade").

Iamque ibat dicto parens et dona Cupido   695
regia portabat Tyriis duce laetus Achate.
cum venit, aulaeis iam se regina superbis
aurea composuit sponda mediamque locavit,
iam pater Aeneas et iam Troiana iuventus
conveniunt, stratoque super discumbitur ostro.   700
dant manibus famuli lymphas Cereremque canistris
expediunt tonsisque ferunt mantelia villis.
quinquaginta intus famulae, quibus ordine longam
cura penum struere et flammis adolere penatis;

695-722. *Cupid (disguised as Ascanius) arrives with gifts and makes Dido fall in love with Aeneas, forgetting her vow to her deceased husband Sychaeus.*

695. **dicto parens:** *dicto* is dative with *parens* (from *pareo*) and refers to Venus' request; the phrase echoes *paret Amor dictis* (689). Despite Venus' flattery about the power of Cupid, he acts rather quickly to do his mother's bidding.

697. **cum venit:** Cupid is subject. **aulaeis...superbis:** ablative of attendant circumstances. *Aulaea* are "tapestries" hung between the columns in a hall (cf. Gr. *aule*), especially at feasts, Cf. Horace, *Odes* 3.29.15 *cenae sine aulaeis et ostro*.

698. **aurea...sponda:** ablative, supply *in*. *Sponda* is a "couch"; *aurea* should be pronounced as two syllables by synizesis (Gr. "a sinking together"), cf. 726-7 n.; 5.352 *aureis*; 6.280 *ferrei*, 412 *alveo*, 678 *dehinc*; 7.609 *aerei*. **mediamque locavit:** Dido placed herself (sc. *se*) "in between" her guests.

699. **pater Aeneas:** Aeneas' position as leader of his people (*Troiana iuventus*) is characterized as that of father to child.

700. **strato...super...ostro:** "on spread-out purple (coverlets)" (cf. 639 n.). **discumbitur:** "they recline" (lit. "it is reclined by them"). For this impersonal use, cf. AG §208. *Discumbo* is a regular word for lying down at meals and can be used of a single person, cf. Juvenal 5.12 *tu discumbere iussus*, "invited to recline" (i.e. to dine).

701. **dant...:** for this description of a feast cf. *Odyssey* 1.136-49, especially 136-7 and 147. **lymphas:** "water," a largely poetic word. **Cererem:** metonymy* for "bread."

702. **tonsis...mantelia villis:** "napkins of smooth texture" (lit. "napkins with close-shorn nap" or "surface"). The phrase *tonsis...villis* is ablative of description or quality (AG §415).

703-4. **quinquaginta intus famulae:** sc. *sunt*; they are presumably in the kitchen (thus *intus* "within"), as opposed to the attendants in the hall, mentioned in 705-6. **quibus...cura:** *quibus* is dative; supply *est*, "whose task is to" (lit. "to whom the task is"); the infinitives *struere* and *adolere* depend on *cura*. See also 705-6 n. **longam...penum struere:** *struere* ("arrange") describes the placing of each course on the *ferculum* or "tray" on which it was served; *penum* ("larder") is feminine, the phrase *longam penum* meaning something like "long (succession of) food." **flammis adolere penatis:** *adolere* ("to burn in sacrifice") is particularly connected to ritual, though here it means "to increase" or "make grow." The *penates* were the gods of the larder (*penus*); images or paintings of them were placed over the kitchen hearth, so that to keep a good fire on it is "to magnify the Penates with fire" (*flammis adolere penatis*).

centum aliae totidemque pares aetate ministri,   705
qui dapibus mensas onerent et pocula ponant.
nec non et Tyrii per limina laeta frequentes
convenere, toris iussi discumbere pictis
mirantur dona Aeneae, mirantur Iulum,
flagrantisque dei vultus simulataque verba,   710
pallamque et pictum croceo velamen acantho.
praecipue infelix, pesti devota futurae,
expleri mentem nequit ardescitque tuendo
Phoenissa, et pariter puero donisque movetur.
ille ubi complexu Aeneae colloque pependit   715

705-6. **centum...qui**: note both how this construction (number followed by relative clause) mirrors *quinquaginta...quibus* in 703-4, and how each relative clause contains two verbs to describe the servants' tasks (704 *struere...adolere*; 706 *onerent...ponant*). The symmetry perhaps conveys the orderliness of Dido's palace and rule, in contrast to the fury that will overwhelm the queen by book 4. **onerent...ponant:** subjunctives in relative clause of purpose.

707. **nec non et:** an unusual connecting phrase that means "likewise" or "furthermore." **laeta:** "festal."

708. **toris...pictis:** i.e. couches adorned with embroidered coverlets, cf. 4.206. **iussi discumbere...:** i.e. Dido's guests. For *discumbere*, cf. 700 n.

709-11. Note the artistry of these lines: the anaphora* of *mirantur*, the asyndeton*, and the chiastic* relationship among *dona* (A), *Iulum* (B), *flagrantisque...verba* (b, i.e. description of Iulus), and *pallam...acantho* (a, i.e. description of the *dona*).

710. **flagrantis:** describes Cupid's appearance (*dei vultus*) but also suggests the burning passion with which he will infect Dido.

711. **pallam...velamen:** these are the items Aeneas told Achates to bring at 648-9.

712. **praecipue infelix:** proleptic*, describing Dido (*Phoenissa*, 714). The wonder of the Carthaginians in general (cf. 709 *mirantur...mirantur*) builds up to Dido's reaction. **devota:** "doomed." The religious connotations of *devota* are especially resonant, given the machinations of Venus and Cupid.

713-14. **expleri mentem:** construe *mentem* as an accusative of respect and *expleri* as passive; or take *mentem* as object of *expleri* understood as a middle. **ardescit:** note the repeated use of fire imagery to describe passion. The placement of *ardescit* both expands and intensifies the idea of *expleri mentem nequit*. **puero donisque:** in chiastic* relation to *dona...Iulum* in 709; cf. 709-11 n. Notice also how effectively Vergil uses a tricolon crescendo* to describe the psychological effect of Cupid on Dido.

715. **ille:** i.e. Cupid disguised as Ascanius. **pependit:** used strictly with *collo* "hung upon the neck" and loosely with *complexu* "in the arms" of Aeneas.

et magnum falsi implevit genitoris amorem,
reginam petit. haec oculis, haec pectore toto
haeret et interdum gremio fovet inscia Dido
insidat quantus miserae deus. at memor ille
matris Acidaliae paulatim abolere Sychaeum 720
incipit et vivo temptat praevertere amore
iam pridem resides animos desuetaque corda.

---

716. **falsi:** because the boy is really Cupid, not Ascanius. **implevit:** usually means "filled," but here "fulfilled" or "satisfied." **amorem:** note the devious way in which Cupid uses filial love to inspire passion in Dido.

717-18. **reginam petit:** after the elaborate description of Ascanius/Cupid with his "father" Aeneas in 715-16, Vergil provides a brief but emphatic statement of the true goal of the god's actions. Note also how the diaeresis after *petit* both underscores Cupid's action and connects it powerfully to the immediate response of *Dido* (*haec*) that follows. **haec oculis, haec…fovet:** the repetition of *haec* (i.e. Dido) and the asyndeton* further convey the intense power of Cupid over her. **inscia Dido:** the queen is thus ignorant both of fate (cf. 299 *fati nescia Dido*) and of the gods' direct involvement in her life.

719. **insidat quantus miserae deus:** indirect question after *inscia* (718); *insidat* means "settles on." The delay and juxtaposition of *miserae deus* help suggest the impossibility of Dido's situation; *miserae* refers to Dido and is proleptic*. **ille:** Cupid.

720. **matris Acidaliae:** i.e. Venus; genitive after *memor* (719). The *fons Acidalius* was a fount sacred to Venus. **abolere Sychaeum:** "to do away with (the memory of) Sychaeus." *Abolere* is a powerful verb.

721. **vivo…amore:** important, because Dido has not experienced love since Sychaeus' death. **praevertere:** "preoccupy."

722. **desueta…corda:** amplifies the idea in *iam pridem resides animos* (theme and variation*). Dido's "heart" is "unaccustomed (to love)" in that she has not allowed herself to fall in love since Sychaeus' death.

Postquam prima quies epulis mensaeque remotae,
crateras magnos statuunt et vina coronant.
fit strepitus tectis vocemque per ampla volutant   725
atria; dependent lychni laquearibus aureis
incensi et noctem flammis funalia vincunt.

723-56. After the feast, the bard Iopas sings a song, and then Dido asks Aeneas to tell the story of his misfortunes and wanderings.

The bard Iopas proceeds to perform a song, much like the Homeric bard Demodocus, who sings three songs in the course of *Odyssey* 8. Unlike Demodocus, however, whose performances deal with the gods and heroic themes (though his second song was interpreted by some in antiquity as an allegory about natural philosophy, as Farrell (1991) 260 shows), Iopas, who performs just one song, treats philosophical ideas. He sings about astrology and cosmogony, topics that on the surface contrast greatly with what has preceded and what will follow. The meaning of Iopas' song is therefore contested. On the one hand, it seems to set Dido's passion for Aeneas within a cosmic context. On the other, it does not introduce any agency by the gods to bring about the events described – an absence made even more striking by the fact that Juno and Aeolus had started the storm with which the epic opened, and that Venus has orchestrated Dido's love for Aeneas.

    Iopas' song has a number of other models. It displays close connections with what Apollonius' Orpheus sings (reported in indirect speech, like Iopas' performance) at *Argonautica* 1.496-511, which as Nelis (2001) has shown is deeply influenced by the ideas of the early Greek philosopher Empedocles on the structuring forces of Love and Strife in the cosmos. Iopas' song also echoes *Georgics* 2.475-82 (cf. 745-6 n.), where Vergil describes the study of nature as the loftiest theme with which the Muses can deal, a passage in which many see an admiration for Lucretius' *De rerum natura*. Indeed some readers have interpreted Iopas as an Epicurean figure, who looks to science rather than *religio* to understand the world. There may also be a recall here of *Eclogues* 6.31-40. On Iopas' song, see Segal (1971, 1981b), Kinsey (1979), Hardie (1986) 52-66, Brown (1990), Farrell (1991) 258-62, Hannah (1993), Putnam (1998) 271-3, Nelis (2001) 96-112, and Adler (2003) 9-16.

723. **Postquam prima quies epulis:** *epulis* is dative of reference; supply a verb such as *erat*. **remotae:** supply *sunt*. For the entire line, cf. 216.

724. **crateras:** "mixing bowls" (Greek accusative plural). **vina coronant:** cf. 3.525-6 *magnum cratera corona| induit*, where "crown the wine" means literally surrounding the bowl with a garland of flowers, although the Homeric phrase on which it is based (e.g. *Iliad* 1.470 "to wreathe the bowls with wine") actually means "to fill them brimming high with wine."

725. **fit strepitus…:** after they have feasted and the wine is brought in, they begin to talk (thus *strepitus*). (Some manuscripts have *it* instead of *fit*.) **tectis:** ablative of place within which, "throughout the palace." **vocem…volutant:** "they roll forth their voice(s)."

726-7. **lychni…incensi:** "burning lamps"; *lychni* is a Greek word. **laquearibus:** "coffered ceilings," ablative. **aureis:** scanned as a disyllable by synizesis (cf. 698 n.). **funalia:** "torches," made of rope covered in wax or fat.

hic regina gravem gemmis auroque poposcit
implevitque mero pateram, quam Belus et omnes
a Belo soliti; tum facta silentia tectis: 730
"Iuppiter, hospitibus nam te dare iura loquuntur,
hunc laetum Tyriisque diem Troiaque profectis
esse velis, nostrosque huius meminisse minores.
adsit laetitiae Bacchus dator et bona Iuno;
et vos, o coetum, Tyrii, celebrate faventes." 735
dixit et in mensam laticum libavit honorem
primaque, libato, summo tenus attigit ore;
tum Bitiae dedit increpitans; ille impiger hausit

---

728. **hic:** adverb, "then." **gravem gemmis auroque...pateram (729):** i.e. a jeweled bowl or dish (*patera*). Such vessels were highly valued at Rome, but were introduced from the East, cf. Cicero, *in Verrem* 4.27.62 *pocula ex auro, quae, ut mos est regius, et maxime in Syria, gemmis erant distincta clarissimis.*

729-30. **quam Belus et omnes/ a Belo soliti:** understand *implere* dependent on *soliti* (*sunt*); *omnes a Belo* probably means "all after Belus" (i.e. his descendants). Belus here would then be the founder of the Tyrian dynasty, not Dido's father (cf. 621 n.). The clause describes the cup (*pateram* 729) as valuable not merely intrinsically but also for its history. **facta:** understand *sunt.*

731. **nam te...:** Dido appeals to Jupiter under his special attribute as "god of strangers," Gr. *Zeus Xenios*. In Latin, he is sometimes called *hospitalis* (note the use of *hospitibus*, which means either "guests" or "hosts"). For *nam*, cf. 65 n.

732. **hunc laetum...diem:** this day will ultimately be problematic for both the Carthaginians and Trojans. For *laetum*, cf. 685 n. **Troia...profectis:** "for those who set out from Troy."

733. **velis:** optative subjunctive (AG §441). **nostrosque...minores:** continues the indirect statement after *velis* with the same level of irony; *minores* = "descendants." **huius:** understand *diei* (cf. 732 *diem*).

734. **adsit:** optative subjunctive; *Bacchus* and *Iuno* are both subjects. **bona Iuno:** note the irony (cf. 732 n.).

735. **coetum:** accusative, "gathering." **faventes:** "being well-disposed" or "showing favor" (presumably to the Trojans).

736-7. **laticum:** here "wine" (cf. 686); it is genitive plural dependent on *honorem*. **prima:** construe adverbially. **libato:** the word alone constitutes an ablative absolute, "the libation having been made," cf. *auspicato, cognito,* and *permisso.* **summo tenus...ore:** *tenus* is a preposition that here governs the ablative *summo ore* and is usually placed after the noun it governs; the phrase literally means "up to the edge of her mouth."

738. **increpitans:** perhaps "prodding him (i.e. Bitias)"; this verb usually involves censure ("scold"), but here it seems more playful. Perhaps Dido is urging Bitias to drink more quickly or enthusiastically, which he seemingly goes on to do.

spumantem pateram et pleno se proluit auro;
post alii proceres. cithara crinitus Iopas   740
personat aurata, docuit quem maximus Atlas.
hic canit errantem lunam solisque labores,
unde hominum genus et pecudes, unde imber et ignes,
Arcturum pluviasque Hyadas geminosque Triones;

739. **pleno...auro:** "from the full gold (i.e. cup)." **se proluit:** "gulped," "swilled" (lit. "drenched onself"). This phrase amplifies *hausit* (738), creating an emphatic and humorous contrast with Dido's sip.

740. **post:** "afterwards," "next," adverb. **cithara:** ablative of means, modified by *aurata* (741). **crinitus:** long hair is a sign of a bard; so too Apollo their patron has "flowing locks" (cf. Horace, *Odes* 3.4.61 *qui rore puro Castaliae lavit/ crinis solutos*; Phemius at *Odyssey* 1.325, and Demodocus at *Odyssey* 8.499).

741. **personat:** "makes the hall ring." **Atlas:** there seems to have been a story that Atlas invented astronomy, as Pliny the Elder notes (*Natural History* 7.203). Vergil here clearly introduces him as locally connected with Africa.

742. **hic...:** Homeric bards sing of heroic deeds, but Vergil makes Iopas a philosopher who had probed the secrets of nature. **errantem lunam:** referring to the moon's revolutions, cf. *Georgics* 1.337 *quos ignis caeli Cyllenius erret in orbes*. **solisque labores:** "solar eclipses" (cf. *Georgics* 2.478 *lunaeque labores*); the strict word for an eclipse, *defectus* ("a failing" or "fading"), is replaced by the poetical word for "suffering," "trouble." The use of the words *errantem* and *labores* also brings to mind both Aeneas and Dido. Vergil employs the noun *labor* to describe especially Aeneas (241, 330, 460, 597) but also Dido (628), while the verb *errare* characterizes Aeneas at 32 and 333, as Nelis (2001) 104 notes. The cosmological events described in Iopas' song may thus reflect on the experiences of Dido and Aeneas. Pöschl (1962) 152, for example, asks: "Is it wrong to connect the moon's wandering and the sun's labors with the fate of Dido and Aeneas and with their past and future wanderings in the true sense of a symbol?"

743. **unde...:** "whence (come)..." This theme of creation forms part of the song of Silenus at *Eclogues* 6.31-41.

744. **Arcturum pluviasque Hyadas geminosque Triones:** are objects of *canit* (742) and are constellations whose risings and settings helped guide the work of sailors and farmers. **Arcturum:** "the brightest star in the constellation Bootes....its rising and setting were associated with stormy weather" (Austin). **pluvias...Hyadas:** the "rainy Hyades" were five stars in the constellation Taurus, also associated with storms. Vergil is fond of placing with a Greek proper name a Latin word which suggests its derivation; here clearly the word *Hyades* is closely connected with the Greek word *huein* "to rain." **geminos...Triones:** the Great and Little Bears.

> quid tantum Oceano properent se tingere soles   745
> hiberni, vel quae tardis mora noctibus obstet.
> ingeminant plausu Tyrii, Troesque sequuntur.
> nec non et vario noctem sermone trahebat
> infelix Dido longumque bibebat amorem,
> multa super Priamo rogitans, super Hectore multa;   750
> nunc quibus Aurorae venisset filius armis,
> nunc quales Diomedis equi, nunc quantus Achilles.
> "immo age et a prima dic, hospes, origine nobis
> insidias" inquit "Danaum casusque tuorum

745-6. Repeated from *Georgics* 2.481-2. There is an artistic contrast between *properent* and *tardis*: the winter suns hurry to plunge into the Ocean, while the nights are so slow that something seems to impede their progress.

745. **quid:** "why?" **properent:** subjunctive in indirect question.

746. **tardis...noctibus:** dative with *obstet*, subjunctive in indirect question.

747. **ingeminant plausu:** "redouble with applause," cf. 9.811 *ingeminant hastis*. The phrase is a variation on the ordinary *ingeminant plausum*, which some manuscripts give. **Tyrii, Troes:** the alliteration* and consonance* of these words placed next to each other suggest the likemindedness of the two peoples at this moment. The enclosing verbs lend the line a chiastic* structure: *ingeminant...Tyrii, Troesque sequuntur.*

748. **nec non et:** "likewise," cf. 707.

749. **infelix Dido:** cf. 712. **longumque bibebat amorem:** i.e. as she listened to Aeneas. *Longus* is a strong adjective in Latin and might here be translated as "everlasting" or "undying," cf. 6.715 *longa oblivia.*

750. **multa super...super...multa:** observe the emphatic (and chiastic*) repetition suggesting Dido's growing excitement; cf. 751-2 n. **super:** "about," "concerning" with ablative (*Priamo...Hectore*).

751-2. With the tricolon* of *nunc* and the interrogatives Vergil again stylistically conveys Dido's excitement, cf. 750 n.

751. **Aurorae...filius:** Memnon, cf. 489 n. His weaponry was made by Vulcan (8.384). **venisset:** subjunctive in indirect question governed by *rogitans* (750).

752. **quales Diomedis equi:** supply *essent*. *Equi* perhaps refers to the horses taken from Rhesus (cf. 469 n.), not to those Diomedes took from Aeneas (*Iliad* 5.323-4). **quantus Achilles:** supply *esset*. *Quantus* primarily involves actual size but also includes the idea of greatness in other respects. Aeneas had fought both Diomedes and Achilles at Troy. Dido asks indiscriminately about everything at Troy.

753. **immo age...:** "no rather, come tell us...," i.e. in preference to answering separate questions, relate the whole story at length. Aeneas does so in the next books, which contain the tale of the sack of Troy (book 2) and of his subsequent wanderings (book 3).

754. **insidias...Danaum:** i.e. the ruse of the Trojan horse.

erroresque tuos; nam te iam septima portat   755
omnibus errantem terris et fluctibus aestas."

755-6. nam te iam septima...aestas: *septima* is problematic, because in Book 5 (roughly
a year later in narrative time) Iris (in the guise of Beroe) says that it is then the seventh
summer since the fall of Troy (5.626 <u>*septima*</u> *post Troiae excidium iam vertitur <u>aestas</u>*).
Unless this is simply a mistake that presumably would have been corrected upon revision,
there is no generally accepted explanation for the inconsistency. Recently, Dyson (1996)
has argued that the line alludes to *Georgics* 4.203-9, a discussion of bees and their devotion
to their community, where *septima aestas* (207) denotes the seventh year when a bee reaches
the full span of life and dies, though the hive continues. "*Tantae molis erat*: what a great
and heavy thing it was to found the empire without end, seemingly immortal, like the
society of bees, but won at the cost of such suffering, as the individual bees are lost while
their community lives on." On this reading, the temporal inconsistency between 1.756
and 5.626 "intentionally marks the phrase *septima aestas* in order to highlight the theme of
sacrificial death."

Appendix A: Vergil's Meter[1]

Dactylic hexameter was the meter of Greek epic, and beginning with Ennius' *Annales* (second century BCE),[2] it became the meter of Roman epic as well. Its basic rhythm can be felt in the following line from the opening of Longfellow's *Evangeline*:

Thís is the fórest prímévál. The múrmuring pínes and the hémlocks

Here five dactyls (búm-ba-ba) are followed by a final disyllabic foot. These metrical units (as with English verse more generally) are created through the use of natural word stress to create patterns of stressed and unstressed syllables. Thus a dactyl in English poetry is a stressed syllable followed by two unstressed syllables (e.g. "Thís is the" and "múrmuring"). Classical Latin meter, however, differs in an important way. Metrical feet are based not on word stress but on the quantity of individual syllables (i.e. whether they are long or short). Thus, in Latin a dactyl contains one long syllable followed by two short ones (– ⌣⌣).

As the name indicates, "dactylic hexameter" literally describes a line that contains six (Gr. *hex*) measures or feet (Gr. *metra*) that are dactylic (– ⌣⌣).[3] In actual practice, however, spondees (– –) could substitute for dactyls within the first four feet,[4] and the line's ending was largely regularized as – ⌣⌣ / –x. The Latin dactylic hexameter can thus be notated as follows:

---

1   For more on Vergil's meter, see Jackson Knight (1944) 232-42, Duckworth (1969) 46-62, Nussbaum (1986), and Ross (2007) 143-52.

2   The early Latin epics by Livius Andronicus and Naevius were composed in Saturnian verse, a meter that is not fully understood.

3   The word "dactyl" comes from the Greek word *dactylos*, "finger." A metrical dactyl with its long and two short syllables resembles the structure of a finger: the bone from the knuckle to the first joint is longer than the two bones leading to the fingertip.

4   More technically the two short syllables of a dactyl are "contracted" into one long; together with the first long syllable, they form a spondee.

$$\_ \; \smile\smile \; / \_ \; \smile\smile \; / \_ \; \smile\smile \; / \_ \; \smile\smile \; / \_ \; \smile\smile \; / \_ \; \times$$

(Here, "/" separates metrical feet; "–" = a long syllable; "$\smile$" = a short syllable; and "x" = an *anceps* ("undecided") syllable, one that is either long or short.)

Very rarely a spondee is used in the fifth foot, in which case the line is called "spondaic."

To *scan* a line (i.e. to identify a line's rhythm and meter), long and short syllables must be identified. A syllable can be *long* in two ways: *by nature*, if it contains a vowel that is inherently long or is a diphthong;[5] or *by position*, if it contains a naturally short vowel followed either by a double consonant (*x* or *z*) or, in most cases, by two consonants.[6] In general, all other syllables are *short*. If, however, a word ending in a vowel, diphthong, or *–m* is followed by a word that begins with a vowel, diphthong, or *h*, the first vowel or diphthong is *elided* (cf. *laeti* in 1.35 below; elided syllables are enclosed in parentheses in the examples below). As a result the two syllables merge and are scanned as one—a phenomenon called *elision*. *Elision* occurs frequently in Vergil.

By applying these rules, we may scan hexameter lines as follows:

> mūltă sŭ/pēr Prĭă/mō rŏgĭ/tāns, sŭpĕr / Hēctŏrĕ / mūltă
>
>   (*Aen.* 1.750)

> prōtrăhĭt / īn mĕdĭ/ōs; quāē / sīnt ĕă / nūmĭnă / dīvŭm
>
>   (*Aen.* 2.123)

> vēlă dă/bānt lāē/t(i) ēt spū/mās sălĭs / āērĕ rŭ/ēbānt
>
>   (*Aen.* 1.35)

A long syllable generally takes twice as long to pronounce as a short, and the first syllable of each foot receives a special metrical emphasis known as the *ictus*.

---

5   One can determine if a vowel is long by nature by looking the word up in a dictionary to see if it has a macron over it or by checking inflected endings in a grammar (for example, some endings, like the first and second declension ablative singular (-*a*, -*o*), are always long; others, like the second declension nominative neuter plural (-*a*), are always short).

6   An exception to this general rule: if a short vowel is followed by a mute consonant (*b, c, d, g, p, t*) and a liquid (*l, r*), the resulting syllable can be either short or long. Cf. 2.663 where *patris* and *patrem* are short and long respectively: *natum ante ora pătris, pātrem qui obtruncat ad aras*. It should also be noted that *h* is a breathing, not a consonant; it therefore does not help make a vowel long by position.

The flow of a line is affected not only by its rhythm but also by the placement of word breaks. A word break between metrical feet is called a *diaeresis:*[7]

> ēt iăcĭt. / ārrēc/tāē mēn/tēs stŭpĕ/fāctăquĕ / cōrdă   (*Aen.* 5.643)

Here, diaereses occurs after *iacit* and after *stupefactaque;*[8] the former helps reinforce the syntactic pause after *iacit.* A word break within a metrical foot is called a *caesura.* When a caesura falls after the first syllable of a foot, it is called "strong" (as after the first *super* in 1.750 above); if it falls after the second syllable in a dactylic foot, it is called "weak" (as after the first *multa* in 1.750). The most important caesura in any given line often coincides with a sense break and is called the *main* or *principal caesura.*[9] It most frequently falls in the third foot, but also occurs not uncommonly in the second or fourth (or sometimes both). The slight pause implied in the main caesura helps shape the movement of each verse by breaking it into two (or more) parts. Here are the first seven lines of the *Aeneid*, scanned and with the principal caesurae marked ("‖"):

> ārmă vĭ/rūmquĕ că/nō, ‖ Trō/iāē quī / prīmŭs ăb / ōrīs
>
> Ītălĭ/ām fā/tō prŏfŭ/gūs ‖ Lā/vīniăquĕ / vēnĭt
>
> lītŏră, / mūlt(um) īl(le) / ēt tēr/rīs ‖ iāc/tātŭs ĕt / āltō
>
> vī sŭpĕ/rūm, ‖ sāē/vāē mĕmŏ/rēm Iū/nōnĭs ŏb / īrăm,
>
> mūltă quŏ/qu(e) ēt bēl/lō pās/sūs, ‖ dūm / cōndĕrĕt / ūrbĕm
>
> īnfēr/rētquĕ dĕ/ōs Lătĭ/ō, ‖ gĕnŭs / ūndĕ Lă/tīnŭm
>
> Ālbā/nīquĕ pă/trēs ‖ āt/qu(e) āltāē / mōēnĭă / Rōmāē.

(Note that in line 2, *Laviniaque* is pronounced as four [not five] syllables, as if the second "*i*" were a consonant.)

---

7   When a *diaeresis* occurs just before the fifth foot, it is often called a *bucolic diaeresis* because this type of diaeresis was used frequently in pastoral poetry: e.g. *nos patriam fugimus: tu, Tityre,* ‖ *lentus in umbra* (*Ecl.* 1.4).

8   In the combinations *qu, gu, su* (e.g. *–que, sanguis, suesco*), note that the *u* is consonantal but that the combinations themselves count as a single consonant for the purpose of scansion.

9   Readers may differ on where (or even if) there is a main caesura in a given line.

In addition to metrical length, words also have a natural accent,[10] which may coincide or clash with the metrical stress (*ictus*), which falls on the first long syllable of each foot. Coincidence of word accent and metrical stress produces fluidity in the verse; clashing of word accent and metrical stress creates tension. For example:

$$x \quad\quad x \quad\quad / \quad\quad x \quad\quad / \quad\quad /$$
īnfān/dūm, rē/gīnă, iŭ/bēs rĕnŏ/vārĕ dŏ/lōrĕm   (*Aen.* 2.3)

(Naturally accented syllables are in boldface; "/" = *ictus* that coincides with word accent; "x" = *ictus* that clashes with word accent.)

In this line, there are several clashes in the first four feet (wherein the word accent generally does not coincide with the verse accent), followed by coincidence in the final two feet.[11] In creating such clashes, the placement of caesurae can be particularly important. For example, "if a word of two or more syllables ends after the first long of a foot (that is, producing a strong caesura), there will be a clash between accent and *ictus* in that foot," because the final syllable of such words is not accented.[12] The strong caesurae in 2.3 (above) and in 2.108, 199 (below) display this principle well.

One of Vergil's artistic feats was to manage the sequence of clash and coincidence of *ictus* and word accent in such a way as to achieve a rhythmically varied and pleasing line. In general we find that Vergilian hexameters are characterized by the clash of *ictus* and word accent in the first four feet and by the coincidence of *ictus* and word accent in the last two feet,[13] which results in a pleasing resolution of stress at line end:

$$/ \quad\quad x \quad\quad x \quad\quad x \quad\quad / \quad\quad /$$
Saēpĕ fŭgām Dănăī Trōiă cŭpĭērĕ rĕlīctā   (2.108)

---

10   Disyllabic words have their accent on their initial syllable: *cáris, dábant, mólis.* If, however, words are three syllables or longer, the word accent falls: on the penultima (second to last syllable), if it is long (*ruébant, iactátos*) but on the antepenultima (the syllable preceding the penultima), if the penultima is short (*géntibus, mária, pópulum*).

11   Classical Latin speakers would presumably have pronounced the word accents in reading lines, while still maintaining the basic rhythm of the hexameter. Otherwise, the *ictus* would have transformed the basic sound of the word.

12   Ross (2007): 146. For word accentuation, see n. 10 (above).

13   Vergil sometimes avoids such resolution for special effect, though he does so rarely. For example, in the following line, a clash between ictus and word accent occurs in the final foot: *sternitur/ exani/misque tre/mens pro/cumbit hu/mi bos* (5.481).

   /   x   x   x   /   /
Hīc ălĭūd māiūs mĭsĕrīs mūltōquĕ trĕmēndŭm   (2.199)

This rhythmical innovation constituted an advance over Vergil's predecessors, who could write such lines as, e.g., Ennius' *spársis/ hástis/ lóngis/ cámpus/ spléndet et/ hórret,* which exhibits a coincidence of *ictus* and word accent throughout the entire line.

Appendix B: Stylistic Terms

Vergil's skillful use of language is a defining element of his artistry. He often employs rhetorical figures and stylistic devices to reinforce the content of his poetry. Careful attention should therefore be paid both to what Vergil says and to how he says it. The following list defines many of the stylistic terms and features that are encountered in studying Vergil. For discussion of the examples cited from Book 1, see the commentary notes. For more information on the terms, see Lanham (1991) and Brogan (1994). Fuller information on Vergilian style can be found in Jackson Knight (1944) 225-341, Camps (1969) 60-74, O'Hara (1997), and Conte (2007) 58-122. Stylistic analyses of Vergilian passages are presented in Horsfall (1995) 237-48 and Hardie (1998) 102-14.

Alliteration: the repetition of the initial consonant sound in neighboring words. E.g., *magno misceri murmure* (1.124). Alliteration is often used to create *onomatopoeia*, and occurs frequently with *assonance* and *consonance*. Cf. 1.55, 81, 83, 115-17, 294-6, 354, 493, 537, 562, 680, 681, 690, 747.

Anaphora (Gr. "bringing back"): the repetition of a word at the beginning of consecutive sentences or clauses. E.g., "*vos et Scyllaeam rabiem penitusque sonantis / accestis scopulos, vos et Cyclopia saxa / experti*" (1.200-2). Cf. 1.78, 106-7, 110, 120, 421, 565, 631-2.

Anastrophe (Gr. "turning back"): the inversion of normal word order, usually involving prepositions and their objects. E.g., *Karthago, Italiam contra Tiberinaque longe* (1.13). *Anastrophe* is a type of *hyperbaton* (see below). Cf. 32, 218, 348, 466.

Aposiopesis (Gr. "becoming silent"): the abrupt stopping of a sentence or a thought. E.g., *iam caelum terramque meo sine numine, venti, / miscere et tantas audetis tollere moles? / quos ego – ! sed motos praestat componere fluctus* (1.133-5). Here, Neptune suddenly cuts short his rebuke of the winds.

Apostrophe (Gr. "turning away"): a sudden shift of address to a figure (or idea), absent or present. E.g., "*sin absumpta salus, et te, pater optime Teucrum,/ pontus habet Libyae*" (1.555-6). Here, Ilioneus in his speech to Dido suddenly addresses Aeneas, who is not present.

Assonance (Lat. "answer with the same sound"): the repetition of vowel sounds in neighboring words or phrases. E.g., *Albanique patres atque altae moenia Romae* (1.7). Note the use of the vowel *a* in this line that concludes the opening of the *Aeneid*. See also *alliteration* and *consonance*. Cf. 1.68, 83, 493, 493.

Asyndeton (Gr. "unconnected"): the omission of connectives between words, phrases, or sentences. In the following example, Aeneas scans the sea after the storm that begins the epic: *navem in conspectu nullam, tris litore cervos/ prospicit errantis* (1.184-5). There is no connective between *nullam* and *tris*. In addition, this particular instance of *asyndeton* implies contrast: "He sees not one ship but three stags wandering on the shore." Cf. 1.105, 106-7, 204, 306, 384, 421, 467-8, 495, 562, 600, 631-2, 657, 709, 717.

Chiasmus (Gr. "crossing"): an arrangement of words whereby parallel constructions are expressed in reverse word order. E.g., *luctantis ventos tempestatesque sonoras* (1.53). Cf. 209, 396, 467-8, 611, 687, 709-11, 747, 750. The word "chiasmus" is derived from the Greek letter "chi" because if the parallel constructions are split in half and placed one over the other, an X is formed when the syntactically related words are connected.

luctantis　　ventos

X

tempestatesque　　sonoras

Consonance (Lat. "concord"): the repetition of consonant sounds in neighboring words or phrases. E.g., *accipiunt inimicum imbrem rimisque fatiscunt* (1.123). Note the use of *c/q* and *m* sounds in this line (and also the assonance involving the vowel *i*). Cf. 68, 574, 747.

Dicolon Abundans: see **Theme and Variation**.

Ellipsis (Gr. "leaving out"): the omission of a syntactically necessary word or words, the meaning of which must be inferred. E.g., *sis felix nostrumque leves, quaecumque, laborem* (1.330). Here, the verb *es* must be understood with *quaecumque*: "whoever you are." Cf. 1.299-300.

Enallage (Gr. "interchange"): a distortion in normal word order, whereby a word, instead of modifying the word to which it belongs in sense, modifies another grammatically. E.g., *odium crudele tyranni* (1.361). Here *crudele* grammatically modifies *odium* but in sense describes *tyranni* (thus "hatred of the cruel tyrant"). Cf. 1.311.

End-stopped lines: see **Enjambment**.

Enjambment (Fr. "crossing over," "spanning"): the continuation of the sense or syntactic unit from one line to the next. E.g., "*Troes te miseri, ventis maria omnia vecti, / oramus*" (1.524-5). Enjambed words are often followed by some kind of pause (here a strong caesura) that adds emphasis. Lines without enjambment are called *end-stopped*. Cf. 1.11, 62, 115, 122, 596.

Epanalepsis (Gr. "taking up again"): the repetition of a syntactically unnecessary word or phrase from a preceding line. E.g., *tris Notus abreptas in saxa latentia torquet / (saxa vocant Itali mediis quae in fluctibus Aras...)* (1.108-9).

Golden Line and Variations: in dactylic hexameter, an artful arrangement of two substantive/adjective phrases with a verb in between. It usually takes the form of ABCab, where Aa and Bb are both adjective-noun phrases, while C is a verb. E.g.,

> A   B   C   a   b
> egressi optata potiuntur Troes harena   (1.172)

The variation ABCba is often called a *silver line*. E.g.,

> A   B   C   b   a
> aeternumque adytis effert penetralibus ignem   (2.297)

Cf. 1.291, 502.

Hendiadys (Gr. "one through two"): the expression of one idea through two terms joined by a conjunction. E.g., *instans operi regnisque futuris* (1.504). Here *operi regnisque futuris* really means "the work of her future kingdom." Cf. 1.61, 111, 293, 648, 654-5.

Hyperbaton (Gr. "transposed"): a distortion of normal word order. E.g., *tris Notus abreptas in saxa latentia torquet / (saxa vocant Itali mediis quae in fluctibus Aras ...)* (1.108-9). Note the deliberate delay of the relative pronoun *quae*. *Hyperbaton* is also used to create artful arrangements of words, such as *golden lines* and *synchysis*.

Hyperbole (Gr. "excess"): exaggeration. E.g., *velum adversa ferit, fluctusque ad sidera tollit* (1.103). Cf. 1.106-7, 129, 465.

Hypotaxis: see **Parataxis**.

Hysteron Proteron (Gr. "later as earlier"): the reversal of the chronological order of events. E.g., *moriamur et in media arma ruamus* (2.353). Technically one must rush to battle before dying in battle.

Interlocking word order: see **synchysis**.

Interpretatio: see **Theme and Variation**.

Irony (Gr. "dissembling"): saying one thing but with its opposite somehow implied or understood. E.g., *ni frustra augurium vani docuere parentes* (1.392). Venus, disguised as a huntress, tells her son Aeneas that his comrades and fleet are now safe, but adds this line (1.392). It is playfully ironic because Venus is a goddess (her father being the king of the gods), and knows that her words are truthful (even if somewhat deceptive). Cf. 1.451-2, 464, 685, 733.

Litotes (Gr. "simplicity"): the description of something by negating its opposite. E.g., *interea ad templum non aequae Palladis ibant* (1.479). Here *non aequae* is used instead of an adjective meaning something like "hostile" or "angry." Cf. 1.130, 136, 630.

Metaphor (Gr. "transference"): the application of a word or phrase from one field of meaning to another, thereby suggesting new meanings. E.g., *donisque furentem / incendat reginam atque ossibus implicet ignem* (1.659-60). Here the passion that Venus would have Cupid inspire in Dido is figured as *fire* (*incendat...ignem*). Cf. 9, 50, 63, 301, 342, 356, 671-2, 675, 688.

Metonymy (Gr. "change of name"): the substitution of one word for another somehow closely related. E.g., *Cereremque canistris / expediunt* (1.701-2). Here Ceres, the goddess of agriculture, is used to mean "bread." *Synecdoche* is a type of *metonymy*. Cf. 1.177, 215, 253, 470, 506.

Onomatopoeia (Gr. "making of a word" or "name"): the use or formation of words that imitate natural sounds. E.g., *perque undas superante salo perque invia saxa* (1.537). Here the *alliteration* and *consonance* of *s/x* suggest the sound of the storm. *Onomatopoeia* often involves other devices such as *alliteration, assonance,* and *consonance*.

Oxymoron (Gr. "pointedly foolish"): the juxtaposition of seemingly contradictory words. E.g., *animum pictura pascit inani* (1.464). Here the idea of feeding (*pascit*) on something that is empty (*inani*) seems contradictory. Cf. also *festina lente* (Gr. *speude bradeos*, Suetonius, *Augustus* 25.4).

Parataxis (Gr. "placing side by side"): the sequential ordering of independent clauses (as opposed to *hypotaxis*, the subordination of one clause to another). A famous example is Caesar's *veni, vidi, vici*. An example from Aeneid 1: *et iam iussa facit, ponuntque ferocia Poeni / corda* (302-3). Though the two halves of the sentence are independent, in sense one is subordinated to the other: "after he has performed the commands, the Phoenicians set aside their fierce hearts." Vergil leaves it to the reader to sense such logical relationships. *Parataxis* is particularly characteristic of Vergil and epic more generally.

Paronomasia (Gr. "slight alteration of name"): a wordplay or pun. E.g., *Vrbs antiqua fuit (Tyrii tenuere coloni)/ Karthago* (1.12). Here there seems to be a wordplay since the word *Karthago* meant *nova urbs* in Punic. Cf. 1.298, 366, 493, 522, 566.

Pleonasm (Gr. "excess"): redundancy, especially for the sake of emphasis. E.g., *arma virumque cano, Troiae qui primus ab oris/ Italiam fato profugus Laviniaque venit / litora — multum ille et terris iactatus et alto...* (1.1-3). Here, the *ille* is techinically unnecessary but draws added attention to the *vir* (10), Aeneas. Cf. 1.372, 392.

Polyptoton (Gr. "in many cases"): the repetition of a word in its inflected cases. E.g., *notos pueri puer indue vultus* (1.684). Cf. 1.106.

Polysyndeton (Gr. "much-connected"): the repetition or excessive use of conjunctions. E.g., *ast ego, quae divum incedo regina Iovisque / et soror et coniunx* (1.46-7). Cf. 1.18.

Prolepsis (Gr. "anticipation"): the use of a word or phrase that anticipates a later event. E.g., *furentem / incendat reginam* (1.659-60). Here the force of *furentem* is not "set the raging queen on fire" but "set her on fire so that she rages." (On the use here of *incendat*, see *metaphor.*) Cf. 1.70, 259, 712, 719.

Rhetorical question: a question that is posed not to receive an answer but for some other purpose or effect. E.g., *et quisquam numen Iunonis adorat / praeterea aut supplex aris imponet honorem?* (1.48-9). Here Juno soliloquizes about the harm her honor has suffered from her inability to destroy the Trojans.

Simile (Lat. "similar"): a figurative comparison between two different things. It is an important component of epic style. E.g., *ac veluti magno in populo cum saepe coorta est / seditio saevitque animis ignobile vulgus; / iamque faces et saxa volant, furor arma ministrat; / tum, pietate gravem ac meritis si forte virum quem / conspexere, silent arrectisque auribus astant; / ille regit dictis animos et pectora mulcet* (1.148-53). In this simile (perhaps the most famous in the *Aeneid*), Neptune's calming of the storm is compared to a pious human leader quelling civil unrest. Cf. 1.316-17, 430-6, 498-502, 592.

Synchysis (Gr. "mingling," "confusion"): an arrangement of two phrases (here Aa and Bb) that interweave their members in an ABab pattern. It is also called *interlocking word order.* E.g.,

A   B   a   b

amissos longo socios sermone requirunt (1.217)

Cf. 1.647, 649.

Synecdoche (Gr. "understanding one thing with another"): a type of *metonymy* that uses the part for the whole (or the reverse). E.g., *atque rotis summas levibus perlabitur undas* (1.147). Here *rotis* ("wheels") really stands in for "chariot."

Theme and Variation: the restatement of an initial phrase in different language. E.g., *vivo temptat praevertere amore / iam pridem resides animos desuetaque corda* (1.721-2). Here *resides animos* essentially reformulates the idea in *desueta corda*. *Theme and variation* is also called *interpretatio* and *dicolon abundans*.

Transferred Epithet: see **Enallage**.

Tricolon (Gr. "having three limbs"): the grouping of three parallel clauses or phrases. When the third element is the longest, the resulting tricolon is called *abundans, crescens,* or *crescendo*. E.g., *tu mihi quodcumque hoc regni, tu sceptra Iovemque / concilias, tu das epulis accumbere divum / nimborumque facis tempestatumque potentem* (1.78-80). In this address by Aeolus to Juno, the three clauses beginning with *tu* increase in length (i.e. *tricolon crescendo*). Cf. 1.57, 100-1,142, 143, 495, 520-60 n., 566, 607, 713-14, 751-2.

Zeugma (Gr. "yoking"): the governing of two words by one verb or adjective, which is strictly appropriate for just one of them. E.g., *crudelis aras traiectaque pectora ferro / nudavit* (1.355-6). Here, Sychaeus figuratively "reveals" his murder at the altar (*aras*) but literally "bares" his pierced chest (*traiectaque pectora*). Cf. 1.426, 447.

Works Cited

Adler, E. (2003) *Vergil's Empire: Political Thought in the Aeneid*. Lanham, MD.

Allen, G. (2000) *Intertextuality*. London.

Anderson, W.S. (2005) *The Art of the Aeneid*. Second edition. Wauconda, IL.

Anderson, W. S. and Quartarone, L. N. (eds.) (2002) *Approaches to Teaching Vergil's Aeneid*. New York.

Armstrong, D., Fish, J., Johnston, P. A., and Skinner, M. (eds.) (2004) *Vergil, Philodemus, and the Augustans*. Austin.

Austin, R. G. (ed.) (1971) *P. Vergili Maronis Aeneidos Liber Primus*. Oxford.

Barchiesi, A. (1984) *La traccia del modello: effetti omerici nella narrazione virgiliana*. Pisa.

_____(1997) "Ecphrasis," in *The Cambridge Companion to Virgil*, ed. C. Martindale. Cambridge: 271-81.

_____(1999) "Representations of suffering and interpretation in the *Aeneid*," in *Virgil: Critical Assessments of Classical Authors*, vol. 3, ed. P. Hardie. London: 324-44. Originally published as "Rappresentazioni del dolore e interpretazione nell'*Eneide*." *Antike und Abendland* 40 (1994): 109–24.

Bartsch, S. (1998) "*Ars* and the man: The politics of art in Virgil's *Aeneid*," *Classical Philology* 93: 322-42.

Braund, S. (2004) "Making Virgil Strange," *Proceedings of the Virgil Society* 25: 135-46.

Briggs, W. W., Jr. (1981) "Virgil and the Hellenistic epic," *Aufstieg und Niedergang der römischen Welt* 2.31.2: 948-84.

Brogan, T. V. F. (ed.) (1994) *The New Princeton Handbook of Poetic Terms*. Princeton.

Brown, R. D. (1990) "The structural function of the song of Iopas," *Harvard Studies in Classical Philology* 93: 315-34.

Cairns, F. (1989) *Virgil's Augustan Epic*. Cambridge.

_____ (2003) "Propertius 3.4 and the *Aeneid* incipit," *Classical Quarterly* 53.1: 309-11.

Camps, W. A. (1969) *An Introduction to Virgil's Aeneid*. Oxford.

Clausen, W. (1987) *Virgil's Aeneid and the Tradition of Hellenistic Poetry*. Berkeley, CA.

_____(1994) *A Commentary on Virgil, Eclogues*. Oxford.

_____(2002) *Virgil's Aeneid: Decorum, Allusion, and Ideology*. Munich and Leipzig.

Clay, D. (1988) "The archaeology of the temple to Juno in Carthage," *Classical Philology* 83: 195-205.

Coleman, R. (1977) *Virgil: Eclogues*. Cambridge.

Conington, J., and Nettleship, H. (eds.) (1858-83) *The Works of Virgil*. Three volumes. London.

Conte, G. B. (1986) *The Rhetoric of Imitation: Genre and Poetic Memory in Virgil and Other Latin Poets*, tr. C. Segal. Ithaca, NY.

_____(1999) "The Virgilian paradox: an epic of drama and sentiment," *Proceedings of the Cambridge Philological Society* 45: 17-42.

_____(2007) *The Poetry of Pathos: Studies in Virgilian Epic*. Oxford.

Conway, R. S. (ed.) (1935) *P. Vergili Maronis Aeneidos Liber Primus*. Cambridge.

Crook, J. (1996) "Political history: 30 B.C. to A.D. 14," in *The Augustan Empire: 43 B.C. – A.D. 69. The Cambridge Ancient History*, vol. X. Second edition, eds. A. Bowman, E. Champlin, and A. Lintott. Cambridge: 70-112.

de Grummond, W. W. (1981) "*Saevus dolor*: the opening and the closing of the *Aeneid*," *Vergilius* 27: 48-52.

Duckworth, G. (1969) *Vergil and Classical Hexameter Poetry: A Study in Metrical Variety*. Ann Arbor.

Dyson, J. (1996) "The puzzle of *Aen.* 1.755-6 and 5.626," *Classical World* 90.1: 41-3.

Edmunds, L. (2001) *Intertextuality and the Reading of Roman Poetry*. Baltimore.

Everitt, A. (2006) *Augustus: The Life of Rome's First Emperor*. New York.

Fagles, R. (1990) *Homer: Iliad*. New York.

Farrell, J. (1991) *Vergil's Georgics and the Traditions of Ancient Epic: The Art of Allusion in Literary History*. Oxford.

_____(1997) "The Virgilian intertext," in *The Cambridge Companion to Virgil*, ed. C. Martindale. Cambridge: 222-38.

_____(2005) "The Augustan Period: 40 BC-AD 14," in *A Companion to Latin Literature*, ed. S. J. Harrison. Oxford: 44-57.

Farron, S. (1989) "The introduction of characters in the *Aeneid*," *Acta Classica* 32: 107-10.

Feeney, D. (1991) *The Gods in Epic: Poets and Critics of the Classical Tradition.* Oxford.

Fowler, D. P. (1991) "Narrate and describe: the problem of ekphrasis," *Journal of Roman Studies* 81: 25-35.

_____ (1997) "On the shoulders of giants: intertextuality and classical studies," *Materiali e discussioni per l'analisi dei testi classici* 39: 13-34.

Frangoulidis, S. A. (1992) "Duplicity and gift-offerings in Vergil's *Aeneid* 1 and 2," *Vergilius* 38: 26-37.

Fratantuono, L. (2007) *Madness Unchained: A Reading of Virgil's Aeneid.* Lanham, MD.

Fredricksmeyer, E. A. (1984) "On the opening of the *Aeneid*," *Vergilius* 30: 10-19.

Gale, M. (2000) *Virgil on the Nature of Things: The Georgics, Lucretius and the Didactic Tradition.* Cambridge.

Galinsky, K. (1988) "The anger of Aeneas," *American Journal of Philology* 109: 321-48.

_____ (1996) *Augustan Culture: An Interpretive Introduction.* Princeton.

_____ (2003) "Greek and Roman drama and the *Aeneid*," in *Myth, History, and Culture in Republican Rome: Studies in Honour of T. P. Wiseman*, eds. D. Braund and C. Gill. Exeter: 275-94.

_____ (ed.) (2005) *The Cambridge Companion to the Age of Augustus.* Cambridge.

Geymonat, M. (ed.) (1973) *P. Vergili Maronis opera. Post Remigium Sabbadini et Aloisium Castiglioni recensuit Marius Geymonat.* Paravia.

George, T. V. (1974) *Aeneid VIII and the Aitia of Callimachus.* Mnemosyne Suppl. 27. Leiden.

Goold, G. P. (ed.) (1999) *Virgil.* Two volumes. Cambridge, MA.

Gordon, P. (1998) "Phaeacian Dido: Lost pleasures of an Epicurean intertext," *Classical Antiquity* 17: 188-211.

Gransden, K. W. (1984) *Virgil's Iliad: An Essay on Epic Narrative.* Cambridge.

Greenwood, M. A. (1989) "Venus intervenes: Five episodes in the *Aeneid*," *Liverpool Classical Monthly* 14: 132-6.

Gurval, R. A. (1995) *Actium and Augustus.* Ann Arbor.

Hannah, R. (1993) "The stars of Iopas and Palinurus," *American Journal of Philology* 114.1: 123-35.

Hansen, P. A. (1972) *"Ille ego qui quondam...*once again," *Classical Quarterly* n.s. 22: 139-49.

Hardie, P. R. (1986) *Virgil's Aeneid: Cosmos and Imperium.* Oxford.

_____(1987) "Aeneas and the omen of the swans," *Classical Philology* 82: 145-50.

_____(1991) "The *Aeneid* and the *Oresteia*," *Proceedings of the Virgil Society* 20: 29-45.

_____(1993) *The Epic Successors of Virgil.* Cambridge.

_____(1997) "Virgil and tragedy," in *The Cambridge Companion to Virgil*, ed. C. Martindale. Cambridge: 312-26.

_____(1998) *Virgil.* New Surveys in the Classics 28. Oxford.

_____(ed.) (1999) *Virgil: Critical Assessments of Classical Authors.* Four volumes. London.

Harrison, E. L. (1972-73) "Why did Venus wear boots? Some reflections on *Aeneid* I, 314 f." *Proceedings of the Virgil Society* 12: 10-25.

_____(1992) "Aeneas at Carthage: The opening scenes of the *Aeneid*," in *The Two Worlds of the Poet: New Perspectives on Vergil*, eds. R. Wilhelm and H. Jones. Detroit: 109-28.

Harrison, S. J. (1988) "Vergil on kingship: the first simile of the *Aeneid*," *Proceedings of the Cambridge Philological Society* n.s. 34: 55-9.

_____(ed.) (1990) *Oxford Readings in Vergil's Aeneid.* Oxford.

_____(1996) "*Aeneid* 1.286: Julius Caesar or Augustus?" *Papers of the Leeds International Latin Seminar* 8: 127-33.

_____(ed.) (2005) *A Companion to Latin Literature.* Oxford.

Heinze, R. (1915) *Vergils epische Technik.* Third edition. Leipzig and Berlin.

_____(1993) *Virgil's Epic Technique*, tr. H. Harvey, D. Harvey, and F. Robertson. Berkeley, CA.

Hexter, Ralph (1992) "Sidonian Dido," in *Innovations of Antiquity*, eds. R. Hexter and D. Selden. London: 332-84.

Heyworth, S. (2005) "Pastoral," in *A Companion to Latin Literature*, ed. S. J. Harrison. Oxford: 148-58.

Hinds, S. (1998) *Allusion and Intertext: Dynamics of Appropriation in Roman Poetry.* Cambridge.

Hirtzel, F. A. (ed.) (1900) *P. Vergili Maronis Opera.* Oxford.

Horsfall, N. (1973-74) "Dido in the Light of History," *Proceedings of the Virgil Society* 13: 1-13. Reprinted in *Oxford Readings in Vergil's Aeneid*, ed. S. J. Harrison (1990). Oxford: 127-44.

_____(1995) *A Companion to the Study of Virgil*. Leiden.

_____(2006) *Virgil, Aeneid 3: A Commentary*. Leiden.

Hunter, R. L. (2006) *The Shadow of Callimachus: Studies in the Reception of Hellenistic Poetry at Rome*. Cambridge.

Jackson Knight, W. F. (1944) *Roman Vergil*. London.

James, S. (1995) "Establishing Rome with the sword: *condere* in the *Aeneid*," *Transactions of the American Philological Association* 116: 623-37.

Johnson, W. R. (1976) *Darkness Visible: A Study of Vergil's Aeneid*. Berkeley.

_____(1999) "*Dis aliter visum*; self-telling and theodicy in *Aeneid* 2," in *Reading Vergil's Aeneid: An Interpretive Guide*, ed. C. Perkell. Norman, OK: 50-63.

_____(2005) "Introduction," in *Virgil: Aeneid*, S. Lombardo, Indianapolis, IN: xv-lxxi.

Johnston, P. A. (1980) *Vergil's Agricultural Golden Age: A Study of the Georgics*. Leiden.

_____(2002) "The anger of Juno in Vergil's *Aeneid*," in *Approaches to Teaching Vergil's Aeneid*, eds. W. S. Anderson and L. N. Quartarone. New York: 123-30.

Jones, A. H. M. (1970) *Augustus*. London.

Kennedy, D. (1992) "'Augustan' and 'Anti-Augustan': reflections on terms of reference," in *Roman Poetry and Propaganda in the Age of Augustus*, ed. A. Powell. Bristol: 26-58.

Khan, H. Akbar (2002): "The boy at the banquet: Dido and Amor in Vergil, *Aen.* I," *Atheneum* 90, 187-205.

_____(2003): "Venus' intervention in the Dido-affair: Controversies and considerations," in *Studies in Latin Literature and Roman History 11*. Collection Latomus 272 (Bruxelles), ed. C. Deroux: 244-74.

Kinsey, T. E. (1979): "The song of Iopas," *Emerita* 47: 77-86.

Knauer, G. N. (1964a) *Die Aeneis und Homer: Studien zur poetischen Technik Vergils mit Listen der Homerzitate in der Aeneis*. Göttingen.

_____(1964b) "Vergil's *Aeneid* and Homer," *Greek, Roman and Byzantine Studies* 5: 61-84. Reprinted in *Oxford Readings in Vergil's Aeneid*, ed. S. J. Harrison (1990). Oxford: 390-412.

Kraggerud, Egil (1994): "Caesar versus Caesar again: A reply," *Symbolae Osloenses* 69: 83-93.

Lanham, R. A. (1991) *A Handlist of Rhetorical Terms*. Second edition. Berkeley, CA.

Leach, E. W. (1988) *The Rhetoric of Space: Literary and Artistic Representations of Landscape in Republican and Augustan Rome*. Princeton.

Levitan, William (1993) "Give up the beginning? Juno's mindful wrath (*Aeneid* 1.37)", *Liverpool Classical Monthly* 18: 14.

Lombardo, S. (1997) *Homer: Iliad*. Indianapolis, IN.

_____(2005) *Virgil: Aeneid*. Indianapolis, IN.

Lowenstam, S. (1993) "The pictures on Juno's temple in the *Aeneid*," *Classical World* 87: 37-49.

Lowrie, Michèle (1999): "Telling pictures: Ecphrasis in the *Aeneid*," *Vergilius* 45: 111-20.

Lyne, R. O. A. M. (1987) *Further Voices in Vergil's Aeneid*. Oxford.

McKay, A. G. (1989) "Vergil's Aeolus episode," in *Daidalion: Studies in Memory of Raymond Schoder*, ed. R. F. Sutton. Wauconda, IL: 249-56.

Mahoney, A. (ed.) (2001) *Allen and Greenough's New Latin Grammar*. Newburyport, MA.

Martindale, C. (1993) "Descent into Hell: reading ambiguity, or Virgil and the critics," *Proceedings of the Virgil Society* 21: 111-50.

_____(ed.) (1997) *The Cambridge Companion to Virgil*. Cambridge.

Mynors, R. A. B. (ed.) (1969) *P. Vergili Maronis Opera*. Oxford.

_____(ed.) (1990) *Virgil: Georgics*. Oxford.

Nappa, C. (2005) *Reading After Actium: Vergil's Georgics, Octavian, and Rome*. Ann Arbor.

Nelis, D. (2001) *Vergil's Aeneid and the Argonautica of Apollonius Rhodius*. Leeds.

Nussbaum, G. B. (1986) *Vergil's Meter: A Practical Guide for Reading Latin Hexameter Poetry*. Bristol.

O'Hara, J. J. (1990) *Death and the Optimistic Prophecy in Vergil's Aeneid*. Princeton.

_____(1994) "Temporal distortions, 'Fatal' ambiguity, and Iulius Caesar at *Aeneid* I. 286-96" *Symbolae Osloenses* 69: 72-82.

_____(1996) *True Names: Vergil and the Alexandrian Tradition of Aetiological Wordplay*. Ann Arbor.

_____(1997) "Virgil's style," in *The Cambridge Companion to Virgil*, ed. C. Martindale. Cambridge: 241-58.

_____(2007) *Inconsistency in Roman Epic: Studies in Catullus, Lucretius, Vergil, Ovid, and Lucan*. Cambridge.

Otis, B. (1964) *Virgil: A Study in Civilized Poetry*. Oxford.

Page, T. E. (ed.) (1892) *P. Vergili Maronis Aeneidos Lib. I*. London.

_____(ed.) (1894, 1900) *Virgil: Aeneid*. Two volumes. London.

Panoussi, V. (2002) "Vergil's Ajax: allusion, tragedy, and heroic identity in the *Aeneid*," *Classical Antiquity* 21: 95-134.

Pavlock, B. (1985) "Epic and tragedy in Vergil's Nisus and Euryalus episode," *Transactions of the American Philological Association* 115: 207-24.

Pease, A. S. (ed.) (1935) *Publi Vergili Maronis Aeneidos Liber Quartus*. Cambridge.

Pelling, C. (1996) "The Triumviral period," in *The Augustan Empire: 43 B.C. – A.D. 69. The Cambridge Ancient History*, vol. X. Second edition, eds. A. Bowman, E. Champlin, and A. Lintott. Cambridge: 1-69.

Perkell, C. (1989) *The Poet's Truth: A Study of the Poet in Virgil's Georgics*. Berkeley.

_____(1994) "Ambiguity and irony: the last resort?," *Helios* 21: 63-74.

_____ (ed.) (1999) *Reading Vergil's Aeneid: An Interpretive Guide*. Norman, OK.

Petrini, M. (1997) *The Child and the Hero: Coming of Age in Catullus and Vergil*. Ann Arbor.

Phillips, O. (1980) "*Aeole, namque tibi*," *Vergilius* 26: 18-26.

Pöschl, V. (1950) *Die Dichtkunst Vergils: Bild und Symbol in der Aeneis*. Innsbruck.

_____(1962) *The Art of Vergil: Image and Symbol in the Aeneid*, tr. G. Seligson. Ann Arbor.

Powell, A. (ed.) (1992) *Roman Poetry and Propaganda in the Age of Augustus*. Bristol.

Purcell, N. (2005) "Romans in the Roman world," in *The Cambridge Companion to the Age of Augustus*, ed. K. Galinsky. Cambridge: 85-105.

Putnam, M. (1965) *The Poetry of the Aeneid*. Cambridge, MA.

_____(1979) *Virgil's Poem of the Earth: Studies in the Georgics*. Princeton.

_____(1993) "The languages of Horace, *Odes* 1.24," *Classical Journal* 88.2: 123-35.

_____(1995) *Virgil's Aeneid: Interpretation and Influence*. Chapel Hill.

_____(1998) *Virgil's Epic Designs: Ekphrasis in the Aeneid*. New Haven.

Quinn, K. (1968) *Virgil's Aeneid: A Critical Description*. London.

Reckford, K. J. (1995-96) "Recognizing Venus I: Aeneas meets his mother," *Arion* 3: 1-42.

Reed, J. D. (2007) *Virgil's Gaze*. Princeton.

Ross, D. O. (1987) *Virgil's Elements: Physics and Poetry in the Georgics*. Princeton.

_____(2007) *Virgil's Aeneid: A Reader's Guide*. Oxford.

Scullard, H. H. (1982) *From the Gracchi to Nero: A History of Rome from 133 B.C. to A.D. 68*. Fifth edition. London.

Segal, C. (1971) "The song of Iopas in the *Aeneid*," *Hermes* 99: 336-49 .

_____(1981a) "Art and the hero: Participation, detachment, and narrative point of view in *Aeneid* 1," *Arethusa* 14.1: 67-83.

_____ (1981b) "Iopas revisited (*Aeneid* I.740 ff.)," *Emérita* 49: 17-25.

Shotter, D. (2005) *Augustus Caesar*. Second edition. London.

Skutsch, O. (ed.) (1985) *The Annals of Q. Ennius*. Oxford.

Smith, R. A. (2005) *The Primacy of Vision in Virgil's Aeneid*. Austin.

Southern, P. (1998) *Augustus*. New York.

Stahl, H.-P. (ed.) (1998) *Vergil's Aeneid: Augustan Epic and Political Context*. London.

Staley, G. A. (1990) "Aeneas' first act: 1, 180-194," *Classical World* 84: 25-38.

Syed, Y. (2005) *Vergil's Aeneid and the Roman Self: Subject and Nation in Literary Discourse*. Ann Arbor.

Syme, R. (1939) *The Roman Revolution*. Oxford.

Thomas, R. (1983) "Virgil's ecphrastic centerpieces," *Harvard Studies in Classical Philology* 87: 175-84

_____(1986) "Virgil's *Georgics* and the art of reference," *Harvard Studies in Classical Philology* 90: 171-98.

_____(1988) *Virgil: Georgics*. Two volumes. Cambridge.

_____(1999) *Reading Virgil and His Texts: Studies in Intertextuality*. Ann Arbor.

_____(2001) *Virgil and the Augustan Reception*. Cambridge.

Van Sickle, J. (1992) *A Reading of Virgil's Messianic Eclogue*. New York.

Vernant, J.-P. and Vidal-Naquet, P. (1988) *Myth and Tragedy in Ancient Greece*, tr. J. Lloyd. New York.

Volk, K. (ed.) (2008a) *Vergil's Eclogues*. Oxford.

_____(ed.) (2008b) *Vergil's Georgics*. Oxford.

Wallace-Hadrill, A. (1993) *Augustan Rome*. London.

Warmington, E. H. (1935-40) *Remains of Old Latin*. Revised edition. Four volumes. Cambridge, MA.

White, P. (1993) *Promised Verse: Poets in the Society of Augustan Rome*. Cambridge, MA.

_____(2005) "Poets in the new milieu: realigning," in *The Cambridge Companion to the Age of Augustus*, ed. K. Galinsky. Cambridge: 321-39.

Wigodsky, M. (1972) *Vergil and Early Latin Poetry*. Wiesbaden.

Wilkinson, L. P. (1963) *Golden Latin Artistry*. Cambridge.

_____(1969) *The Georgics of Virgil: A Critical Survey*. Cambridge.

Williams, G. W. (1983) *Technique and Ideas in the Aeneid*. New Haven and London.

Williams R. D. (1960) "The pictures on Dido's temple (*Aeneid* I, 450-493)," *Classical Quarterly* 10: 145-51.

_____ (1965-66) "The opening scenes of the *Aeneid*," *Proceedings of the Virgil Society* 5: 14-23.

_____ (1972-73) *Virgil: Aeneid*. Two volumes. London.

Wlosok, A. (1999) "The Dido tragedy in Virgil: a contribution to the question of the tragic in the *Aeneid*," transl. of Wlosok (1976), in *Virgil: Critical Assessments of Classical Authors*, vol. 4, ed. P. Hardie. London: 158-81. Originally published as "Vergils Didotragödie: ein Beitrag zum Problem des Tragischen in der *Aeneis*," in *Studien zum antiken Epos*, eds. H. Görgemanns and E. A. Schmidt. Meisenheim: 228-50.

Wyatt, W. (ed.) *Homer: Iliad*. Two volumes. Cambridge, MA.

Zanker, P. (1988) *The Power of Images in the Age of Augustus*, tr. A. Shapiro. Ann Arbor.

List of Abbreviations

abl.	= ablative
acc.	= accusative
adj.	= adjective
adv.	= adverb
cf.	= *confer*, i.e. compare
comp.	= comparative
conj.	= conjunction
dat.	= dative
dep.	= deponent
f.	= feminine
gen.	= genitive
i.e.	= *id est*, that is
indecl.	= indeclinable
indef.	= indefinite
interj.	= interjection
intr.	= intransitive
interrog.	= interrogative
m.	= masculine
n.	= neuter
nom.	= nominative
num.	= numeral
opp.	= opposed
part.	= participle
pass.	= passive
perf.	= perfect
pers.	= personal
pl.	= plural
poss.	= possessive
prep.	= preposition
pron.	= pronoun
rel.	= relative
sc.	= *scilicet*, i.e. understand, supply
sing.	= singular
subst.	= substantive
superl.	= superlative
tr.	= transitive
v.	= verb
viz.	= *videlicet*, namely

Vocabulary

(In general, macrons are placed only over long vowels in metrically indeterminate positions.)

A

ā, ab, prep. with abl. *from, by*

Abās, -ntis, m. *a Trojan*

abdō, -ere, -didī, -ditum, tr. *put away; hide*

abeō, -īre, -īvī or **-iī, -itum,** intr. *go away*

aboleō, -ēre, -ēvī, -itum, tr. *make to grow less; take away, destroy*

abripiō, -ere, -ripuī, -reptum, tr. *snatch away*

absistō, -ere, -stitī, —, intr. *stand away; leave off*

absum, -esse, -fuī, intr. *am away, absent*

absūmō, -ere, -sūmpsī, -sūmptum, tr. *take away*

ac, see **atque**

acanthus, -ī, m. *the plant acanthus,* also called *bear's-foot*

accēdō, -ere, -cessī, -cessum, intr. and tr. *go to, approach*

accendō, -ere, -cendī, -censum, tr. *kindle; rouse, enrage*

accingō, -ere, -cinxī, -cinctum, tr. *gird on, girdle;* **sē accingere,** *gird oneself, make oneself ready*

accipiō, -ere, -cēpī, -ceptum, tr. *receive; hear*

accītus, -ūs, m. *summoning*

accumbō, -ere, -cubuī, -cubitum, intr. with dat. *recline at*

ācer, ācris, ācre, adj. *sharp, fierce*

acerbus, -a, -um, adj. *sharp, bitter; cruel*

Acestēs, -ae, m. king in Sicily, son of Sicilian river-god Crimisus and the Trojan Egesta

Achātēs, -ae, m. the faithful companion of Aeneas

Achillēs, -is and **-ī,** m. son of Peleus and Thetus, the bravest and most beautiful of the Greeks; slew Hector

Achīvī, -ōrum and **-um,** m. *Greeks*

Acīdalius, -a, -um, adj. *belonging to the Acidalian fountain* in Boeotia where Venus and the Graces bathed

aciēs, -ēī, f. *edge; line of battle; battle*

acūtus, -a, -um, adj. *sharp*

ad, prep. with acc. *to, towards; at*

addō, -ere, -didī, -ditum, tr. *add, join to*

adeō, -īre, -iī, -itum, intr. and tr. *go to, approach*

adeō, adv. *to such an extent; so*

adflīgō, -ere, -flixī, -flictum, tr. *strike down, crush*

adflō, -āre, -flāvī, -flātum, tr. *breathe upon*

(adfor), -fārī, -fātus sum, dep. tr. *speak to*

adhūc, adv. *hitherto*

adloquor, -ī, -locūtus sum, dep. tr. *speak to, address*

adnītor, -ī, -nixus or **-nīsus sum,** dep. intr. *lean upon; labor*

adnō, -āre, -nāvī, -nātum, intr. and tr. *swim to*

adnuō, -ere, -nuī, -nūtum, intr. and tr. *nod assent; grant by a nod*

adoleō, -ēre, -oluī, -ultum, tr. *make to grow* (see 703-4 n.)

adōrō, -āre, -ōrāvī, -ōrātum, tr. *pray to, entreat*

adsum, -esse, -fuī, intr. *am present*

adsurgō, -ere, -surrexī, -surrectum, intr. *rise up*

adultus, -a, -um, adj. *full-grown*

advehō, -ire, -vexī, -vectum, tr. *carry to*

adveniō, -īre, -vēnī, -ventum, intr. and tr. *come; arrive; arrive at*

adversus, -a, -um, adj. *opposite*

advertō, -ere, -vertī, -versum, tr. and intr. *turn towards*

Aeacidēs, -ae, m. patronymic, son or descendant of Aeacus, king of Aegina; *Achilles,* whose father Peleus was son of Aeacus

aeger, -gra, -grum, adj. *sick, weary*

Aeneadae, -ārum or **–um,** m. patronymic *children* or *followers of Aeneas*

Aenēās,-ae, m. *Aeneas*

aēnum, -ī, n. *caldron*

aēnus, -a, -um, adj. *of brass* or *copper*

Aeolia, -ae, f. the country of Aeolus

Aeolus, -ī, m. king of the winds

aequō, -āre, -āvī, -ātum, tr. *make equal*

aequor, -oris, n. *level surface, sea*

aequus, -a, -um, adj. *level; fair, favorable*

āēr, -eris, m. *air; the lower air; mist*

aereus, -a, -um, adj. *of bronze*

aes, aeris, n. *bronze* or *copper*

aestās,-ātis, f. *summer*

aestus, -ūs, m. *heat; billows, surge*

aetās,-ātis, f. *time of life; time, an age*

aeternus, -a, -um, adj. *everlasting*

aethēr, -eris, m. *the bright upper air, ether*

aetherius, -a, -um, adj. *belonging to the upper air; heavenly*

Agēnor, -oris, m. a king of Phoenicia

ager, -grī, m. *field*

agger, -eris, m. *bank, mound*

agmen, -inis, n. *army on line of march; line; troop, array*

agnoscō, -ere, -nōvī, -nitum, tr. *recognize*

agnus, -ī, m. *lamb*

agō, -ere, ēgī, actum, tr. *drive, move; deal with;* **age,** *come now, come*

Aiax, -ācis, m. *Ajax,* see 41 n.

āiō, v. defect. *say;* 3rd pers. sing. **ait**

āla, -ae, f. *wing*

Alba, -ae, f. a city on the Alban mount 15 m. S.E. of Rome, see 271 n.

Albānus, -a, -um, adj. *belonging to Alba, Alban*

āles, alitis, adj. *winged;* then as subst. m. and f. *bird*

Alētēs, -ae, m. proper name

āliger, -era, -erum, adj. *winged*

aliquis or **aliquī, aliqua, aliquid** or **aliquod,** indef. pron. and adj. *any, some*

aliter, adv. *otherwise*

alius, alia, aliud, adj. *another, other;* **aliī...aliī,** *some...others*

alligō, -āre, -ligāvī, -ligātum, tr. *bind to, bind*

almus, -a, -um, adj. *nurturing; kindly*
altē, adv. *on high*
alter, altera, alterum, adj. *one of two, another, a second*
altus, -a, -um, adj. *lofty; deep;* **altum, -ī,** n. as subst. *the deep; the sky*
amāracus, -ī, m. and f. *marjoram*
Amazonis, -idis, f. *an Amazon.* The Amazons were a community of female warriors dwelling in Pontus by the river Thermodon
ambāgēs, -is, f. rare in sing.; gen. pl. **ambagum;** *a going round; devious tale*
ambiguus, -a, -um, adj. *doubtful*
ambō, -ae, -ō, adj. *both*
ambrosius, -a, -um, adj. *ambrosial,* from **ambrosia,** the unguent used by the gods
amiciō, -īre, amicuī or **amixī, amictum,** tr. *wrap around, clothe*
amictus, -ūs, m. *clothing, cloak*
amīcus, -ī, m. *friend*
āmittō, -ere, -mīsī, -missum, tr. *let go, lose*
amor, -ōris, m. *love;* **Amor,** *Love, Cupid,* the son of Venus
amplexus, -ūs, m. *embrace*
amplius, comp. adv. *more*
amplus, -a, -um, adj. *spacious*
an, conj. *whether, or*
Anchīsēs, -ae, m. *Anchises,* father of Aeneas
anchora, -ae, f. *anchor*
anima, -ae, f. *breath, life*
animus, -ī, m. *mind;* in plur. *spirits, wrath*
annālis, -e, adj. *belonging to a year;* as plur. subst. m. **annālēs, -ium,** *annals, records*
annus, -ī, m. *year*
ante, adv. and prep. with acc. *before*

Antēnor, -oris, m. a Trojan who after the fall of Troy founded Patavium (Padua)
Antheus, -eī, m. follower of Aeneas
antīquus, -a, -um, adj. *old; ancient*
antrum, -ī, n. *cave*
aper, -prī, m. *wild boar*
aperiō, -īre, -uī, -ertum, tr. *open*
apertus, -a, -um, adj. *open*
apis, -is, f. *bee*
appāreō, -ēre, -pāruī, -pāritum, intr. *appear*
appellō, -ere, -pulī, -pulsum, tr. *drive to*
applicō, -āre, -plicuī or **-plicāvī, -plicitum** or **-plicātum,** tr. *drive to*
aptō, -āre, -āvī, -ātum, tr. *make fit, shape*
apud, prep. with acc. *with, among*
aqua, -ae, f. *water*
Aquilō, -ōnis, m. *North Wind*
āra, -ae, f. *altar*
arbor, -oris, f. *tree*
arboreus, -a, -um, adj. *belonging to a tree; tree-like*
arcānus, -a, -um, adj. *secret*
arceō, -ēre, -uī, —, tr. *shut up, confine; ward off*
Arctūrus, -ī, m. The Bear-Warden, the brightest star in Bootes
arcus, -ūs, m. *bow*
ardeō, -ēre, arsī, arsum, intr. *blaze, burn; am eager*
ardescō, -ere, arsī, —, v. inceptive intr. *begin to glow* or *burn*
argentum, -ī, n. *silver*
Argos, n. sing. only in nom. and acc., also **Argī, -ōrum,** plur. m. *Argos,* capital town of Argolis in the Peloponnesus
Argīvus, -a, -um, adj. *belonging to Argos, Greek;* **Argīvī, -ōrum,** m. plur. *Argives, Greeks*

āridus, -a, -um, adj. *dry*

arma, -ōrum, n. plur. *arms*

armentum, -ī, n. *herd*

arrigō, -ere, -rexī, -rectum, tr. *raise up; rouse, cheer*

ars, artis, f. *art, skill; cunning*

artifex, -icis, m. and f. *cunning workman, contriver*

artus, -a, -um, adj. *made close; close, tight, narrow*

artus, -ūs, m. *joint, limb*

arvum, -ī, n. *ploughed land, field*

arx, arcis, f. *place of defense, citadel*

Ascanius, -iī, m. son of Aeneas and Creusa, also called Iulus

ascendō, -ere, -cendī, -censum, intr. and tr. *climb*

Asia, -ae, f. *Asia Minor*

aspectō, -āre, -spectāvī, -spectātum, tr. *gaze at, view*

aspectus, -ūs, m. *sight; appearance*

aspiciō, -spicere, -spexī, -spectum, tr. *behold; examine*

aspīrō, -āre, -spirāvī, -spirātum, intr. *breathe upon*

Assaracus, -ī, m. king of Phrygia, son of Tros, grandfather of Anchises

ast, see at

astō, -āre, -stitī, —, intr. *stand by; halt by* or *at*

astrum, -ī, n. *star*

at or **ast,** conj. *but, yet, however*

āter, ātra, ātrum, adj. *black, gloomy*

Atlās, Atlantis, m. a king of Mauritania; a high mountain in Mauritania

atque or **ac,** conj. *and*

Atrīdēs, -ae, m. patronymic *son of Atreus.* The *Atridae* were Agamemnon and Menelaus, leaders of the Greeks against Troy

ātrium, -iī, n. *hall*

ătrox, -ōcis, adj. *fierce, savage*

attingō, -ere, -tigī, -tactum, tr. *touch, touch lightly*

attollō, -ere, —, —, *lift up*

audeō, -ēre, ausus sum, semi-dep. *dare*

audiō, -īre, -īvī or **–iī, -ītum,** tr. *hear*

augurium, -iī, n. *omen by the utterance of birds; omen*

aula, -ae, f. *court, hall*

aulaea, -ōrum, n. plur. *curtains*

aura, -ae, f. *air, breeze, breath*

aurātus, -a, -um, adj. *gilded*

aureus, -a, -um, adj. *golden*

auris, -is, f. *ear*

Aurōra, -ae, f. goddess of the dawn

aurum, -ī, n. *gold*

Auster, -trī, m. the *south wind*

aut, conj. *or*

auxilium, -iī, n. *help*

avārus, -a, -um, adj. *greedy*

āvehō, -ere, -vexī, -vectum, tr. *carry away*

āversus, -a, -um, adj. *turned away*

āvertō, -ere, -vertī, versum, tr. *turn away*

avidus, -a, -um, adj. *eager, longing*

B

bācātus, -a, -um, adj. *adorned with pearls*

Bacchus, -ī, m. god of wine; *wine*

barbarus, -a, -um, adj. *speaking an unknown tongue, barbarous*

beātus, -a, -um, adj. *happy*

bellātrix, -īcis, f. *female warrior*

bellō, -āre, -āvī, -ātum, intr. *carry on war*

bellum, -ī, n. *war* (= **duellum,** *a contest between two*)

Bēlus, -ī, n. proper name

benignus, -a, -um, adj. *kind*

bibō, -ere, -ī, -itum, tr. *drink*

bilinguis, -e, adj. *having two tongues* or *a double tongue*

bīnī, -ae, -a, distrib. num. adj. *two of each*

birēmis, -e, adj. *with two oars* or *rows of oars;* as subst. f. (supply **navis**) *ship with two rows of oars on each side*

bis, num. adj. *twice*

Bitiās, -ae, m. proper name

blandus, -a, -um, adj. *smooth, winning*

bonus, -a, -um, adj. comp. **melior,** superl. **optimus,** *good; favorable*

brevis, -e, adj. *short; shallow*

breviter, adv. *shortly, briefly*

Byrsa, -ae, f. see 367-8 n.

C

cadō, -ere, cecidī, cāsum, intr. *fall*

cadus, -ī, n. *wine-jar*

caecus, -a, -um, adj. *blind; dark; secret, hidden*

caedēs, -is, f. *slaughter*

caelestis, -e, adj. *heavenly;* **caelestēs,** as pl. subst. *the inhabitants of heaven*

caelō, -āre, -āvī, -ātum, tr. engrave

caelum, -ī, n. *heaven*

Caesar, -aris, m. a cognomen of the *gens Julia;* applied to the Emperor Augustus as the adopted son of Julius Caesar (cf. Czar, Shah, Kaiser)

caesariēs, -ēī, f. *flowing locks*

Caīcus, -ī, n. proper name

caleō, -ēre, -uī, —, intr. *am hot, glow*

campus, -ī, m. *plain, field*

canistra, -ōrum, n. plur. *basket* woven from reeds

canō, -ere, cecinī, cantum, tr. and intr. *sing*

cantus, -ūs, m. *singing*

cānus, -a, -um, adj. *gray; hoary, ancient*

capessō, -ere, capessīvī, capessītum, tr. *take; undertake, perform*

capiō, -ere, cēpī, captum, tr. *take, seize*

caput, -itis, n. *head; top*

Capys, -yos, m. proper name

carcer, -eris, m. *prison*

cardō, -inis, m. *hinge, pivot, socket*

carpō, -ere, carpsī, carptum, tr. *pluck, take*

cārus, -a, -um, adj. *dear, beloved*

castra, -ōrum, n. plur. *camp*

cāsus, -ūs, m. *fall; accident, hazard*

caterva, -ae, f. *crowd*

cavō, -āre, -āvī, -ātum, tr. *make hollow*

cavus, -a, -um, adj. *hollow*

causa, -ae, f. *cause*

celebrō, -āre, -āvī, -ātum, tr. *make crowded, throng; celebrate*

celer, -eris, -ere, adj. *swift*

celerō, -āre, -āvī, -ātum, tr. *make quick, hasten*

cella, -ae, f. *cell, chamber*

cēlō, -āre, -āvī, -ātum, tr. *hide, conceal*

celsus, -a, -um, adj. *lofty*

centum, num. adj. indecl. *hundred*

Cereālis, -e, adj. *belonging to Ceres*

Cerēs, -eris, f. goddess of agriculture; *corn*

cernō, -ere, crēvī, crētum, tr. *distinguish* (e.g. with the eyes)

certē, adv. *assuredly*

certō, -āre, -āvī, -ātum, intr. *contend, strive*

certus, -a, -um, adj. *the other*

cervix, -vīcis, f. *neck*

cervus, -ī, m. *stag*

cessō, -āre, -āvī, -ātum, tr. *am idle, inactive*

cēterus, -a, -um, adj. *the other*

chorus, -ī, m. *dance; band of singers; troop*

cieō, -ēre, cīvī, citum, tr. *set in motion, rouse*

cingō, -ere, cinxī, cinctum, tr. *put
round; gird*

cingulum, -ī, n. *belt*

circum, adv. and prep. with acc.
around

circumdō, -are, -dedī, -datum, tr. *put
around; surround*

circumfundō, -ere, -fūdī, -fūsum, tr.
pour around

circumtexō, -ere, -texuī, -textum, tr.
weave around

cithara, -ae, f. *lyre; harp*

cito, adv. *quickly*

citus, -a, -um, adj. *quick*

clam, adv. *secretly*

clāmor, -ōris, m. *shout*

clārus, -a, -um, adj. *clear, bright;
glorious*

classis, -is, f. *fleet*

claudō, -ere, -sī, -sum, tr. *shut; shut in*

claustrum, -ī, n. *bar*

Cloanthus, -ī, m. proper name

coepī, -isse, v. defective tr. and intr.
begin

coetus, -ūs, m. *gathering*

cognōmen, -inis, n. *surname; name*

cognoscō, -ere, -nōvī, -nitum, v.
inceptive tr. *begin to recognize,
learn*

cōgō, -ere, coēgī, coactum, tr. *drive
together, compel*

colligō, -ere, -lēgī, -lectum, tr. *gather
together*

collis, -is, m. *hill*

collum, -ī, n. *neck*

colō, -ere, -uī, cultum, tr. *take care of;
till; cherish*

colōnus, -ī, m. *tiller; settler*

columna, -ae, f. *column, post*

coma, -ae, f. *hair*

comitor, -ārī, -ātus sum, dep. tr.
accompany; **comitātus** often
passively, *accompanied*

commissum, -ī, n. *offence, crime*

committō, -ere, -mīsī, -missum, tr.
incur or *do a wrong*

commoveō, -ēre, -mōvī, -mōtum, tr.
move strongly, stir up

compāgēs, -is, f. *fastening*

compellō, -āre, -āvī, -ātum, tr. *address*

compellō, -ere, -pulī, -pulsus, tr. *drive*

complector, -ī, -plexus sum, dep. tr.
embrace

complexus, -ūs, m. *embrace*

compōnō, -ere, -posuī, -positum or
-postum, tr. *lay to rest, arrange,
calm*

conciliō, -āre, -āvī, -ātum, tr. *bring
together; procure*

conclūdō, -ere, -clūsī, -clūsum, tr. *shut
in*

concurrō, -ere, -currī, -cursum, intr.
run together; meet (in battle)

concursus, -ūs, m. *meeting, assembly*

condō, -ere, -didī, -ditum, tr. *put
together; build; found*

confīdō, -ere, confīsus sum, semi-dep.
intr. *trust in*

confugiō, -ere, -fūgī, -fugitum, intr.
fly for refuge

congredior, -ī, -gressus sum, dep. intr.
come together, fight

coniungō, -ere, -iunxī, -iunctum, tr.
join together

coniunx, coniugis, m. and f. *one
joined; husband, wife*

conscendō, -ere, -scendī, -scensum, tr.
climb, mount; embark on

conscius, -a, -um, adj. *knowing* or
conscious of (with gen.)

consīdō, -ere, -sēdī, -sessum, intr.
settle down

consilium, -iī, n. *counsel, plan*

consistō, -ere, -stitī, -stitum, intr.
stand still; settle; rest

conspectus, -ūs, m. *sight*

conspiciō, -ere, -spexī, -spectum, tr.
 behold, view
constituō, -ere, -stituī, -stitūtum, tr.
 establish; determine
contendō, -ere, -tendī, -tentum, intr.
 strive, use eager effort
contingō, -ere, -tigī, -tactum, tr. *touch*
contrā, prep. with acc. *against,
 opposite;* adv. *in answer*
contrārius, -a, -um, adj. *opposite*
contundō, -ere, -tudī,- tūsum or
 -tunsum, tr. *crush*
cōnūbium, -iī, n. *marriage*
convellō, -ere, -vellī, -vulsum, tr. *tear
 or pluck vigorously; shatter*
conveniō, -īre, -vēnī, -ventum, intr.
 come together, assemble
convertō, -ere, -vertī, -versum, tr.
 turn; turn towards
convexus, -a, -um, adj. *vaulted,
 rounded;* as subst. **convexum,**
 rounded, arched spot; valley; slope
convīvium, -iī, n. *banquet*
coorior, -īrī, -ortus sum, dep. intr.
 collect and rise up, arise
cōpia, -ae, f. *plenty; opportunity*
cor, cordis, n. *heart*
cōram, adv. *before anyone; face to face*
cornū, -ūs, n. *horn*
corōnō, -āre, -āvī, -ātum, tr. *crown*
corpus, -oris, n. *body*
corripiō, -ere, -ripuī, -reptum, tr.
 snatch eagerly; seize
corrumpō, -ere, -rūpī, -rūptum, tr.
 break up, cause to decay; spoil
coruscus, -a, -um, adj. *vibrating;
 flashing*
costa, -ae, f. *rib*
coturnus, -ī, m. *high hunting-boot*
crātēr, -ēris, m. *mixing-bowl*
crēber, -bra, -brum, adj. *frequent*
crēdō, -ere, -didī, -ditum, intr. *believe*
crīnis, -is, m. *hair*

crīnītus, -a, -um, adj. *long-haired*
crispō, -āre, -āvī, -ātum, tr. *make to
 quiver, brandish*
cristātus, -a, -um, adj. *crested*
croceus, -a, -um, adj. *saffron-colored,
 yellow*
crūdēlis, -e, adj. *cruel*
cruentus, -a, -um, adj. *bloody*
cum, conj. *when*
cum, prep. with abl. *with;* always put
 after the personal pronouns **mē, tē,
 sē, nōbīs, vōbīs,** e.g. **mēcum**
cumulus, -ī, m. *heap*
cunctus, -a, -um, adj. *all*
Cupīdō, -inis, m. Cupid, son of Venus
 (=*desire,* **cupiō**)
cūr, adv. *why?*
cūra, -ae, f. *care, anxiety*
currō, -ere, cucurrī, cursum, intr. *run*
currus, -ūs, m. *chariot*
cursus, -ūs, m. *running, course*
cuspis, -idis, f. *spear*
custōs, ōdis, m. *guard*
Cyclōpius, -a, -um, adj. *Cyclopean,
 connected with the Cyclops,* one-
 eyed monsters in Sicily
cycnus, -ī, m. *swan*
Cymothoē, -ae, f. ocean nymph
Cynthus, -ī, m. mountain in Delos
Cyprus, -ī, f. large island in the E.
 of the Mediterranean, sacred to
 Venus
Cythēra, -ōrum, n. an island at the
 S. of Laconia, sacred to Venus,
 because near it she rose from the
 sea
Cytherēa, -ae, f. the goddess of
 Cythera, Venus

D

Danaī, -ōrum or –um, m. *the Greeks;*
 so called from Danaus, an old king
 of Argos

daps, dapis, f. *feast;* usually in pl.

Dardanidae, -ārum, m. patronymic, *children of Dardanus, Trojans*

Dardanius, -a, -um, adj. *connected with Dardanus,* the ancestor of the Trojans; *Trojan*

dator, -ōris, m. *giver*

dē, prep. with abl. *from, down from; in accordance with*

dea, -ae, f. *goddess*

decōrus, -a, -um, adj. *graceful*

decus, -oris, n. *grace, beauty; ornament*

dēfetiscor, -ī, -fessus sum, dep. intr. *become weary;* **dēfessus,** *weary*

dēfīgō, -ere, -fixī, -fixum, tr. *fix on*

dēfluō, -ere, -fluxī, -fluxum, intr. *flow down*

dehinc (usually monosyllable), adv. *after this, thereafter*

dehiscō, -ere, -hīvī, —, intr. *yawn apart, gape*

deinde, (often two syllables) adv. *thereafter, then*

Dēiopēa, -ae, f. a nymph

dēmittō, -ere, -mīsī, -missum, tr. *send down*

dēmum, adv. *at length*

dēnī, -ae, -a, distribut. num. adj. *ten each*

dependeō, -ēre, —, —, intr. *hang down*

dēripiō, -ere, -ripuī, -reptum, tr. *tear off*

dēsertum, -ī, n. *desert*

dēsistō, -ere, -stitī, -stitum, intr. *stand apart, leave off*

despectō, -āre, -āvī, -ātum, tr. *look down on*

despiciō, -ere, -spexī, -spectum, tr. *look down on*

dēsuescō, -ere, -suēvī, -suētum, tr. *render unaccustomed,* **dēsuētus,** *unaccustomed*

dēsuper, adv. *from above*

dētrūdō, -ere, -trūsī, -trūsum, tr. *push off*

deus, -ī, m. *god;* gen. pl. **deum** or **deōrum; dī** and **dīs** are often used for **deī** and **deīs. dea, -ae,** f. *goddess*

dēveniō, -īre, -vēnī, -ventum, intr. and tr. *come down to*

dēvoveō, -ēre, -vōvī, -vōtum, tr. *vow to, doom*

dextera or **dextra, -ae,** f. *the right hand*

Dǐāna, -ae, f. a goddess, sister of Apollō, presided over hunting

diciō, -ōnis, f. *power, rule*

dīcō, -ere, dixī, dictum, tr. *say, speak; call; name*

dico, -āre, -āvī, -ātum, tr. *dedicate*

dictum, -ī, n. *word*

Dīdō, -ōnis, f. Dīdō, daughter of Belus king of Tyre, wife of Sychaeus; founded Carthage

diēs, -ēī, m. (in. sing. often fem.) *day; time*

diffundō, -ere, -fūdī, -fūsum, tr. *pour or scatter apart*

dignor, -ārī, -ātus sum, tr. *deem worthy*

dignus, -a, -um, adj. *worthy*

dīlectus, -a, -um, adj. *chosen, dear*

dīmittō, -ere, -mīsī, -missum, tr. *send away or in different directions*

Diomēdēs, -is, m. *son of Tydeus, one of the Greek heroes of the siege of Troy*

dīrigō, -ere, -rexī, -rectum, tr. *direct, guide*

dīrus, -a, -um, adj. *fearful, terrible*

discō, -ere, didicī, —, tr. *learn*

discrīmen, -inis, n. *that which divides; critical moment, danger* discumbō, -ere, -cubuī, -cubitum, intr. *lie loosely; recline*

disiciō, -ere, -iēcī, -iectum, tr. *fling apart; scatter*

disiungō, -ere, -iunxī, -iunctum, tr. *disjoin, separate*

dispellō, -ere, -pulī, -pulsum, tr. *drive apart*

dissimulō, -āre, -āvī, -ātum, tr. *hide, conceal*

distendō, -ere, -tendī, -tentum, tr. *stretch out, cause to swell out*

diū, adv. *for a long time*

dīva, -ae, f. *goddess*

dīversus, -a, -um, adj. *different*

dīves, -itis, comp. dītior, superl. dītissimus, adj. *rich*

dīvidō, -ere, -vīsī, -vīsum, tr. *divide*

dīvīnus, -a, -um, adj. *divine*

dīvus, -ī, m. *deity* (gen. plur. often dīvom)

dō, dare, dedī, datum, tr. *give; give forth; place*

doceō, -ēre, -uī, doctum, tr. *teach, instruct*

doleō, -ēre, -uī, -itum, intr. *grieve; am angry*

dolor, -ōris, m. *grief; indignation*

dolus, -ī, m. *guile*

dominor, -ārī, -ātus sum, dep. intr. *hold sway*

dominus, -ī, m. *master, land*

domus, -ī and –ūs, f. *house*

dōnec, conj. *until*

dōnum, -ī, n. *gift*

dorsum, -ī, n. *back, ridge*

dubius, -a, -um, adj. *doubtful*

dūcō, -ere, duxī, ductum, tr. *draw, lead, draw out*

ductor, -ōris, m. *leader*

dulcis, -e, adj. *sweet*

dum, conj. *while; until*

duplex, -icis, adj. *two-fold, double*

dūrō, -āre, -āvī, -ātum, tr. and intr. *make hard; endure*

dūrus, -a, -um, adj. *hard; cruel*

dux, ducis, m. *leader*

E

ē, ex, prep. with abl. *from, out of*

ebur, -oris, n. *ivory*

ēdūcō, -ere, -duxī, -ductum, tr. *lead out*

efficiō, -ere, -fēcī, -fectum, tr. *make, complete*

effodiō, -ere, -fōdī, -fossum, tr. *dig out*

effundō, -ere, -fūdī, -fūsum, tr. *pour forth*

egēnus, -a, -um, adj. *needy, in want of* (with gen.)

egeō, -ēre, -uī, —, intr. *am needy, lack*

ego, meī, pers. pron. *I*

ēgredior, -gredī, -gressus sum, intr. *go out; go out from*

ēgregius, -a, -um, adj. *distinguished* (from the flock; e and grex)

ēiciō, -ere, -iēcī, -iectum, tr. *cast out*

ēlābor, -lābī, -lapsus sum, dep. intr. *glide out, slip from*

ēmittō, -ere, -mīsī, -missum, tr. *send out*

ēn, interj. *lo!*

enim, conj. *for*

eō, īre, īvī or iī, itum, intr. *go*

Ēōus, -a, -um, adj. *eastern*

epulum, -ī, n.; epulae, -ārum, f. pl. *feast, banquet*

equidem, adv. *verily, truly*

equus, -ī, m. *horse*

ergō, adv. *therefore*

ēripiō, -ere, -ripuī, -reptum, tr. *snatch away, forth*

errō, -āre, -āvī, -ātum, intr. *wander*

error, -ōris, m. *wandering*

ērumpō, -ere, -rūpī, -ruptum, intr.
and tr. *burst forth; burst forth from*
Eryx, -ycis, m. a mountain on the
Western coast of Sicily famous for
a temple of Venus
et, conj. *and; even;* et...et, *both...and*
etiam, conj. *also*
Eurōpa, -ae, f. *Europe*
Eurōtās,-ae, m. the chief river of
Laconia (SE part of Peloponnese)
Eurus, -ī, m. *East wind*
ēvertō, -ere, -vertī, -versum, tr.
overthrow
ex, see ē
exanimus, -a, -um, adj. *breathless,
lifeless*
exaudiō, -īre, -audīvī, -audītum, tr.
and intr. *hear*
excēdō, -ere, -cessī, -cessum, intr. *go
forth* or *away*
excidium, -iī, n. *destruction, collapse*
excidō, -ere, -cidī, —, intr. *fall out,
escape*
excīdō, -ere, -cīdī, -cīsum, tr. *cut* or
hew out
excipiō, -ere, -cēpī, -ceptum, tr. *take
from some one else; take in turn*
excūdō, -ere, -cūdī, -cūsum, tr. *strike
out, make by striking*
excutiō, -ere, -cussī, -cussum, tr. *shake
off* or *out*
exeō, -īre, -iī or īvī, -itum, intr. *go out,
forth,* or *away*
exerceō, -ēre, -uī, -itum, tr. *keep busy;
busy oneself at, practice*
exhauriō, -īre, -hausī, -haustum, tr.
drink up; drain
exigō, -ere, -ēgī, -actum, tr. *lead out;
complete, brings to an end*
eximō, -ere, -ēmī, -emptum, tr. *take
away*

expediō, -īre, -pedīvī or –pediī,
-pedītum, tr. *set free; make ready*
expellō, -ere, -pulī, -pulsum, tr. *drive
out*
experior, -īrī, -pertus sum, dep. tr. *try;
test*
expleō, -ēre, -plēvī, -plētum, tr. *fill up*
explōrō, -āre, -āvī, -ātum, tr. *search
out, explore*
exspīrō, -āre, -āvī, -ātum, tr. *breathe
out*
extrēmus, -a, -um, superl. adj. *outmost;
utmost, last*
exuō, -ere, -uī, -ūtum, tr. *put off*
exūrō, -ere, -ussī, -ustum, tr. *burn up*

F

faciēs, -ēī, f. *face; appearance*
facilis, -e, adj. *easy*
faciō, -ere, fēcī, factum, tr. *do; make;
cause.* Passive fīō, fierī, factus
sum, *am made; become*
factum, -ī, n. *deed*
fallō, -ere, fefellī, falsum, tr. *make to
err, deceive*
falsus, -a, -um, adj. *false*
fāma, -ae, f. *report, rumor*
famēs, -is, f. *hunger*
famulus, -ī, m. and famula, -ae, f.
servant, attendant
fandus, -a, -um, gerund of fārī, *to be
spoken; right*
fās, n. indecl. *divine law; what is lawful*
fastīgium, -iī, n. *gable roof, roof; point*
fateor, -ērī, fassus sum, dep. tr. *confess*
fatīgō, -āre, -āvī, -ātum, tr. *make
weary; harass*
fatiscō, -ere, —, —, intr. *gape, break
into cracks*
fātum, -ī, n. *that which is spoken;
oracle; fate*

fātur, 3rd sing. pres. ind. of v. defect. tr.
  for, fārī, fātus sum, *speak, say, tell*
faveō, -ēre, fāvī, fautum, intr. *am*
  favorable, well disposed to
fax, facis, f. *torch*
fēlix, -īcis, f. adj. *happy; propitious*
fēmina, -ae, f. *woman*
fera, -ae, f. *wild beast* (**ferus**)
ferīna, -ae, f. *flesh of wild beast; venison*
  (really f. adj. **carō,** *flesh,* being
  supplied)
feriō, -īre, —, —, tr. *strike*
ferō, ferre, tulī, lātum, tr. *bear, carry,*
  bring; say, relate; **sē ferre,** *advance*
ferox, -ōcis, adj. *fierce*
ferrum, -ī, n. *iron; sword*
ferveō, -ēre, ferbuī, —, intr. *am aglow*
fessus, -a, -um, adj. *weary*
fētus, -a, -um, adj. *pregnant, filled with*
fētus, -ūs, m. *offspring*
fidēs, -eī, f. *faith, honor*
fīdūcia, -ae, f. *confidence*
fīdus, -a, -um, adj. *faithful*
fīgō, -ere, fixī, fixum, tr. *fix; fasten*
fīlius, -iī, m. *son*
fīnis, -is, m. *end;* in plur. *boundaries*
fīō, see **faciō**
flagrō, -āre, -āvī, -ātum, intr. *blaze*
flamma, -ae, f. *flame*
flammō, -āre, -āvī, -ātum, tr. *set on fire*
flāvus, -a, -um, adj. *yellow*
flectō, -ere, flexī, flexum, tr. *bend, turn*
flōreus, -a, -um, adj. *flowery*
flōs, flōris, m. *flower*
fluctus, -ūs, m. *wave*
flūmen, -inis, n. *river*
fluō, -ere, fluxī, fluxum, intr. *flow*
fluvius, -iī, m. *stream*
foedus, -eris, n. *bond of faith, treaty*
folium, -iī, n. *leaf*
fōmes, -itis, m. *chip*
fons, -tis, m. *fountain*

foris, -is, f. *door*
forma, -ae, f. *form, shape; beauty*
fors, f. *chance,* used only in nom. and
  abl. **forte** *by chance*
fortis, -e, adj. *brave*
fortūna, -ae, f. *fortune*
fortūnātus, -a, -um, adj. *having good*
  fortune, lucky
foveō, -ēre, fōvī, fōtum, tr. *cherish;*
  fondle
fragor, -ōris, m. *breaking, crash*
frāgrō, -āre, -āvī, —, intr. *am of sweet*
  smell, scented
frangō, -ere, frēgī, fractum, tr. *break*
fremō, -ere, -uī, -itum, intr. *roar, shout*
frēnō, -āre, -āvī, -ātum, tr. *control with*
  reins; curb
frequens, -ntis, adj. *crowded, in crowds*
fretum, -ī, n. *strait, sound, channel*
frīgus, -oris, n. *cold*
frondeus, -a, -um, adj. *leafy*
frons, -tis, f. *forehead; front*
frustrā, adv. *in vain*
frustum, -ī, n. *piece, morsel*
(**frux, -ūgis**) f. mostly in plur. **frūgēs,**
  fruit of the earth, corn
fūcus, -ī, m. *drone*
fuga, -ae, f. *flight*
fugiō, -ere, fūgī, fugitum, intr. and tr.
  flee; escape
fugō, -āre, -āvī, -ātum, tr. *put to flight,*
  rout
fulmen, -inis, n. *thunderbolt*
fulvus, -a, -um, adj. *yellow, tawny*
fūnāle, -is, n. *thing made of rope; torch*
fundāmentum, -ī, n. *foundation*
fundō, -ere, fūdī, fūsum, tr. *pour;*
  spread out
fūnus, -eris, n. *funeral, death*
furiae, -ārum, f. plur. *rage, madness*
furō, -ere, -uī, —, intr. *rave, rage*
furor, -ōris, m. *rage, madness*

G

galea, -ae, f. *helmet*

Ganymēdēs, -is, m. son of Tros king of Troy, a beautiful youth carried off to heaven by the eagle to be the cupbearer of Jupiter

gaudeō, -ēre, gāvīsus sum, intr. *rejoice*

gaudium, -iī, n. *joy*

gāza, -ae, f. *treasure*

geminus, -a, -um, adj. *twin*

gemitus, -ūs, m. *groan, roar*

gemma, -ae, f. *jewel*

gemō, -ere, -uī, -itum, intr. and tr. *groan; groan for, lament*

genetrix, -īcis, f. *mother*

genitor, -ōris, m. *father*

gens, -tis, f. *family, race*

genū, -ūs, n. *knee*

genus, -eris, n. *race, kin*

germāna, -ae, f. *sister*; **germānus, -ī,** m. *brother*

gerō, -ere, gessī, gestum, tr. *carry, wear; carry on*

gestō, -āre, -āvī, -ātum, tr. *keep carrying; wear*

gignō, -ere, genuī, genitum, tr. *bring forth, bear*

glaeba, -ae, f. *clod*

glomerō, -āre, -āvī, -ātum, tr. *form into a ball; gather together*

gradior, -ī, gressus sum, dep. intr. *step, advance*

gradus, -ūs, m. *step*

Grāius, -a, -um, adj. *Grecian*; **Grāiī** or **Grāī,** as subst. *Greeks*

grandaevus, -a, -um, adj. *of great age*

grātēs, -ium, f. pl. *thanks*

gravis, -e, adj. *heavy; weighty; heavy with child*

graviter, adv. *heavily*

gremium, -iī, n. *bosom, lap*

gressus, -ūs, m. *step*

gurges, -itis, m. *whirlpool*

gustō, -āre, -āvī, -ātum, tr. *taste*

Gyās,-ntis, m. proper name

H

habēna, -ae, f. *the holding thing, rein*

habeō, -ēre, -uī, -itum, tr. *have; hold, regard*

habilis, -e, adj. *easily handled, handy*

habitus, -ūs, m. *a holding oneself, bearing*

hāc, sc. **viā,** adv. *by this way*

haereō, -ēre, -sī, -sum, intr. *cling, remain steadfast*

hālō, -āre, -āvī, -ātum, intr. *am fragrant*

harēna, -ae, f. *sand, shore*

Harpalycē, -ēs, f. daughter of Thracian king Harpalycus, brought up as a warrior

hasta, -ae, f. *spear*

hastīle, -is, n. *spear-shaft*

haud, adv. *not at all; not*

hauriō, -īre, hausī, haustum, tr. *drink up*

Hector, -oris, m. son of Priam, bravest of the Trojans, slain by Achilles

Hectoreus, -a, -um, adj. *belonging to Hector*

Helena, -ae, f. wife of Menelaus, king of Sparta, carried off to Troy by Paris

herba, -ae, f. *grass*

hērōs, -ōis, m. *hero*

Hesperia, -ae, f. *the land of the West, Italy*

heus, interj. *ho!*

hībernus, -a, -um, adj. *wintry*; **hīberna** (sc. **castra**) as subst. *winter camp*

hīc, adv. *here; hereupon*

hic, haec, hoc, dem. pron. *this*

hiems, hiemis, f. *winter, storm*
hinc, adv. hence, *from hence;*
henceforth; hinc...hinc, *on the one*
side...on the other
homō, -inis, m. *man*
honōs or honor, -ōris, m. *honor; offering*
horreō, -ēre, —, —, intr. *am rough,*
bristle
horridus, -a, -um, adj. *bristling,*
dreadful
hospes, -itis, m. and f. *host, guest*
hospitium, -iī, n. *hospitality, welcome*
hostia, -ae, f. *victim*
hostis, -is, m. *stranger, enemy*
hūc, adv. *hither*
hūmānus, -a, -um, adj. *belonging to*
men, human
humus, -ī, f. *ground;* humī *is the*
locative case used adverbially, on
the ground
Hyades, -um, f. pl. seven stars on the
head of Taurus
Hymenaeus, -ī, m. god of marriage;
marriage

I

ibīdem, adv. *in the same place*
iaceō, -ēre, -uī, -itum, intr. *lie, am*
prostrate
iactō, -āre, -āvī, -ātum, tr. *keep*
throwing, toss, move up and down;
sē iactāre, *boast*
iaculor, -ārī, -ātus sum, dep. tr. *fling,*
hurl
iam, adv. *already*
iamdūdum, adv. (*already*) *some time*
since
iamprīdem, adv. (*already*) *long since*
Īdalia, -ae, f. and Idalium, -iī, n. city
and grove in Cyprus sacred to Venus
ignārus, -a, -um, adj. *not knowing,*
ignorant

ignāvus, -a, -um, adj. *lazy*
ignis, -is, m. *fire*
ignōbilis, -e, adj. *unknown, mean*
ignōtus, -a, -um, adj. *unknown*
Īlia, -ae, f. proper name, see 274 n.
Īliacus, -a, -um, adj. *belonging to Ilium*
Īlias, -adis, f. *woman of Ilium*
Īlionē, -ēs, f. daughter of Priam,
married Polymnestor king of
Thrace
Īlium, -ī, n. the citadel of Troy
Īlius, -a, -um, adj. *belonging to Ilium*
Īlus, -ī, m. old name of Iulus
ille, -a, illud, dem. pron. *that; that*
famous; that man
illīc, adv. *there*
Īllyricus, -a, -um, adj. *belonging to*
Illyria, roughly modern Dalmatia
on the Adriatic sea
imāgō, -inis, f. *phantom; form*
imber, -bris, m. *rain; water*
immānis, -e, adj. *huge, vast, monstrous;*
wicked
immineō, -ēre, —, —, intr. *overhang*
immītis, -e, adj. *not gentle, fierce*
immō, adv. *nay rather*
immōtus, -a, -um, adj. *unmoved*
impār, imparis, adj. *uneven, unequal;*
ill-matched
impellō, -ere, -pulī, -pulsum, tr. *drive*
on; push
imperium, -ī, n. *military command;*
empire
impiger, -gra, -grum, adj. *not indolent,*
vigorous
impius, -a, -um, adj. *unholy*
impleō, -ēre, -plēvī, -plētum, tr. *fill up*
impōnō, -ere, -posuī, -positum, tr.
place on
imprōvīsus, -a, -um, adj. *unforeseen*
īmus, -a, -um, adj. *lowest,* used as
superl. of inferus

implicō, -āre, -plicuī or –plicāvī,
-plicitum or -plicātum, tr. *enfold,*
wrap in

in, prep with acc. *towards; into, against;*
with abl. *in, on*

inānis, -e, adj. *empty*

incautus, -a, -um, adj. *not taking*
precautions, careless

incēdō, -ere, -cessī, -cessum, tr. *move,*
advance

incendium, -iī, n. *burning, fire*

incendō, -ere, -cendī, -censum, tr.
kindle, fire

inceptum, -ī, n. *beginning; design*

incessus, -ūs, m. *gait*

incipiō, -ere, -cēpī, -ceptum, tr. and
intr. *begin*

incognitus, -a, -um, adj. *unknown*

inconcessus, -a, -um, adj. *not granted,*
forbidden

increpitō, -āre, -āvī, -ātum, intr. and
tr. *make a noise at, challenge*

incubō, -āre, -cubuī, -cubitum, intr.
lie upon; brood over

incultus, -a, -um, adj. *uncultivated;*
desert

incūsō, -āre, -āvī, -ātum, tr. *blame*

incutiō, -ere, -cussī, -cussum, tr. *strike*
into, dash into

inde, adv. *thence; after that*

indīcō, -ere, -dīxī, -dictum, tr.
proclaim

indignor, -ārī, -ātus sum, dep. intr.
think unworthy; am wrathful

induō, -ere, -duī, -dūtum, tr. *put on*

inermis, -e, adj. *unarmed*

infandus, -a, -um, adj, *unutterable;*
awful

infēlīx, -īcis, adj. *unhappy*

inferō, -ferre, -tulī, -lātum, tr. *bring*
in; sē inferre, *enter*

infīgō, -ere, -fīxī, -fīxum, tr. *fix on*

ingeminō, -āre, -gemināvī,
-geminātum, tr. and intr. *redouble*

ingemō, -ere, -gemuī, —, intr. *groan*

ingens, -tis, adj. *huge*

inhumātus, -a, -um, adj. *unburied*

inimīcus, -a, -um, adj. *unfriendly*

inīquus, -a, -um, adj. *unfair, hostile*

iniūria, -ae, f. *injustice, wrong*

inlīdō, -ere, -līsī, -līsum, tr. *dash into*
or upon

inquam, v. defect. *say*

inrigō, -āre, -āvī, -ātum, tr. *convey*
water to, irrigate

inscius, -a, -um, adj. *ignorant*

inscrībō, -ere, -scripsī, -scriptum, tr.
write on

insequor, -ī, -secūtus sum, dep. tr.
follow

insidiae, -ārum, f. *ambush, plot*

insīdō, -ere, -sēdī, -sessum, intr. *settle*
on

insignis, -e, adj. *marked out,*
distinguished

inspīrō, -āre, -spīrāvī, -spīrātum, tr.
breathe in

instō, -āre, -stitī, —, intr. *press on*

instruō, -ere, -struxī, -stuctum, tr.
build up, equip

insula, -ae, f. *island*

insuper, adv. *on the top*

intactus, -a, -um, adj. *untouched;*
virgin

intentō, -āre, -āvī, -ātum, tr. *direct*
against, threaten

inter, prep. with acc. *among*

interdum, adv. *sometimes*

intereā, adv. *meanwhile*

interfor, -fārī, fātus sum, dep. intr.
interrupt

interior, -us, comp. adj. *inner*
intimus, -a, -um, superl. adj. *inmost*
intonō, -āre, -tonuī, —, intr. *thunder*
intrā, prep. with acc. *within*
intractābilis, -e, adj. *hard to deal with*
intrōgredior, -ī, -gressus sum, dep.
    intr. *enter in*
intus, adv. *from within, within*
invehō, -ere, -vexī, -vectum, tr. *bear in*
    or *on;* in passive, *ride*
invīsus, -a, -um, adj. *hated*
invius, -a, -um, adj. *pathless*
Iōpās,-ae, m. proper name
ipse, -a, -um, pron. *self; him-, her-,*
    itself
īra, -ae, f. *anger*
Ĭtalia, -ae, f. *Italy*
Ĭtalus, -a, -um, adj. *Italian;* Ĭtalī, *the*
    Italians
iter, itineris, n. *road, journey*
iubeō, -ēre, iussī, iussum, tr. *bid,*
    command
iūdicium, -iī, n. *judgment*
iūgō, -āre, -āvī, -ātum, tr. *yoke, join*
iugum, -ī, n. *that which joins; yoke;*
    mountain-ridge
Iūlius, -iī, m. name of Roman family to
    which C. Julius Caesar belonged
Iūlus, -ī, m. son of Aeneas
iungō, -ere, iunxī, iunctum, tr. *join*
Iūnō, -ōnis, f. queen of heaven, wife of
    Jupiter, the bitter enemy of Troy
Iūnōnius, -a, -um, adj. *belonging to*
    Juno
Iuppiter, Iovis, m. the greatest of gods;
    Jupiter
iūs, -ūris, n. *right; law; ordinance*
iussum, -ī, n. *command*
iussus, -ūs, m. *command*
iustitia, -ae, f. *justice*
iustus, -a, -um, adj. *just*
iuvenis, -is, m. and f. originally adj.

young, then used as subst. *youth,*
    young man
iuventa, -ae, f. *youth*
iuventūs, -ūtis, f. *youth; group of young*
    men
iuvō, -āre, iūvī, iūtum, tr. *assist;* iuvat
    impersonally, *it delights*

K

Karthāgō, -inis, f. *Carthage* in N.
    Africa near the modern Tunis

L

labor, -ōris, m. *toil; trouble; work*
lābor, -ī, lapsus sum, dep. intr. *glide*
labōrō, -āre, -āvī, -ātum, intr. and tr.
    toil; make with toil
lacrima, -ae, f. *tear*
lacrimor, -ārī, -ātus sum, dep. intr.
    weep
laedō, -ere, -sī, -sum, tr. *hurt, injure*
laetitia, -ae, f. *gladness*
laetor, -ārī, -ātus sum, dep. intr. *rejoice*
laetus, -a, -um, adj. *glad; joyous*
laevus, -a, -um, adj. *on the left;* laeva,
    -ae, f. (sc. manus) *left hand*
laquear and laqueāre, -āris, n. *panelled*
    ceiling
largus, -a, -um, adj. *plentiful,*
    abundant
lātē, adv. *far and wide*
lateō, -ere, -uī, —, intr. *lie hid*
latex, -icis, m. *liquid, wine*
Latīnus, -a, -um, adj. *belonging to*
    Latium, Latin
Latium, -iī, n. district of Italy in which
    Rome was situated
Lātōna, -ae, f. mother of Apollo and
    Diana
lātus, -a, -um, adj. *broad*
latus, -eris, n. *side*
laus, -dis, f. *praise, renown*

Lăvīnium, -iī, n. city of Latium
founded by Aeneas
Lāvīnus or **Lāvīnius,** adj. *belonging to
Lavinium*
laxus, -a, -um, adj. *loose*
Lēda, -ae, f. *wife of Tyndareus, mother
of Castor and Pollux, also of Helen*
legō, -ere, lēgī, lectum, tr. *choose*
lēniō, -īre, -īvī or **-iī, -ītum,** tr. *soothe*
levis, -e, adj. *light*
levō, -āre, -āvī, -ātum, tr. *make light,
easy; remove; lift up, raise*
lex, lēgis, f. *law*
lībō, -āre, -āvī, -ātum, tr. *take small
portion of, touch, taste; pour a
libation*
Liburnī, -ōrum, m. a people in Illyria
on the E. coast of the Adriatic
Libya, -ae, f. *Libya, Africa*
Libycus, -a, -um, adj. *Libyan*
licet, -ēre, -uit and **licitum est,**
impersonal intr. *it is lawful*
līmen, -inis, n. *threshold*
linquō, -ere, līquī, tr. *leave*
līquor, -ī, —, dep. intr. *flow, am liquid*
lītus, -oris, n. *shore*
locō, -āre, -āvī, -ātum, tr. *place*
locus, -ī, m. (in pl. also n.) *place,
position*
longē, adv. *afar*
longus, -a, -um, adj. *long*
loquor, -ī, locūtus sum, dep. intr. and
tr. *speak; say*
lōrum, -ī, n. *thong*
luctor, -ārī, -ātus sum, dep. intr.
struggle
lūcus, -ī, m. *grove*
lūdō, -ere, -sī, -sum, tr. and intr. *play;
treat playfully, mock*
lūmen, -inis, n. *light*
lūna, -ae, f. *moon*

lūnātus, -a, -um, adj. *moon-shaped;
crescent- shaped*
luō, -ere, -ī, —, tr. *get rid of; set free;
atone for*
lupa, -ae, f. *she-wolf*
lustrō, -āre, -āvī, -ātum, tr. *go around;
transverse; survey*
lustrum, -ī, n. *expiatory offering;
purification; a solemn purification
held at Rome by the Censors every
five years; a space of five years*
lux, -ūcis, f. *light*
luxus, -ūs, m. *luxury*
Lyaeus, -ī, m. god who releases from
care; *Bacchus*
lychnus, -ī, m. *lamp*
Lycius, -a, -um, adj. *belonging to Lycia*
in Asia Minor
Lycus, -ī, m. proper name
lympha, -ae, f. *water*
lynx, -cis, f. *lynx*

M

maculōsus, -a, -um, adj. *spotted*
maereō, -ēre, —, —, intr. *mourn*
maestus, -a, -um, adj. *sad*
māgālia, -ium, n. plur. *huts*
magis, comp. adv. *more*
magister, -trī, m. *master;* of a ship *pilot*
magistrātus, -ūs, m. *magistrate*
magnanimus, -a, -um, adj. *great-
souled*
magnus, -a, -um, adj. *great; large;
important, mighty,* comp. **māior;**
superl. **maximus**
malus, -a, -um, adj. *bad, evil;* comp.
pēior; superl. **pessimus**
mamma, -ae, f. *breast*
maneō, -ēre, mansī, mansum, intr.
remain
mantēle, -is, n. *napkin*
mare, -is, n. *sea*

Mars, -tis, m. god of War

māter, -tris, f. *mother*

mātūrō, -āre, -āvī, -ātum, tr. *perform
in good time; hasten*

Māvortius, -a, -um, adj. *belonging to
Mavors or Mars*

maximus, see magnus

meditor, -ārī, -ātus sum, dep. intr.
ponder over; plan

medius, -a, -um, adj. *middle, in the
middle*

membrum, -ī, n. *limb*

meminī, -isse, v. defect. tr. *remember*

Memnōn, -onis, m. son of Tithonus
and Aurora, king of the Ethiopians

memor, -oris, adj. *mindful*

memorō, -āre, -āvī, -ātum, tr. *relate*

mens, -tis, f. *mind*

mensa, -ae, f. *table*

mensis, -is, m. *month*

mercor, -ārī, -ātus sum, dep. tr. *buy*

meritum, -ī, n. *merit, desert*

merus, -a, -um, adj. *alone, pure;*
merum, -ī, n. *undiluted wine*

mēta, -ae, f. cone-shaped *column*
placed at end of the course in the
circus; *goal, limit*

metuō, -ere, metuī, metūtum, tr. *fear*

metus, -ūs, m. *fear*

meus, -a, -um, poss. adj. *my*

micō, -āre, micuī, —, intr. *move
quickly to and fro; glitter*

mille, num. adj. indecl. *a thousand;*
as subst. n. with plur. mīlia
thousands

minister, -trī, m. *attendant*

ministrō, -āre, -āvī, -ātum, tr. *serve,
supply*

minor, -ārī, -ātus sum, dep. intr. *jut
forth; threaten*

minor, -us, adj. comp. of parvus, *less;*
minōrēs as subst. *those who are
younger*

minus, comp. adv. *less*

mīrābilis, -e, adj. *wonderful*

mīror, -ārī, -ātus sum, dep. intr. and
tr. *wonder; wonder at*

mīrus, -a, -um, adj. *wonderful*

misceō, -ēre, miscuī, mistum and
mixtum, tr. *mingle; confound*

miser, -era, -erum, adj. superl.
miserrimus, *wretched*

miserābilis, -e, adj. *pitiable, wretched*

miseror, -ārī, -ātus sum, dep. tr. *pity*

mītescō, -ere, —, —, intr. *grow mild* or
gentle

mittō, -ere, mīsī, missum, tr. *send*

modō, adv. *only*

modus, -ī, m. *manner*

moenia, -ium, n. plur. *walls, a fortress*

mōlēs, -is, f. *mass; difficulty*

mōlior, -īrī, molītus sum, dep. tr.
perform with toil or *effort; build,
rear; attempt*

molliō, -īre, mollīvī or molliī,
mollītum, tr. *soften*

mollis, -e, adj. *soft*

monīle, -is, n. *neckless*

mons, montis, m. *mountain*

monstrō, -āre, -āvī, -ātum, tr. *show*

mora, -ae, f. *delay*

moror, -ārī, morātus sum, dep. tr.
delay

mors, mortis, f. *death*

morsus, -ūs, m. *bite*

mortālis, -e, adj. *mortal, human*

mōs, mōris, m. *custom*

moveō, -ēre, mōvī, mōtum, tr. *move*

mulceō, -ēre, mulsī, mulsum, tr.
soothe

multus, -a, -um, adj. *much, many a;* in
plur. *many*

mūniō, -īre, mūnīvī or mūniī,
mūnītum, tr. *fortify*

mūnus, -eris, n. *gift*

murmur, -uris, n. *murmur*
mūrus, -ī, n. *wall*
Mūsa, -ae, f. one of the nine muses, *Muse*
mūtō, -āre, -āvī, -ātum, tr. *change; exchange*
Mycēnae, -ārum, f. the royal city of Agamemnon in Argolis

N

nam, namque, conj. *for*
nascor, -ī, nātus sum, dep. intr. *am born*
nāta, -ae, f. *daughter*; **nātus, -ī,** m. *son*; **nātī,** *children*
nāvigō, -āre, -āvī, -ātum, intr. and tr. *sail; sail over*
nāvis, -is, f. *ship*
nē, conj. *lest*
-ne, interrogative particle appended to other words
nebula, -ae, f. *mist*
nec, see **neque**
necdum, conj. *nor yet*
nectar, -aris, n. the drink of the gods, *nectar*
nectō, -ere, nexuī, nexum, tr. *weave*
nefandus, -a, -um, adj. *unutterable; impious*
nemus, -oris, n. *grove*
Neptūnus, -ī, m. the god of the sea
neque or **nec,** conj. *neither, nor*
nequeō, -īre, nequīvī or **nequiī, nequitum,** tr. *am unable*
nesciō, -īre, nescīvī or **nesciī, nescītum,** tr. *am ignorant of*
nescius, -a, -um, adj. *ignorant*
neu = nēve, conj. *and that...not, and lest, or lest*
nī, conj. = **nisi,** *if not, unless*
niger, -gra, -grum, adj. *black*
nihil or **nīl, nihilī,** n. *nothing*

nimbōsus, -a, -um, adj. *stormy*
nimbus, -ī, m. *rain-cloud*
niteō, -ēre, nituī, —, intr. *am bright*
niveus, -a, -um, adj. *snowy*
nō, nāre, nāvī, —, intr. *swim*
nōdus, -ī, m. *knot*
nōmen, -inis, n. *name*
nōn, adv. *not*
noster, -tra, -trum, pronominal adj. *our*
nōtus, -a, -um, adj. *well-known*
Notus, -ī, m. the south wind
novem, cardinal num. adj. *nine*
novitās,-ātis, f. *newness*
novus, -a, -um, adj. *new*
nox, noctis, f. *night*
noxa, -ae, f. *guilt*
nūbēs, -is, f. *cloud*
nūdō, -āre, -āvī, -ātum, tr. *lay bare*
nūdus, -a, -um, adj. *bare*
nullus, -a, -um, adj. *not any, no*
nūmen, -inis, n. *nod; divine will; deity*
numerus, -ī, m. *number*
nunc, adv. *now*
nuntiō, -āre, -āvī, -ātum, tr. *announce*
nūtrīmentum, -ī, n. *nourishment, food*
nūtrix, -īcis, f. *nurse*
Nympha, -ae, f. *Nymph,* half divine being dwelling in seas, rivers, or forests

O

ō, interj. *O!*
ob, prep. with acc. *on account of*
obiectus, -ūs, m. *a throwing across; barrier*
oblātus, see **offerō**
obruō, -ere, -ruī, -rutum, tr. *overwhelm*
obscūrus, -a, -um, adj. *shady, obscure*
obstipescō, -ere, -stupuī, —, intr. *become amazed, confounded*

obstō, -āre, -stitī, -stātum, intr. with
dat. *stand in the way, hinder*
obtundō, -ere, -tudī, -tūsum or
tunsum, tr. *make blunt* or *dull*
obtūtus, -ūs, m. *gaze*
obvius, -a, -um, adj. *in the way,
opposite*
occāsus, -ūs, m. *fall, destruction*
occubō, -āre, —, —, intr. *lie* (in the
grave)
occulō, -ere, occuluī, occultum, tr.
hide
occumbō, -ere, -cubuī, -cubitum, intr.
fall (esp. in death)
occurrō, -ere, occurrī, occursum, intr.
run against, thwart
Ōceanus, -ī, m. *ocean*
oculus, -ī, m. *eye*
odium, -iī, n. *hate*
odor, -ōris, m. *scent*
Oenōtrus, -a, -um, adj. *belonging to
Oenotria*, a district in the extreme
S.E. of Italy, from which all Italy
was sometimes called Oenotria
offerō, -ferre, obtulī, oblātum, tr. *put
before, present*
officium, -iī, n. *duty; act of courtesy*
Oīleus, -eī, n. father of the lesser Ajax
ōlim, adv. *at that time; some day;
hereafter; formally*
Olympus, -ī, m. a lofty mountain in
Thessaly, the seat of the gods;
heaven
ōmen, -inis, n. *prognostic, omen*
omnipotens, -tis, adj. *almighty*
omnis, -e, adj. *all*
onerō, -āre, -āvī, -ātum, tr. *laden, load*
onus, -eris, n. *burden*
onustus, -a, -um, adj. *laden*
opīmus, -a, -um, adj. *rich, fertile*
opperior, -īrī, opperitus and oppertus
sum, dep. tr. *await*

oppetō, -ere, -petīvī, or –petiī,
-petītum, tr. *go to seek;* then with
mortem understood, *die*
opprimō, -ere, -pressī, -pressum, tr.
crush, overwhelm
[ops], opis, f. *aid, power;* in pl. opēs,
opum, *wealth*
optō, -āre, -āvī, -ātum, tr. *desire*
opulentus, -a, -um, adj. *wealthy*
opus, -eris, n. *work*
ōra, -ae, f. *shore, coast*
orbis, -is, m. *circle; the* (round) *world*
ordior, -īrī, ortus sum, dep. tr. and
intr. *begin*
ordō, -inis, m. *order, row*
Oreās, -adis, f. mountain-nymph
Oriens, -tis, m. *the rising sun; the East*
orīgō, -inis, f. *source, beginning*
Orīon, -ŏnis or -ōnis, m. a mighty
hunter changed into a constellation
orior, -īrī, ortus sum, dep. intr. *arise*
ornātus, -ūs, m. *decoration*
Orontēs, -is, m. proper name
ōs, ōris, n. *mouth; face*
os, ossis, n. *bone*
osculum, -ī, n. *little mouth; lips; kiss*
ostendō, -ere, ostendī, ostensum and
ostentum, tr. *show*
ostium, -iī, n. *mouth* (of river)
ostrum, -iī, n. *purple*

P

pābulum, -ī, n. *food, pasture*
paenitet, -uit, v. impers. with acc. *it
repents*
palla, -ae, f. *loose shawl, robe*
Pallas, -adis, f. Greek name for
Minerva, the goddess of war and
wisdom
pallidus, -a, -um, adj. *pale*
palma, -ae, f. *palm* (of the hand)

pandō, -ere, pandī, pansum and
passum, tr. *open;* **passus,** of the
hair, *flung loose, disheveled*
Paphos, -ī, f. *city of Cyprus sacred to
Venus*
pār, paris, adj. *equal*
Parca, -ae, f. *one of the three Fates;
their names were Clotho, Lachesis,
and Atropos*
parcō, -ere, pepercī, parcitum or
parsum, intr. with dat. *spare; cease*
parens, -tis, m. and f. *parent*
pāreō, -ēre, pāruī, pāritum, intr. with
dat. *obey*
pariō, -ere, peperī, partum, tr.
produce, bring forth
Paris, -idis, m. *the beautiful son of
Priam who in the famous contest
between Juno, Minerva, and Venus
adjudged the golden apple to Venus,
carried Helen from Menelaus, and
so caused the Trojan War.*
pariter, adv. *equally*
Parius, -a, -um, adj. *belonging to Paros,
one of the Cyclades in the Aegaean
sea, famous for its white marble*
parō, -āre, -āvī, -ātum, tr. *make ready*
pars, partis, f. *part;* often= *some*
partior, -īrī, partītus sum, dep. tr.
divide
partus, -ūs, m. *bringing forth, birth*
pascō, -ere, pāvī, pastum, tr. *feed*
passus, see **pandō** or **patior**
Patavium, -iī, n. *a city in Cisalpine
Gaul, now Padua*
pateō, -ēre, patuī, —, intr. *am open*
pater, patris, m. *father*
patera, -ae, f. *open goblet; cup*
patior, patī, passus sum, dep. tr. *suffer,
endure*
patria, -ae, f. *fatherland*
patrius, -a, -um, adj. *belonging to a
father*

paucus, -a, -um, adj. *small;* in plur. *few*
paulātim, adv. *little by little*
pax, pācis, f. *peace*
pectus, -oris, n. *breast*
pecus, -oris, n. *flock, throng*
pecus, -udis, f. *beast*
pelagus, -ī, n. *sea*
Pelasgī, -ōrum, m. *the oldest
inhabitants of Greece;* **Pelasgus,
-a, -um,** as adj. *Greek*
pellō, -ere, pepulī, pulsum, tr. *drive*
pelta, -ae, f. *small crescent-shaped
shield*
Penātēs, -ium, m. *gods of the household*
pendeō, -ēre, pependī, —, intr. *hang*
penetrō, -āre, -āvī, -ātum, tr. *go into
the inmost part of, enter, penetrate*
penitus, adv. *from within, deeply*
Penthesilēa, -ae, f. *queen of the
Amazons*
penus, -ūs and **–ī,** m. and f. *store, food,
provisions*
peplus, -ī, m. *robe* worn by Greek
women, esp. one offered to Pallas
per, prep. with acc. *through, among,
along*
peragrō, -āre, -āvī, -ātum, tr. *traverse,
roam over*
percutiō, -ere, -cussī, -cussum, tr.
strike
perferō, -ferre, -tulī, -lātum, tr. *carry
through*
perflō, -āre, -āvī, -ātum, tr. *blow
through*
Pergama, -ōrum, n. pl. *the citadel of
Troy*
pergō, -ere, perrexī, perrectum, intr.
go forward, proceed
perīculum, or **periclum, -ī,** n. *danger*
perlābor, -lābī, -lapsus sum, dep. tr.
glide over
permisceō, -ēre, -miscuī, -mixtum,
tr. *mingle*

permittō, -ere, -mīsī, -missum, tr.
allow

persolvō, -ere, -solvī, -solūtum, tr.
loosen; pay in full

personō, -āre, -sonuī, -sonitum, intr.
and tr. *sound* (through a place); *fill
with sound*

pertemptō, -āre, -āvī, -ātum, tr. *try;
search out*

pēs, pedis, m. *foot*

pestis, -is, f. *plague*

petō, -ere, petīvī or petiī, petītum, tr.
seek

pharĕtra, -ae, f. *quiver*

Phoebus, -ī, m. poetic name of Apollo,
lit. 'the radiant one'

Phoenix, -īcis, m. *Phoenician
inhabitant of the district of Syria
and Tyre*

Phoenissa, -ae, f. adj. or subst.
Phoenician (woman), esp. *Dido*

Phrygius, -a, -um, belonging to
Phrygia in the N.W. of Asia Minor
near Troy, Trojan

Phryx, Phrygis, m. and f. *a Phrygian*

Phthīa, -ae, f. city of Thessaly,
birthplace of Achilles

pictūra, -ae, f. *painting*

pietās, -ātis, f. *dutiful behavior, holiness*

pingō, -ere, pinxī, pictum, tr. *paint;
embroider*

pinguis, -e, adj. *fat*

pius, -a, -um, adj. *dutiful, pious,
righteous*

placeō, -ēre, placuī, placitum, intr.
please; placet imper. with perf.
placitum est, *it is pleasing, resolved*

placidus, -a, -um, adj. *calm*

plācō, -āre, -āvī, -ātum, tr. *appease*

plaga, -ae, f. *region*

plausus, -ūs, m. *clapping*

plēnus, -a, -um, adj. *full*

plūs, gen. plūris, in plural plūrēs,
plūra, comp. adj. *more*

plūrimus, -a, -um, superl. adj. *very
much, great;* in plur. *very many*

pluvius, -a, -um, adj. *rainy*

pōculum, -ī, n. *goblet*

poena, -ae, f. *punishment*

Poenī, -ōrum, m. *Phoenicians or
Carthaginians*

polliceor, -ērī, pollicitus sum, dep. tr.
promise

polus, -ī, m. *the pole, heaven*

pondus, -eris, n. *weight*

pōnō, -ere, posuī, positum, tr. *put,
place; put aside*

pontus, -ī, m. *sea*

populō, -āre, -āvī, -ātum, tr. *lay waste*

populus, -ī, m. *people, nation*

porta, -ae, f. *gate*

portō, -āre, -āvī, -ātum, tr. *carry*

portus, -ūs, m. *harbor*

poscō, -ere, poposcī, —, tr. *demand;
beg, ask for urgently*

possum, posse, potuī, —, intr. irreg.
am able

post, prep. with acc. *after,* adv.
afterwards

posthabeō, -ēre, -habuī, -habitum, tr.
hold as inferior, despise

postquam, conj. *after that*

potens, -tis, adj. *powerful;* with gen.
powerful over

potentia, -ae, f. *power*

potior, -īrī, potītus sum, dep. with abl.
gain, possess; enjoy

praecipuē, adv. *chiefly*

praeda, -ae, f. *booty*

praemittō, -ere, -mīsī, -missum, tr.
send forward

praemium, -iī, n. *reward*

praeruptus, -a, -um, adj. *broken off in
front, rugged*

praesens, -tis, adj. *present, immediate*
praesēpe, -is, n. *fenced in place;*
    enclosure, hive
praestō, -are, -stitī, -stitum, intr. *stand*
    before, excel; **praestat,** impers. *it is*
    better; **praestans,** as adj. *excelling*
praetereā, adv. *besides; after this*
praevertō, -ere, -vertī, -versum,
    tr. *outstrip, anticipate, seize*
    beforehand
premō, -ere, pressī, pressum, tr. *press;*
    keep down or *in; overwhelm*
Priamus, -ī, m. *king of Troy during the*
    siege
prīdem, adv. *for a long time*
prīmum, adv. *first, firstly*
prīmus, -a, -um, superl. adj. *first*
princeps, -cipis, m. and f. *chief, leader*
prior, -us, comp. adj. *former, before*
    another
priusquam, conj. *before that*
prō, prep. with abl. *for; on behalf of;*
    instead of
procax, -ācis, adj. *wanton*
procella, -ae, f. *tempest*
procer, -eris, m. *nobleman*
procul, adv. *at a distance*
prōdō, -ere, -didī, -ditum, tr. *put*
    forward; betray
proficiscor, -ī, profectus sum, dep.
    intr. *set forth*
profor, -fārī, -fātus sum, dep. tr. and
    intr. *speak out*
profugus, -a, -um, adj. *exiled*
profundus, -a, -um, adj. *deep, high*
prōgeniēs, -ēī, f. *offspring*
prohibeō, -ēre, -hibuī, -hibitum, tr.
    keep off
prōlēs, -is, f. *offspring*
prōluō, -ere, -luī, -lūtum, tr. *rinse out,*
    wash out

prōmittō, -ere, -mīsī, -missum, tr.
    hold out, promise
prōnus, -a, -um, adj. *headlong*
properō, -āre, -āvī, -ātum, intr. *hasten*
propior, -ius, comp. adj. *nearer,*
    propius, comp. adv. *nearer*
proprius, -a, -um, adj. *one's own*
prōra, -ae, f. *prow*
prōrumpō, -ere, -rūpī, -ruptum, tr.
    cause to burst forth
prospectus, -ūs, m. *outlook*
prospiciō, -ere, -spexī, -spectum, tr.
    see in front, see
proximus, -a, -um, superl. adj. *nearest*
pūbēs, -is, f. *youth, group of youths*
puer, -erī, m. *boy*
pugna, -ae, f. *fight*
pulcher, -chra, -chrum, adj. *fair*
pulvis, -eris, m. *dust*
Pūnicus, -a, -um, adj. *Carthaginian*
puppis, -is, f. *stern, poop*
purgō, -āre, -āvī, -ātum, tr. *clear*
purpureus, -a, -um, adj. *purple; with*
    the sheen of purple, dazzling
Pygmaliōn, -ōnis, m. *brother of Dido*

Q

quā, adv. *by what way; where*
quaerō, -ere, quaesīvī, quaesītum, tr.
    seek; inquire
quālis, -e, adj. *of what sort*
quam, conj. *than;* adv. *how*
quandō, adv. *when;* conj. *since*
quantus, -a, -um, adj. *how great; as*
    great as
quārē, adv. *wherefore*
quassō, -āre, -āvī, -ātum, tr. *keep*
    shaking, shake strongly
quater, num. adv. *four times*
queror, -ī, questus sum, dep. *complain*
quīcumque, quaecumque, quodcumque,
    relative pronoun, *whoever*

quid, interrog. adv. *why?*
quiēs, -ētis, f. *rest, repose*
quiescō, -ere, quiēvī, quiētum, intr. *become at rest, repose*
quiētus, -a, -um, adj. *peaceful, calm*
quīn, adv. *nay more*
quinquāgintā, num. adj. *fifty*
quippe, conj. *for surely, for indeed*
Quirīnus, -ī, m. name of Romulus when deified
quis, quae, quid, interrog. pron. *who? what?*
quisquam, quaequam, quicquam, indef. pron. *any one*
quisquis, quicquid, indef. pron. *whoever, whatever*
quō, adv. *whither*
quōcircā, adv. *wherefore*
quondam, adv. *at a certain time, once*
quoque, conj. *also*

R

rabiēs, no gen. or dat., **rabiem, rabiē,** *rage*
rapidus, -a, -um, adj. *hurrying, rapid*
rapiō, -ere, rapuī, raptum, tr. *seize, snatch*
raptō, -āre, -āvī, -ātum, tr. *snatch violently, drag*
rārus, -a, -um, adj. *not frequent, scattered*
ratis, -is, f. *ship*
recens, -tis, adj. *fresh*
recipiō, -ere, -cēpī, -ceptum, tr. *take back, recover*
reclūdō, -ere, -clūsī, -clūsum, tr. *open*
recondō, -ere, -condidī, -conditum, tr. *hide (far back)*
rectus, -a, -um, adj. *straight, right*
recursō, -āre, -āvī, -ātum, intr. *run back, return*

reddō, -ere, reddidī, redditum, tr. *give back, restore*
redoleō, -ēre, -doluī, —, intr. *am fragrant*
redūcō, -ere, -duxī, -ductum, tr. *lead back, draw back*
redux, -ucis, adj. *returned*
referō, -ferre, rettulī, relātum, tr. *carry* or *take back; relate*
refulgeō, -ēre, -fulsī, —, intr. *shine out*
refundō, -ere, -fūdī, -fūsum, tr. *pour back*
rēgālis, -e, adj. *royal*
rēgīna, -ae, f. *queen*
regiō, -ōnis, f. *district*
rēgius, -a, -um, adj. *royal*
regnō, -āre, -āvī, -ātum, intr. *hold sway, rule*
regnum, -ī, n. *kingdom*
regō, -ere, rexī, rectum, tr. *rule*
relātus, see **referō**
rēliquiae, -ārum, f. *that which is left, remnant*
rēmigium –iī, n. *oarage*
remordeō, -ēre, —, -morsum, tr. *bite far back, gnaw deeply*
removeō, -ēre, -mōvī, -mōtum, tr. *take away*
rēmus, -ī, m. *oar*
Remus, -ī, m. brother of Romulus
rependō, -ere, -pendī, -pensum, tr. *weigh back* or *against something else*
repente, adv. *suddenly*
repetō, -ere, -petīvī, or **–petiī, -petītum,** tr. *reseek, seek back*
repōnō, -ere, -posuī, -positum, tr. *place back, place far back, store up*
requīrō, -ere, -quīsīvī, -quīsītum, tr. *seek again; regret*
rēs, reī, f. *thing; affair*
reses, -idis, adj. *sitting still, sluggish*

resīdō, -ere, -sēdī, -sessum, intr. *sit down*

resistō, -ere, restitī, —, intr. *stand back; stand against, stand out* from anything

respectō, -āre, -āvī, -ātum, tr. *look back at, regard*

respondeō, -ēre, -spondī, -sponsum, tr. and intr. *answer; answer to*

restō, -āre, -stitī, —, intr. *remain, am left*

resupīnus, -a, -um, adj. *bent backwards, face upwards*

resurgō, -ere, -surrexī, -surrectum, intr. *rise again*

retegō, -ere, -texī, -tectum, tr. *uncover, reveal*

revīsō, -ere, —, —, tr. *revisit*

revocō, -āre, -āvī, -ātum, tr. *recall*

rex, rēgis, m. *king*

Rhēsus, -ī, m. *a Thracian prince*

rigeō, -ēre, riguī, —, intr. *am stiff*

rīma, -ae, f. *crack*

rīpa, -ae, f. *bank*

rōbur, -oris, n. *oak-wood, oak; strength*

rogitō, -āre, -āvī, -ātum, tr. *keep asking*

Rōma, -ae, f. *Rome*

Rōmānus, -a, -um, adj. *Roman;* Rōmānī, -ōrum, m. *Romans*

Rōmulus, -ī, m. *founder of Rome*

roseus, -a, -um, adj. *rosy*

rota, -ae, f. *wheel*

rudens, -tis, m. *cable*

ruīna, -ae, f. *downfall, ruin*

ruō, -ere, ruī, rutum, intr. and tr. *rush; cause to rush, drive*

rūpēs, -is, f. *rock*

rūs, rūris, n. *country*

Rutulī, -ōrum, m. pl. *a people of Latium*

S

Sabaeus, -a, -um, adj. *belonging to Saba,* the chief town in Arabia Felix

sacerdōs, -ōtis, m. and f. *priest, priestess*

sācrō, -āre, -āvī, -ātum, tr. *make holy, hallow*

saeculum, -ī, n. *generation, age*

saepe, adv. *often*

saepiō, -īre, saepsī, saeptum, tr. *hedge in, enclose, surround*

saeviō, -īre, saeviī, saevītum, intr. *am fierce, wrathful*

saevus, -a, -um, adj. *fierce, cruel*

sagitta, -ae, f. *arrow*

sal, salis, m. *salt; sea*

saltem, adv. *at least*

salum, -ī, n. *brine; sea*

salūs, -ūtis, f. *safety*

Samos, -ī, f. *Samos,* large island on the W. of Asia Minor sacred to Juno

sanctus, -a, -um, adj. *holy, reverend*

sanguis, -inis, m. *blood*

Sarpēdōn, -onis, m. *king of Lycia, slain at Troy*

sator, -ōris, m. *sower, father*

Sāturnius, -a, -um, adj. *belonging to Saturn,* an Italian god of 'sowing' identified with Kronos; father of Jupiter and Juno

saxum, -ī, n. *rock, stone*

scaena, -ae, f. *background, stage*

scelus, -eris, n. *guilt*

sceptrum, -ī, n. *staff, scepter*

scīlicet, adv. *one may know, doubtless*

scindō, -ere, scidī, scissum, tr. *cleave, tear*

scintilla, -ae, f. *spark*

sciō, -īre, scīvī, scītum, tr. *know*

scopulus, -ī, m. *rock, crag*

scūtum, -ī, n. *shield*
Scyllaeus, -a, -um, adj. *belonging to Scylla*, a monster who devoured ships opposite Charybdis in the straits between Italy and Sicily
sēcessus, -ūs, m. *retreat, recess*
sēclūdō, -ere, sēclūsī, sēclūsum, tr. *shut off, banish*
secō, -āre, secuī, sectum, tr. *cut*
secundus, -a, -um, adj. *following; favorable; obedient*
sēcūrus, -a, -um, adj. *careless*
sed, conj. *but*
sedeō, -ēre, sēdī, sessum, intr. *sit*
sēdēs, -is, f. *seat; abode*
sedīle, -is, n. *seat*
sēditiō, -ōnis, f. *going apart, discord*
sēmita, -ae, f. *by-path*
semper, adv. *always*
senātus, -ūs, m. *assembly of elders, senate*
sēnī, -ae, -a, distribut. num. adj. *six each*
sententia, -ae, f. *opinion, judgment*
sentiō, -īre, sensī, sensum, tr. *feel, perceive*
septem, num. adj. *seven*
septimus, -a, -um, ordinal adj. *seventh*
sequor, -ī, secūtus sum, dep. intr. and tr. *follow*
serēnō, -āre, -āvī, -ātum, tr. *make cloudless, calm*
Serestus, -ī, m. *proper name*
Sergestus, -ī, m. *proper name*
seriēs, no gen. or dat., -em, -ē, f. *row, succession*
sermō, -ōnis, m. *conversation*
sertum, -ī, n. *wreath*
servitium, -iī, n. *slavery*
servō, -āre, -āvī, -ātum, tr. *keep, preserve*
seu, see **sī**

sī, conj. *if;* sīve (seu)...sīve (seu) *whether...or*
sīc, adv. *in this way, so*
Sīcania, -ae, f. *old name for* Sicily
Siculus, -a, -um, adj. *belonging to* Sicily
Sīdōn, -ōnis, f. *city of Phoenicia which founded* Tyre
Sīdŏnius, -a, -um, adj. *belonging to* Sidon
sīdus, -eris, n. *star, constellation*
signum, -ī, n. *sign, figure*
silentium, -iī, n. *silence*
sileō, -ēre, siluī, —, intr. *am silent*
silex, -icis, m. *flint*
silva, -ae, f. *wood*
similis, -e, adj. *like;* superl. **simillimus**
Simoīs, -entis, m. *river near Troy*
simul, adv. *at the same time*
simulō, -āre, -āvī, -ātum, tr. *imitate*
sīn, conj. *but if*
sine, prep. with abl. *without*
singulī, -ae, -a, distribut. adj. *one each, one at a time*
sinō, -ere, sīvī, situm, tr. *let be; permit, allow*
sinus, -ūs, m. *bend; bay; fold*
sīve, see **sī**
sociō, -āre, -āvī, -ātum, tr. *make a companion* or *partner*
socius, -iī, m. *companion*
sōl, sōlis, m. *the sun*
soleō, -ēre, solitus sum, intr. *am accustomed*
solium, -iī, n. *throne*
sōlor, -ārī, sōlātus sum, dep. tr. *console*
solum, -ī, n. *ground*
sōlus, -a, -um, adj. *alone*
solvō, -ere, solvī, solūtum, tr. *unloose; relax; dispel*
somnus, -ī, m. *sleep*
sonō, -āre, sonuī, sonitum, intr. *sound, resound*

sonōrus, -a, -um, adj. *loud, noisy*

sōpiō, -īre, sopīvī or **sopiī, sopītum,** tr. *lull to sleep*

soror, -ōris, f. *sister*

sors, -tis, f. *lot; fate*

spargō, -ere, sparsī, sparsum, tr. *scatter*

Spartānus, -a, -um, adj. *belonging to Sparta, the chief city of Laconia*

speculor, -ārī, speculātus sum, dep. intr. *look out*

spēlunca, -ae, f. *cavern*

spernō, -ere, sprēvī, sprētum, tr. *despise*

spērō, -āre, -āvī, -ātum, tr. *hope, hope for*

spēs, -eī, f. *hope; expectation*

spīrō, -āre, -āvī, -ātum, intr. *breathe*

splendidus, -a, -um, adj. *bright, brilliant*

spolium, -iī, n. *spoil*

sponda, -ae, f. *couch*

spūma, -ae, f. *foam*

spūmō, -āre, -āvī, -ātum, intr. *foam*

stabilis, -e, adj. *steadfast, firm*

stāgnum, -ī, n. *standing-water, pool*

statuō, -ere, statuī, statūtum, tr. *set up*

sternō, -ere, strāvī, strātum, tr. *stretch out, lay low*

stīpō, -āre, -āvī, -ātum, tr. *press close, throng*

stirps, -pis, f. *stock*

stō, stāre, stetī, statum, intr. *stand*

strātus, -a, -um, adj. *laid down, paved*

strepitus, -ūs, m. *din*

strīdō, -ere (also **strīdeō, -ēre**), **strīdī, —,** intr. *creak, grate, rustle*

strīdor, -ōris, m. *creaking, rattling*

stringō, -ere, strinxī, strictum, tr. *strip; cut off*

struō, -ere, struxī, structum, tr. *build*

studium, -iī, n. *zeal*

stupeō, -ēre, stupuī, —, intr. *am amazed*

suādeō, -ēre, suāsī, suāsum, tr. *advise*

sub, prep. with acc. *to, beneath, towards;* with abl. *under*

subdūcō, -ere, -duxī, -ductum, tr. *draw up* (on shore, of vessels)

subeō, -īre, -īvī or **-iī, -itum,** intr. and tr. *go under, come up, approach, enter*

subigō, -ere, -ēgī, -actum, tr. *drive under; subdue*

subitō, adv. *suddenly*

subitus, -a, -um, adj. *sudden*

sublīmis, -a, adj. *on high*

subnectō, -ere, —, -nexum, tr. *weave or bind beneath*

subnītor, -ī, -nīsus or **-nixus sum,** dep. intr. with abl. *rest upon*

subrīdeō, -ēre, -rīsī, -rīsum, intr. *laugh slightly, smile*

subvolvō, -ere, —, —, tr. *roll up* (from below)

succēdō, -ere, -cessī, -cessum, intr. *go beneath*

succinctus, -a, -um, adj. *girt up*

succurrō, -ere, -currī, -cursum, intr. *run up to, aid*

suffundō, -ere, -fūdī, -fūsum, tr. *pour up from below, suffuse*

sulcus, -ī, m. *furrow*

summergō, -ere, -mersī, -mersum, tr. *sink*

summus, -a, -um, superl. adj. *highest,* see **superus**

super, prep. with acc. *to upon, to;* with abl. *above;* as adv. *in addition*

superbia, -ae, f. *pride*

superbus, -a, -um, adj. *proud*

superēmineō, -ēre, -uī, —, tr. *stand out above*

superō, -āre, -āvī, -ātum, tr. *overcome*

supersum, -esse, -fuī, intr. *am over, survive*

superus, -a, -um, adj. *that is above;* superl. **sūprēmus,** *last,* and **summus,** *highest;* **superī, -ōrum,** m. *those above; the gods*

supplex, -icis, adj. *bending the knee, suppliant*

suppliciter, adv. *in suppliant fashion*

sūra, -ae, f. *calf of the leg*

surgō, -ere, surrexī, surrectum, intr. *rise*

sūs, suis, m. and f. *pig*

suscipiō, -ere, -cēpī, -ceptum, tr. *catch up, take up*

suspendō, -ere, -pendī, -pensum, tr. *hang*

suspiciō, -ere, -spexī, -spectum, tr. *look up at*

suspīrō, -āre, -āvī, -ātum, intr. *sigh*

suus, -a, -um, possess. adj. *his-, her-, its-, their own*

Sychaeus, -ī, m. *husband of Dido*

syrtis, -is, f. *sandbank*

T

tābeō, -ēre, —, —, intr. *melt away, drip*

tabula, -ae, f. *plank*

tacitus, -a, -um, adj. *silent*

tālis, -e, adj. *of such kind, such*

tam, adv. *so*

tamen, adv. *notwithstanding*

tandem, adv. *at length*

tangō, -ere, tetigī, tactum, tr. *touch*

tantus, -a, -um, adj. *so great;* **tantum,** as adv. *only*

tardus, -a, -um, adj. *slow*

taurīnus, -a, -um, adj. *belonging to a bull*

taurus, -ī, m. *bull*

tectum, -ī, n. *roof; house*

tegmen, -inis, n. *covering; skin*

tellūs, -ūris, f. *the earth; country*

tēlum, -ī, n. *weapon*

temnō, -ere, —, —, tr. *despise*

temperō, -āre, -āvī, -ātum, tr. and intr. *check; refrain*

tempestās, -ātis, f. *storm*

templum, -ī, n. *temple*

temptō, -āre, -āvī, -ātum, tr. *try, attempt*

tempus, -oris, n. *time*

tendō, -ere, tetendī, tensum, tr. *stretch; strive; direct one's course*

teneō, -ēre, tenuī, tentum, tr. *hold, occupy*

tentōrium, -iī, n. *tent*

tenus, prep. with abl. put after its case, *as far as*

ter, num. adv. *thrice*

tergum, -ī, n. *back;* also **tergus, -oris,** n. *covering of the back, hide*

terminō, -āre, -āvī, -ātum, tr. *limit, bound*

ternī, -ae, -a, num. adj. *three each*

terra, -ae, f. *earth, dry land*

terreō, -ēre, terruī, territum, tr. *terrify*

tertius, -a, -um, ordinal adj. *third*

testūdō, -inis, f. *tortoise;* anything shaped like a tortoise shell, *vaulted roof*

Teucer, -crī, m. *a king of Troy, whence* **Teucrī, -ōrum,** m. *the Trojans;* also a brother of Ajax, see 619 n.

theātrum, -ī, n. *theater*

thēsaurus, -ī, m. *treasure*

Thrēissa, -ae, f. adj. of **Thrax,** *Thracian*

thymum, -ī, n. *thyme*

Tiberīnus, -a, -um, adj. *belonging to the River Tiber at Rome*

Timāvus, -ī, m. *a river in Istria at the north of the Adriatic*

timeō, -ēre, timuī, —, tr. *fear*

timor, -ōris, m. *fear*

tinguō, -ere, tinxī, tinctum, tr. *wet; drip*

togātus, -a, -um, adj. *wearing the toga, a large gown or robe specially worn at Rome*

tollō, -ere, sustulī, sublātum, tr. *raise*

tondeō, -ēre, totondī, tonsum, tr. *shear*

torqueō, -ēre, torsī, tortum, tr. *twist, whirl*

torreō, -ēre, torruī, tostum, tr. *roast*

torus, -ī, m. *couch*

tot, num. adj. indecl. *so many*

totidem, num. adj. indecl. *just so many*

totiēns, adv. *so many times*

tōtus, -a, -um, adj. *whole*

trabs, trabis, f. *beam*

trahō, -ere, traxī, tractum, tr. *drag, draw along*

trāiciō, -ere, -iēcī, -iectum, tr. *throw through, pierce*

transeō, -īre, transīvī or **transiī, transitum,** intr. *pass by*

transferō, -ferre, -tulī, -lātum, tr. *carry across, remove*

transfīgō, -ere, -fixī, -fixum, tr. *pierce*

tremō, -ere, tremuī, —, intr. *tremble, quiver*

trēs, tria, num. adj. *three*

tridens, tridentis, m. *trident, a fork with three teeth carried by Neptune*

trīgintā, num. adj. *thirty*

Trīnacrius, -a, -um, adj. *belonging to Trinacria, the land with three promontories, i.e. Sicily*

Triōnēs, -um, m. pl. see 744 n.

tristis, -e, adj. *sad; stern*

Trītōn, -ōnis, m. *a sea god, son of Neptune*

Trōēs, -um, m. *Trojans*

Trōia, -ae, f. *Troy,* the famous city, the siege of which by the Greeks forms the subject of the *Iliad*. **Trōiānus, -a, -um,** and **Trōius, -a, -um,** adj. *Trojan*

tueor, -ērī, tuitus or **tūtus sum,** dep. tr. *see; defend*

tum, adv. *at the time, then*

tumidus, -a, -um, adj. *swelling*

tundō, -ere, tutudī, tunsum, tr. *beat*

turba, -ae, f. *crowd*

turbō, -āre, -āvī, -ātum, tr. *throw into confusion, disturb*

turbō, -inis, m. *whirlwind*

tūs, tūris, n. *frankincense, incense*

tūtus, -a, -um, adj. *safe*

tuus, -a, -um, possess. adj. *your*

Tȳdīdēs, -ae, m. *son of Tydeus, Diomedes*

Typhōeus, -a, -um, adj. *belonging to Typhoeus,* a giant slain by Jupiter and placed beneath Etna

tyrannus, -ī, m. *tyrant*

Tyrius, -a, -um, adj. *belonging to Tyre,* and so *Carthaginian*

Tyrrhēnī, -ōrum, m. original inhabitants of Etruria; **Tyrrhēnus, -a, -um,** adj. *Tyrrhenian, Etruscan*

Tyrus, -ī, f. *Tyre,* a famous city on the coast of Phoenicia, 20 miles S. of Sidon

U

ūber, -eris, n. *udder; richness*

ubi, adv. *where, when*

ubīque, adv. *everywhere*

ullus, -a, -um, adj. *any*

umbra, -ae, f. *shade*

ūmectō, -āre, -āvī, -ātum, tr. *wet*

umerus, -ī, m. *shoulder*

ūnā, adv. *at one time, together*

uncus, -a, -um, adj. *crooked*

unda, -ae, f. *wave*

unde, adv. *whence*

ūnus, -a, -um, num. adj. *one*

urbs, urbis, f. *city*

urgeō, -ēre, ursī, —, tr. *press hard, drive*

ūrō, -ere, ussī, ustum, tr. *burn*

usquam, adv. *anywhere, at any time, ever*

ut, adv. and conj. *as, when, how; so that, in order that*

utī = **ut,** *how*

utinam, adv. *O that! Would that!*

ūtor, ūtī, ūsus sum, dep. with abl. *use*

V

vacō, -āre, -āvī, -ātum, intr. *am at leisure;* **vacat,** impers. *there is leisure*

vadum, -ī, n. *shallow, shoal*

validus, -a, -um, adj. *strong*

vallis, -is, f. *valley*

vānus, -a, -um, adj. *empty, vain, false*

varius, -a, -um, adj. *different, changing, various*

vastō, -āre, -āvī, -ātum, tr. *lay waste*

vastus, -a, -um, adj. *huge, vast*

vehō, -ere, vexī, vectum, tr. *carry*

vel, conj. *or*

vēlāmen, -inis, n. *covering thing, veil*

vēlivolus, -a, -um, adj. *flying with sails, studded with sails*

vēlum, -ī, n. *sail*

velut, velutī, adv. *just as*

vendō, -ere, vendidī, venditum, tr. *sell*

venēnum, -ī, n. *poison*

venia, -ae, f. *favor, pardon*

veniō, -īre, vēnī, ventum, intr. *come*

ventus, -ī, m. *wind*

Venus, -eris, f. goddess of Love and Beauty; mother of Aeneas

verbum, -ī, n. *word*

vereor, -ērī, veritus sum, dep. tr. and intr. *fear*

vērō, adv. *assuredly, indeed*

verrō, -ere, verrī, versum, tr. *sweep*

versō, -āre, -āvī, -ātum, tr. *keep turning, ponder*

vertex, -icis, m. *whirl, eddy, whirlpool; top, head*

vertō, -ere, vertī, versum, tr. *turn, overturn*

veru, -ūs, n. *spit*

vērus, -a, -um, adj. *true, genuine*

vescor, -ī, —, dep. with abl. *feed on*

vesper, -eris or **-erī,** m. *evening, the evening star*

Vesta, -ae, f. goddess of the hearth

vester, vestra, vestrum, possess. adj. *your*

vestis, -is, f. *raiment, dress*

vetō, -āre, vetuī, vetitum, tr. *forbid*

vetus, -eris, adj. *old;* superl. **veterrimus**

via, -ae, f. *road*

victor, -ōris, m. *conqueror*

victus, -ūs, m. *food*

videō, -ēre, vīdī, vīsum, tr. *see*

vīgintī, num. adj. *twenty*

villus, -ī, m. *tuft of hair*

vinciō, -īre, vinxī, vinctum, tr. *bind*

vincō, -ere, vīcī, victum, tr. *conquer*

vinculum or **vinclum, -ī,** n. *chain*

vīnum, -ī, n. *wine*

vir, virī, m. *man, hero*

virgō, -inis, f. *maiden*

virtūs, -ūtis, f. *manliness, virtue*

vīs, vis, f. *violence, force;* plur. **vīrēs, -ium,** *strength*

vītālis, -e, adj. *belonging to life, vital*

vīvō, -ere, vixī, victum, intr. *live*

vīvus, -a, -um, adj. *living*

vix, adv. *scarcely*

vocō, -āre, -āvī, -ātum, tr. *call, summon*

volō, -āre, -āvī, -ātum, intr. *fly*

volō, velle, voluī, —, v. irreg. intr. *wish*

volucer, -cris, -cre, adj. *swift*

volūtō, -āre, -āvī, -ātum, tr. *keep rolling; ponder*

volvō, -ere, volvī, volūtum, tr. and intr. *roll; arrange in a circle; ponder*

vorō, -āre, -āvī, -ātum, tr. *devour*

vōtum, -ī, n. *vow*

vox, vōcis, f. *voice*

vulgō, -āre, -āvī, -ātum, tr. *make known*

vulgus, -ī, n. but sometimes m. *common people, multitude*

vulnus, -eris, n. *wound*

vultus, -ūs, m. *countenance*

X

Xanthus, -ī, m. river near Troy

Z

Zephyrus, -ī, m. *West wind*

Index

This index lists grammatical, metrical, and stylistic items mentioned in the commentary; numbers refer to lines in the Latin text and the corresponding commentary notes.